IF I AM MISSING OR DEAD

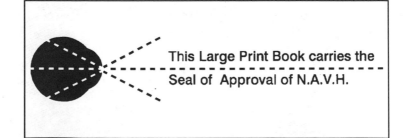

If I Am Missing or Dead

A SISTER'S STORY OF LOVE, MURDER, AND LIBERATION

Janine Latus

THORNDIKE PRESS

An imprint of Thomson Gale, a part of The Thomson Corporation

Detroit • New York • San Francisco • New Haven, Conn. • Waterville, Maine • London

362.829
LAT

THOMSON

---✶--- TM

GALE

LIBRARY OF CONGRESS CATALOGING-IN-PUBLICATION DATA

Latus, Janine, 1959–
  If I am missing or dead / by Janine Latus.
    p. cm. — (Thorndike Press large print basic)
  ISBN-13: 978-0-7862-9660-6 (hardcover : alk. paper)
  ISBN-10: 0-7862-9660-7 (hardcover : alk. paper)
    1. Latus, Janine, 1959– 2. Latus, Amy, 1965– 3. Abused women — United States — Biography. 4. Large type books. I. Title.
  HV6626.2.L383 2007
  362.82'92092273—dc22
  [B]   2007014955

Published in 2007 by arrangement with Simon & Schuster, Inc.

Printed in the United States of America on permanent paper
10 9 8 7 6 5 4 3 2 1

A12004704540

A NOTE TO THE READER

Some names and identifying features of individuals in this book have been changed, but the events depicted are true to the best of my memory.

For Amy

Thou shalt not be a victim. Thou shalt not be a perpetrator. Above all, thou shalt not be a bystander.
— AN INSCRIPTION AT THE HOLOCAUST
        MUSEUM IN WASHINGTON, D.C.

Most of us would rather claim to have always been perfect than admit how much we've grown.
— FROM *BLOOD DONE SIGN MY NAME* BY
        TIM TYSON

July 9, 2002
Two months ago I left my husband, and now, for the first time in years, I am neither scared nor angry. My heart is light. My career is blossoming. My child is happy. Life is full of possibility.

I am talking with a friend when my cell phone rings.

Janine? my sister Jane says. Have you heard from Amy?

No, I say, my skin already prickling from adrenaline. What's up?

I got a call from Kimberly-Clark. Amy hasn't been to work in three days.

My eyes dart to the man standing next to me.

What's wrong? he asks.

He killed her, I say into the phone. That bastard killed her.

My friend looks shocked, then starts shaking his head.

I know, Jane says quietly. But we're not thinking that.

I look around the room. My heart is pounding.

We can't think that yet. I understand that. If we let it gel into a thought it might be true. That is beyond what I can stand.

CHAPTER 1

Amy is born a fighter, six weeks early and a wispy five pounds. Her blood is incompatible with Mom's, so the doctors replace it, draining out the old while infusing the new. Her heart stops anyway. So they pump her tiny baby chest and blow air into her tiny baby lungs until she squalls, and then send her home to round out our family of seven.

The year is 1965, and it is my parents'

third go-round with babies and death. The first had come in 1960, when I woke my mother before dawn, crying for a bottle. At four months and four days old, I was a blue-eyed Gerber baby, the spitting image of my father. Across the room slept my exact replica, my twin sister, Janette. A few weeks earlier our picture had made the front page of the local paper when a smiling mayoral candidate held us up for the cameras. He later complained about the fuzz our blanket left on his black suit coat.

My mother put her hand on Janette's back to feel her breathing. Then she yelled for Dad, who came running. He blew air into her mouth and pressed on her chest, but it was too late. Janette was dead. An errant air bubble or an electrical glitch stopped her heart. Crib death. Cause unknown.

Mom gave birth to Pat barely a year later. Pat was a month early and on the light side at five and a quarter pounds, but within days the local paper announced that mother and daughter were at home and doing fine. Ten days later, though, Mom was in the kitchen warming up a bottle when blood started pouring down her legs. It soaked through her clothes and puddled on the floor. An ambulance came, siren wailing, and rushed her to the hospital. Doctors elevated the foot of her bed and covered her head with an oxygen tent. Through the muffling of the plastic tent she could hear my father and the doctors and nurses, but she couldn't respond. She heard, too, the eerie chant of the priest giving her last rites. "God, the father of mercies, through the death and resurrection of His Son has reconciled the world to himself and sent the Holy Spirit among us for the forgiveness of sins; through the ministry of the church may God give you pardon and peace."

Still she bled, until she was drained, until her heart had nothing left to pump, until it stopped.

"I absolve you from your sins, in the name of the Father, and the Son, and of the Holy Spirit. Through the holy mysteries of our redemption, may almighty God release you from all punishments in this life and in the life to come. May He open to you the gates of paradise and welcome you to everlasting joy."

Long moments passed as doctors scrambled to get it to pump again. Then they rushed her, bed and all, into the operating room. They scraped out the inside of her uterus and gave her half a dozen blood transfusions. When she finally came home, she had to stay in bed for three months, her children pestering for attention.

As an adult I ask my father why he kept getting her pregnant if it was so hard on Mom.

Do you and your husband have sex? he asks.

I hesitate, trying to decide what and whether to answer.

Of course, I say finally.

Then you know, he answers. Men . . . have . . . needs.

By the time Amy is a toddler we live in Kalamazoo, in a two-story box of a house on a double lot, the yard framed by a pair of the huge maple trees that give the street its name. There is a screened-in front porch and a fire escape to one of the girls' bedrooms that scares us all, so we push our bunk beds against it to protect against the boogeyman.

Steve is the eldest and most responsible. He cemented his reputation in the family one Easter when he was about seven by saying, "If we don't get organized, we won't have any fun." I worship him, usually from afar, but sometimes on Saturdays my sisters and I leap onto him as he's stretched out on the floor watching sports, secure that he will be careful even then to throw us off onto cushions or soft rugs, avoiding as much as possible the hard edges of tables and bookcases.

There is Jane, brown-eyed and cherubic, who in high school will cling to the balance beam with her toes, refusing to fall off. She succeeds by sheer force of will. It is Jane's hand-me-downs I wear and her bed I climb into during thunderstorms.

Then there is me. I take ballet lessons instead of piano, try out for plays instead of sports. I don't realize until later that I am the classic middle child, doing what I can to get attention. I am not as good as my older siblings and not as cute as the younger, so I strive mostly to be different.

Next is Patty, and then Amy, the baby, lanky and blue-eyed, the only one with mounds of curls, chasing after all of us, forever trying to keep up.

My father is proud of his family in a Catholic, fill-the-pew sort of way. His children sit in descending order, Steve in an ironed shirt and clip-on tie, the girls in poof-sleeved dresses, veils of lace bobby-pinned to our hair. My mother is proud, too. Straight-backed and beautiful, she holds Amy, always the baby. There we sit, our patent leathers swinging and sometimes kicking, as the priest walks down the aisle in his embroidered brocade, swinging his censer, the rich incense stinging our eyes.

Dad sells insurance for Metropolitan Life. Mom, a registered nurse, stays home with us kids, washing and folding, and carrying in bag after bag of groceries. For a while my Uncle Sandy lives in our basement, his bed and tin clothes cabinet separated off by curtains and a rug. On Sunday mornings we thunder down the stairs and jump on him as he tries to sleep off his Saturday night. He is our favorite uncle, mostly because he lives with us, but also because he has a magical way with broken-spoked bikes and skates without keys. He fixes Amy's favorite push toy without her even asking, though taking out the popping balls that make so much noise that his head hurts. When he is at work, up to his knuckles in the grease from someone's car, we jump on his bed and try to peek at the covers of the *Playboy*s he has hidden on the top of his clothes cabinet, always straightening his blankets and pillow afterward, and giggling with guilt.

In the summer we barely clear our dinner dishes before disappearing down the block for our nightly games of Kick the Can and

Capture the Flag, the older kids forced by parents to let us little ones play. In the winter we switch to King of the Mountain on the hard-packed snowbanks, or build igloos out of the chunks the snowplows leave on the curb.

The year I am in kindergarten the whole family climbs into the station wagon for the drive to Borgess Hill. It is the steepest and iciest in town, and we pile as many as we can fit onto the sled, me in front, Pat behind me, Jane behind her, and Uncle Sandy in the back. Steve runs behind, pushing, his boots churning on the snow, and then jumps on as we fly, the wind ripping screams from our mouths. Halfway down we tip, and the metal runner of the sled slices over my boot and breaks my ankle. For weeks Steve, four years older, has to drag me to school on the same sled, my cast in a plastic bread bag to keep it from getting wet. One day he stops at the top of a hill and gives the sled a shove, and I hurtle down the sidewalk, luge-like, between the snowbanks.

The year I am seven the snow is so deep that drivers put orange Styrofoam balls on the tips of their car antennas so they can see each other at intersections. We kids dig a tunnel from our house to the neighbors', then burrow back home for hot chocolate, our scarves and mittens dripping in the hall.

At Christmas we line up every year, oldest to youngest, Amy standing on tiptoe and still not reaching high enough to hang her stocking on the hooks that line the mantel. In the summers we pose again, draped on the sign of the year's campground or national park, our beagle Penny out front.

Don't you take the picture, Dad says to Mom. You always cut off everyone's head.

By the time I am twelve we are living in Haslett, Michigan, where I spend the summer bored, experimenting with blue eye shadow and giving myself hickeys in the hollow of my elbow as I practice kissing.

Over Labor Day weekend Mom breaks out in a rash so fierce she has to be rushed to a doctor. Her body is covered in hives. It's hard for her to breathe. Later we find out why. Without telling anyone, she has interviewed for a job in a doctor's office. Dad isn't making much money, the bills are piling up, we kids keep growing and needing clothes and shoes and ever more groceries, and besides, doesn't she deserve validation? Doesn't she deserve respect and a paycheck and recognition for her intelligence and training and skills?

Still, the anticipation of telling Dad has

made her so anxious that she gets hives.

Dad harrumphs.

So I got the job, Mom says.

Wow, I say.

Cool, Steve says.

We all look to Dad.

Don't forget you still have responsibilities around here, he says.

I babysit for the Johnstons, who live down the street. Easy-to-entertain kids, an early bedtime, color TV, and a selection of snacks. Like a lot of families in the neighborhood, the Johnstons called my house to see if any of the Latus girls could babysit, and my parents told them I'd be happy to. They don't ask me first.

At ten 'til six I say good-bye to my mom and dad, who are in their room dressing for a party at the country club. Tomorrow I'm going to the mall with my girlfriends, where we will dip hot pretzels in mustard while we thumb through Partridge Family posters. I'm saving up for a glow-in-the-dark bead curtain that I saw last week in Spencer Gifts.

Bedtime is at eight, Mrs. Johnston says. They don't need baths, but you do need to help them with their teeth.

More quietly she adds, It's okay if you can't get them down until 8:30, and once they're asleep you can help yourself to anything in the fridge. And there are cookies in the breadbox. I got you some Coke, too.

I love these kids and want some just like them, plump and soft and adoring. They hold tight to my fingers as we walk around the yard looking at bugs and dandelions. We wave as their parents drive off, then go inside, where the kids tackle me and we fall to the floor, wrestling and laughing, playing Hide-and-Seek and Tag.

At eight o'clock I shepherd them into their bedroom and help them into their pajamas, then into the bathroom to brush their teeth.

Please, one more monster game, the younger one asks.

What? I say, rising up to my full five feet one. You want the monster?

And with that I stamp toward them, my hands high, my fingers clawed. They run away, screaming and laughing, and I chase them down the hall and into the living room. We are wrestling again when the door opens and Mr. Johnston walks in.

I am on the floor, flushed and disheveled.

I forgot something, he says, and walks past us to his bedroom.

The kids and I look at each other, and then they leap onto me again, and I flail and pretend to scream as they attack.

Mr. Johnston comes out of the bedroom and looks down at us.

I wonder if the babysitter is ticklish, he says.

He gets down on all fours and the children jump on their daddy's back, squealing, joining in. I scoot to the side to give them space, but an instant later he is on top of me. Pressing his erection against my pelvis, grinding it into me. I can feel his gin breath on my face, in my ear. He moves against me as a man does a woman, except I am just a girl.

For a second I am paralyzed.

He wants me, I think.

I cannot breathe, cannot get free.

I am going to hell.

I push against him with my palms, try to plant my feet flat on the floor so I can get traction to squirm out from under him. It doesn't work.

Knee him.

That's right. That's what the gym teacher said to do if you were attacked. Knee him where it counts, even though she never explained what was there for me to knee. But there's no room. He is bigger and stronger, and I am pinned.

He is grinding into me, making animal

sounds in my ear while I pummel his back with my flailing fists. I look for the children. *Can they jump on his back and help me?* But they are huddled against each other against the couch, their eyes wide, staring.

Think.

Then it comes to me, and I do what my father has done to me when he needs to get my attention. I grab the tiny hairs at the back of his neck and yank.

You little bitch, he says. He spits the words onto my face. You little shit.

He rolls off me and rubs the back of his neck, and I scramble to my feet and behind a chair. He glares at me before getting up and slamming out the door.

When the Johnstons return hours later, Mr. Johnston stays in the car. Mrs. Johnston doles out three dollar bills and two quarters for the seven-hour job. I can't even look at her.

I'm fine getting home.

Goodness no, she answers. My husband will take you.

Honestly, I'll be okay, I say. I like to walk.

It's no trouble, Mrs. Johnston says. Besides, your mom would kill me if I let you go alone this late.

I can't figure out what to say, so I walk

out to the car, my eyes on my feet as I open the door. The interior light flips on, but I don't look at him. Instead I climb in, close the door, and press myself against it. His hand in the sudden darkness finds my knee, holds it.

We'll never tell anyone what we did, Mr. Johnston says.

I pull my leg away, don't answer, even though he's a grown-up, and sit utterly silent and hard against my door during the drive. I jump out before the car's fully stopped and scurry up the walk, thankful that the front door is unlocked.

My mother will be awake, I know, until each of her children is home and safe. My father will be snoring, his pale chest exposed above the covers. At least I hope so. My mom has told me that when I was little he paced the floor for nights that seemed endless, singing and crooning and patting my back. He changed my diapers, as he reminds me so often and so publicly. He taught me to ride a bike, to swim. Now, though, he disgusts me, still pulling me onto his lap, still squeezing my pimples, still insisting on kissing me on the lips. He tickles me until I cry, and pits the siblings against each other, egging us on to do the same. I dread my birthdays, when he lays me over his knees and paddles me once for every year of age and one more — much harder — to grow on, followed by a pinch to grow an inch. He does it in front of my aunts and uncles and cousins, who laugh nervously. Even his side of the family has stopped the birthday spankings, allowing their pubescent children some degree of dignity. So tonight I lean against the wall as I climb the stairs, hoping he's not awake, wanting only my mommy.

Unfortunately, he's sitting up in bed. My parents have just gotten back from the same party as the Johnstons, and they smell of cigarette smoke and gin. Mom's hair is in its party beehive, her blue eye shadow all the way up to her plucked eyebrows. Dad is bleary-eyed and in a hurry to fall asleep. I sit on the edge of their bed and tell my story, how Mr. Johnston had come home, pinned me down, ground his, his thing into me, and how I had triumphed and gotten away. I wait for their pride and sympathy.

There is a long pause as my mom and I look to my dad.

If you tell anyone what happened, Dad says, you'll be known as a slut.

Mom strokes my hair and doesn't say anything. Neither do I.

It is two decades before I learn that she wrote Mr. Johnston a letter.

Stay away from my daughter, it said. And tell your wife what you've done.

CHAPTER 2

A few weeks later I start eighth grade. I stand in the back of the band room playing the drums, which gives me the camaraderie of membership without the effort of learning to read music.

Jane and Steve are off in high school half a mile away, and Pat and Amy are still in elementary. Every day I enter a world of clanging lockers, Kotex machines, and a tinsel-toothed best friend who says that if my parents really loved me, they'd get me braces. It is my first time in a school with no other Latus children. Their ghosts are there, though, in the teachers who expect me to be able to master algebra like Steve or sit still and pay attention like Jane. There are shuffled dances to "Stairway to Heaven" in the cafeteria and formaldehyde-soaked frogs in the science labs, mine so full of eggs that I leave the room gagging. The year cannot pass quickly enough.

The next summer we pack into the family station wagon, me at a disadvantage in the rear-facing backseat, as we race to see who can find each letter of the alphabet on signs and passing license plates. Q is the hardest, followed by J. Amy sleeps with her head in my lap, nauseated by my father's cigar smoke and the ever-receding landscape. We sing "Deep in the Woods" and "Three Little Fishies."

You sound like a dog in heat, Dad says to Mom.

We are on our way to another state park, where my mother for a week will heat up SpaghettiOs and wieners and beans and Dinty Moore beef stew. My father will slyly mix gin and tonics in a Thermos, the quartered limes littering the fire pit in the morning.

I have brought a stack of Harlequin romances, and the next morning I hide behind one, trying to block out my father walking around the campsite in his baggy underwear. The summer before, I had asked him why, knowing he would have a reason, and a damn good one at that.

This is no worse than you girls walking around with your cheeks hanging out of those little bathing suits, he'd said, snapping the elastic in my bikini bottoms before I could jump away.

This year I am pretending he doesn't exist.

I am not the prettiest girl here. That position is already taken by Cathy, in her pale blue two-piece that doesn't quite conceal her new breasts. Cathy has been here since Tuesday and has chosen Tim, the most desirable of the brothers from lot 98, down by the rope swing. It is rumored that she holds hands with him at the camp amphitheater while the projector whirrs and ticks and the ranger lectures brightly about bats and fish and poison ivy.

I am not the ugliest. On our drive in — slouched into the vinyl seat, forehead against the window, eyes just above the sill — I saw a lumpy girl picking at a zit in lot 18. Her suit is half caught in her crack, revealing a doughy butt and a scabbed-over mosquito bite. Her license plates say Nebraska. *At least I am not her.*

Even so, I am not a girl who makes boys nervous. They don't hold their towels in front of their swimsuits or abruptly jump into the water when they look at me. They don't get into shoving matches or do dangerous stunts off the rope swing to impress me. Nor do they spill pop down my back or accidentally splash my T-shirt with cold water down at the spigot where we all go to fill our families' water jugs.

I am too much like them. I can carry a full jug all the way back to lot 24, while the other girls drag theirs down the dirt road, leaving a trail like a tortoise. I am a tomboy, short and sturdy, my sparrow-brown hair parted in the middle and hanging straight to my shoulders, my teeth gapped and my feet too big. I go headlong into all things physical and have already had two casts and uncountable stitches. My mother calls it an awkward phase, but I believe it's going to last forever.

I am not cool in school, either, but I make up for it by being something of a suck-up, a brainiac, the kind who doesn't need a hall pass because she can't possibly be misbehaving. It wouldn't occur to the adults in the school that a Latus kid might be getting in trouble. It doesn't really occur to me, either. Not yet.

But here at the campground, my school persona doesn't help. Here the only contest is in the category of "cute."

Tonight I wait until my father is on his third Thermos before I ask permission to wander up to the Teen Pavilion, an over-lit, tin-roofed cinderblock building that houses two pinball machines and a beat-up foosball table. I have promised to meet Cathy there, and Tim, who asked me earlier in the afternoon. I had been in the water, holding onto the raft, and he'd swum up behind me and held on next to me. Then he had reached around me and held onto the raft on the other side, his body cradling mine in the water, so that I had to quit treading water and grab the slick wood in order not to kick him.

Come to the teen shed tonight, he'd said, into my wet hair.

I had nodded, confused by the attention, and he had put one big hand on my head and pushed me under the green water.

My father says I can go, but not before

lecturing me about how he shouldn't let me out of the camper dressed as I am, in my paisley halter top and cutoff shorts.

You look like a floozy, he says. You girls need to realize that when you dress that way, you're asking for it.

Then he looks me up and down.

You better lay off the chips, too, he says.

Then he goes back to laying out another hand of humidity-warped solitaire cards on the sticky vinyl tablecloth. The Coleman lamp hisses overhead and he cusses at the bugs it attracts. I fade into the shadows and start walking up the dirt road.

Walking in the dark like this, between confusions, is comforting. I pass an Airstream, its air conditioner buzzing in the night. Through the window I see the blue flicker of a television. My family thinks Airstreams with televisions are a crime against camping. We think tents flat on the bare ground are barbaric. We have what is called a pop-up camper, although it doesn't pop up. The new ones do, but old ones like ours have to be wrestled up, all five kids and both parents grabbing a pole and hoisting on the count of three, and harsh words to the one who doesn't quite get hers up on time.

We camp for a week each year, my parents sleeping in one bed and Pat and Amy in another. Steve, who has all the luck, is in his own pup tent outside, and Jane and I sleep in the camper's zip-on Add-a-Room on aluminum and canvas bunk beds, across a hip-wide aisle from the tin fold-up table lined with boxes of cereal, sleeves of Chips Ahoy and bags of Jay's potato chips, all of which will be soggy by the first night. The games are on end in another box, and the extra toilet paper and calamine lotion are closed up in a homemade cabinet. The whole thing smells like canvas and dust and perhaps a bit like urine, because of when Amy used to wet the bed. There is an enameled pot for peeing in during the night. I prefer to grope for the flashlight I keep in my sleeping bag, struggle down from my bunk, unzip the heavy-duty door flap and walk to the outhouse if we're roughing it or to the eyeball-searing bathrooms if we're in a campground with electricity.

The air here between the extremes of Airstreams and pup tents is clean, and I am torn between wanting to rush to the teen shed and wanting to lag back. Inevitably, though, I arrive, and it is loud inside with the clang of pinball and the frantic energy

34

of adolescents. The light is wholesomely bright, and the kids cluster. He is there, of course. Tim, with the unruly curls he constantly flips from his face and the gray eyes he locks on mine. I try not to notice that while he is looking at me his hand is groping in the back pocket of Cathy's plaid shorts.

I look away, fish a quarter out of my pocket, and walk over to a machine. Its frenzied music and panicked pace feel right. I pound the knobs, shake the machine, jerk it half off its legs, using my hips, my arms, my whole body. I advance to the bonus level. I am winning, or at least surviving long enough to stay in the game. But no, suddenly the buttons flail uselessly, the last silver ball rolls away. Game over.

I am sweating, and Tim, I find, is standing next to me.

I have someone for you to meet, he says. You'll like him.

He leads me to the foosball table, where a stocky, black-haired boy I have never seen is spinning the poles and jerking the table off the floor as he battles an older, smoother player.

This is Gary, Tim says. I look to the younger boy, but it is the older one who glances up, nods.

Hi, I say, but he has turned back to his game, his hands selecting and working the rods like a church organist I once saw in a cathedral. I stand still and watch. He is wearing cutoffs and a blue T-shirt. From the back he's cuter than Tim, who now shoves me slightly so I bump up against the older boy's back.

Sorry, I mumble, then scowl at Tim, who laughs as he saunters back to Cathy. I want to crawl under the table, but Gary doesn't seem to notice. He doesn't even know I'm here, I think, but then he spins one last rod and drives the ball into the other guy's goal.

Game, he says, but calmly. He turns and looks straight at me then.

Hi, he says. His eyes are blue.

His shirt pocket bulges with a pack of Salems, his shorts pocket with a wallet, so perhaps he's old enough to drive. He is half a head taller than I, his sandy blond hair hanging to his shoulders.

Hi, I say. You're good at that.

Thanks, he says. Then, It's not exactly rocket science. Just four years after the moon landing this is still a fresh and witty thing to say.

He is from Paw Paw, a town in Michigan's fruit belt famous for its football team and the enormous Christmas tree its Kiwanis

Club decorates each year on the town square, where he plays all three sports and picks cherries and peaches in the summer for a local grower. In a state where everyone uses their hand for a map, he lives between the wrist and the lake and I live closer to the palm. We are now halfway up the pinkie, within a few miles of famous sand dunes. We are camping on Clear Lake, one of nine so-named lakes in the state. The second most common name is Deep Lake. Not original, perhaps, but accurate.

He pulls two quarters from his pocket. Want to play pinball?

Sure, I say. I'm not very good.

It is a lie, but it will cover me if I play poorly and get me praise if I play well. I step up for my turn, and he stands half behind me, half to my side. I can see him on the periphery, feel his proximity. I know if I play as I usually do, thrusting and jerking and flinging my body, I will brush against him, and I almost hope I do, but then I feel guilty. It is hard to concentrate, and I quickly lose my turn.

He, on the other hand, plays gracefully, tapping the buttons rather than pounding them, his hips moving in smaller circles, and he makes it to the sixth level.

My subsequent turns go better, as I surreptitiously try his technique. It works. I rack up the points and relax into it. The game goes on and on, until he flusters me by leaning in until his shirt front brushes my bare shoulders and his breath touches my neck. My ball slides past the flippers. Gary has won.

We walk outside into the spilled-out light, where we sit on top of a picnic table and listen to the night noise of crickets, peepers, and bullfrogs, and voices skittering over the lake. The people over there are arguing, in fact, calling each other selfish bitch and lazy asshole, which is embarrassing.

Must be my parents, he says, and smiles.

Or mine, I answer.

We smile at each other. We talk until eleven, when the lights in the teen shed automatically snap off, leaving us wide-eyed in the dark.

Tim and Cathy come around the corner of the building.

We better get going, Tim says. He and Gary are cousins, staying on adjoining lots, their parents sitting around the fire pit and murmuring as they have every summer since the boys were little and the only things they were hunting after dark were tadpoles and fireflies.

Tim and Cathy walk away, holding hands.

They stop, still within sight, and face each other. Cathy goes up on her tiptoes for a small kiss. I have to look away, and even Gary coughs. He puts his hand on my warm arm and turns me toward him, but I won't look up, focusing instead on my dirty toes, on the ground, on the cigarette butts around my feet.

See you, he says. Tomorrow, maybe? At the rope swing?

If I can, I say.

I still won't look up, so he squeezes my arm, lets go, and I walk away into the cooling night. I feel guilty for wanting more.

The next morning I roll out of my bunk bed and grab the Kellogg's Variety Pack before anyone else can get the Frosted Flakes.

I can see my breath, so I pull on a sweatshirt and shoes before quietly unzipping the door. I cherish this time alone, without siblings or parents, when I can eat my cereal and read my book and drink the sugary milk from the bottom of the bowl without having my manners corrected.

I want to sneak in and get the Froot Loops before my sisters wake up, but I don't want to risk trading in my solitude, and I definitely don't want to hear from Dad again that I'm getting fat. Instead I read.

Not more than ten pages later, though, the tent is unzipped from the inside and my father steps out, scratching his hairy white belly, his swimming trunks clinging high up on his butt in back and sagging low beneath his gut in front. Suits on, Polar Bears! he bellows into the camper. It's a beautiful morning for a swim.

I duck behind the milk, hoping he'll not notice that I'm missing, not make me take that early-morning plunge into the icy water.

You, too, Janine, he said. Since you're up, you can take them their suits.

I grumble about the idiocy of swimming in weather like this as I shuffle around the campsite gathering the cold, damp swimsuits off the tent ropes and take them in to my reluctant sisters, who give me shoot-the-messenger looks.

Mom raises her head and rolls her eyes before flopping face-first back into the pillow and gathering it around her ears. She hates the morning ritual of her kids being forced out into the cold, but she can't stop it. All she can do is put her foot down just enough to keep herself from having to go, too. Early in their marriage she had done it, to prove to him that she could, that she loved him, that she was a good sport. Now she refuses, but we kids don't have that option, so now we are tugging dew-chilled polyester over our thighs and rear ends while our father whistles impatiently outside.

Your mother's a wimp, Dad says.

Amy is riding on his broad back, her toes pointed skyward to keep her flip-flops from falling off.

There's frost on the ground, Dad, Jane says. I swear.

It's dew, he says. Quit being a wienie.

Mist is rising off the lake. Steve dives in first, then my sisters and I drop our towels, run to the end of the dock and dive. We all dive and swim effortlessly, a gift we owe our father, who had passed the genes and done the teaching. Today the water is green and clear, like an old 7-Up bottle, and I slip like an otter under the dock. Underwater I feel graceful.

By the time we return, Mom will have pulled on pedal pushers and a sweatshirt and started bacon and eggs on the stove. The smell will be her compensation for our swim.

I can't slip away to the rope swing until well after lunch, and I worry that Gary will have gotten tired of waiting. If, that is, he was serious. He might not be. He might have just been bored, so he flirted with me, even though he wasn't really interested.

Maybe I should take Amy. Colt-legged and giggly, she'd be good camouflage. She's only eight, so I could pretend I'm babysitting instead of looking like I am going to meet a boy. I can't ask Jane, because she'd disapprove. But Amy would have gone anywhere I asked. I think about going back, but I convince myself to keep going. I am going to meet a boy. No point in making a big deal about it. Other girls make big deals about such things, but I am sensible, emotionally sturdy, too, in spite of the hair I now chew as I make my way under the pines and birches that ring the lake.

As I get closer, I can hear squeals and splashes and threats, although I can't differentiate the voices. The path comes out on the shore far enough away that I can watch the other kids as I approach. Cathy is there, on a pink air mattress, just past the reach of the rope, and Tim is yodeling like Tarzan as he hurtles toward her.

Don't you dare! Cathy squeals just before Tim lets go and lands, his tsunami-like wave threatening to capsize her raft. When he surfaces and sees she hasn't been dumped, he swims underwater and comes up underneath her, lifting one side of the mattress so she flops over the other. They come up kissing.

All this I see as I walk, self-consciously, hoping everyone else is watching the antics in the water and not my slow approach.

It is Gary who catches the rope after Tim's performance. He stands with one leg on the foot-traffic-smooth trunk of the sycamore that serves as the launchpad. The tree has grown or tipped or been knocked out over the water, as if it is reaching toward the center of the lake. Its trunk runs parallel to the surface for about six feet, and then, drawn by the sun and survival, curves back upward, so its branches stretch out over the water and shade the pool below. Someone years ago had scrambled up the tree and tied a thick, knotted rope onto just the right branch, and now the rope rests in Gary's hand.

He passes it off to a tow-headed, gap-toothed boy, then lifts the boy by the hips, as if he is starting him on a playground swing. The boy lifts his feet and soars out over the water.

Now! Gary yells, and the boy lets go and falls, his arms wheeling, into the water.

He comes up beaming. That was a good

one! he calls, shaking the water out of his face.

Gary again catches the rope, hands it off to a little girl, and then holds her as she plants her muddy feet on the big knot at the bottom.

Ready? he asks, then lets her go.

I am smiling as I watch from the shore. *Gary is nice,* I think. *Nice.*

Hi, he says, and smiles.

Hi, I answer, then toss my towel onto a nearby picnic table and strip out of my shorts and T-shirt, worrying and hoping he is looking. It is all too confusing. What I need is a boylike banshee yell launch off the rope swing. What I get instead is the sight of Gary taking his own turn, swinging high out over the water, feet to the sky, then flipping over backward to drop feet first into the water. The little kids scramble to give him a hand out of the water, but they are all too light. He can pull any of them over his head into the water in a move Tim, for one, will think is funny. But he doesn't.

You want to try this, Janine? he asks.

Sure, I say. I am embarrassed when I get next to him, though, because I'm not tall enough to get a good grip on the best hand knot without jumping or having someone help. Gary is holding the rope. If I reach for the good knot, I might fall forward, off the bank, and die of humiliation. If Gary helps, I might die anyway. He smiles at me, then looks startled as a pair of strong hands close on my hips and hoist me toward the rope. I grab it as I fall forward, then pull my feet up and swing high out over the water before I let go and sink blissfully out of sight. I stay under until I will die if I don't come up for air.

When I surface I see Gary angrily shoving Tim, who shoves right back.

Just keep your hands off her, Gary says.

I'm sure *you* will, Tim says. Mr. Nice Guy, won't go past first base without permission.

I shake the water out of my ears, missing Gary's answer, and see the cousins glare at each other, so I swim to the side and start to scramble up the bank. Gary reaches out a hand to help, but Tim hip-checks him and puts out his own hand. I pretend not to notice and climb the bank by myself.

Get back out here, Cathy orders from her air mattress, in the voice such girls use when summoning their boyfriends. Tim snatches the rope from the next kid in line and leaps out over the water, landing with a cannon ball that douses everyone waiting in line. I catch the rope on its backswing, look at Gary, and roll my eyes.

Sorry, he says, and I smile and hand him the rope. He helps the next kid in line get situated, then sends him out over the water.

You all are lame, Tim calls. We're going out to the raft.

He and Cathy lie on their bellies across the air mattress and kick their feet, propelling it toward the main swimming area and the raft anchored there.

Gary and I watch them for a moment, and then he offers me the rope. I take it and he lifts me by the waist as he had the little kids. I am embarrassed, but also thrilled. I soar out over the water and let go at the top of the arc. It is like flying.

By dinnertime, I can flip backward off the rope. Gary and I help each other up the bank time and again, laughing and shaking water out of our hair. Amy would have had fun, I think, clowning around in line with the other kids, clinging to the rope like a squirrel monkey. Then I remember; Amy would have told — not on purpose — but she would have let the tiniest thing slip, and my afternoon with Gary would be turned into teasing and knowing asides. My laugh would be mimicked, my mistakes amplified, my teeny crush on a slightly older boy mocked. When I didn't laugh, my father would say, What's the matter with you? You're a Latus. You're supposed to have a sense of humor.

It wouldn't be Amy's fault, though. Amy adores me and would be mum and loyal as long as she could, but little things would slip out and then she would be cajoled and encouraged and threatened with the limelight if she didn't give up her secrets. I am starting to believe there'll be secrets to keep.

I guess I better head home now, I say. I am in the water, holding on to a low branch and letting my legs float with the fish, but it is past time for me to be back at the campsite. Dusk has deepened the shadow under the tree to near darkness, and most of the kids have scattered. A wind has come up, promising rain. It chills me as I climb up the bank.

Still, I am in no hurry. Gary offers a hand, giving a little tug as I get near the top so that I accidentally on purpose bump against him. His other hand lands on my waist and I gasp, even though his hand is warmer than my skin and I had been hoping for it. I stay still, my chilled body against his dry one. I shiver, my cheek miraculously against his chest. He puts both arms around me, which almost makes me shake more.

His smell of lake and sunshine mixes with

that of the pines. Again I can't raise my head, so he settles for kissing my wet hair before loosening his arms.

See you tonight? he asks. I'll beat you at pinball.

If you're lucky, I say, and glance up quickly to smile. His blue eyes are right there, looking into mine, so I tilt back my head and feel the soft press of his lips. I duck my head again and pull away.

I've got to go, I say.

I walk to the picnic table, pick up my towel, and start to dry myself off, self-conscious because he is watching and because I want to run down the shore leaping and yelling like an idiot. I don't want to pull on my shorts and T-shirt because they will become immediately soaked with the shape of my two-piece, but I don't want to walk away in just the suit, either, because I am afraid my butt wiggles. I try wrapping the towel around my hips like a sarong, but that makes me walk like a Hollywood geisha, so I give up, laughing at myself, and pull on my shorts. Life was easier a week ago. Less exciting, maybe, but easier.

I have a boyfriend. I play with the thought like a loose tooth. I have a boyfriend. A boy. Who likes me. Not just as a good buddy or teammate, but as a girlfriend. He holds my hand, he kisses my lips and hair, he lies softly baking next to me in the sunlight that reflects off the water. He does cannonballs and jackknifes and wild stunts to impress me. Only me. In the evenings I sneak away from the family poker games — penny ante, with a cheat sheet for the younger kids who can't remember whether a full house beats a straight or whether three of a kind beats two pair.

By the third day my family becomes suspicious and the teasing begins.

Do you have a boyfriend? they ask. Then, Janine's got a boyfriend, Janine's got a boyfriend, repeated in the singsong lilt of a jump rope cadence.

Do you? Mom asks quietly, as we stand side by side doing dishes in the plastic bins that pass as sinks. Mom had left water heating on the propane stove all through dinner and now it is hot and sudsy, although much too shallow for dishes for seven. My job is to dry while the other kids hunt in the woods for fallen branches for the fire. It is my only time alone with my mom.

Maybe, I say, glancing up to see how she reacts.

Mom looks at me carefully and keeps washing dishes. Maybe you should cover it a little better, she says. I'm not sure your father's ready to deal with the idea.

It is a warning: You know how your father is. Females are temptresses, while males are mere victims of biology. They can't help themselves. If something happens, we have no one to blame but ourselves. Don't let your father know. She doesn't have to explain any of this. Ever.

As soon as we are done with the dishes, I ask my mom if I can go.

Be back by eleven, she says.

I flash her a grateful smile, throw my wet dish towel over the tent line, and fade into the trees.

Behind me I hear, Honey? Can you come help me with this Thermos? and see my father disappear into the tent.

I have a good idea how my dad would respond if he knew about Gary. He would insist on meeting him, insist on saying something embarrassing like, Don't even think of trying anything funny. I was a young man myself once, and I know what it is you want. Or, You touch her and I'll shoot you, and then in his deep growl, and I could, you know.

The next morning Dad once again rousts us out of our sleeping bags and heads us down to the lake. When we get back Mom is breaking eggs into the bacon grease. Our lips are blue and our teeth are chattering as we rush into the tent and burrow back into our sleeping bags, wet hair and all.

Five minutes, girls, she says. And don't leave your wet towels on the beds.

We dress in our sleeping bags. On normal mornings we have to be asked again and again to get moving, but for bacon and eggs and hot chocolate after a swim, we rush. I bring out the plastic plates and napkins and Jane grabs the garage-sale silverware. Amy gets the multicolored metal cups that make milk and KoolAid taste like tin, and Pat brings the salt and pepper. Steve is out walking our dog, BoJo.

Breakfast is the best part of camping together. Everyone is wide awake and grateful, if for nothing more than a warm sweatshirt and the smell of bacon and pine. The air is crisp and Mom and Dad are cheerful, smiling secretly at each other over their children's heads.

After breakfast we will break camp, cramming dirty clothes in with clean, since they all smell like smoke, rolling up sleeping bags, shaking out rugs, our parents fitting the cabinets and lawn chairs and boxes of supplies back together like a puzzle, until we lower the poles of the camper and close it down for another season. Then my dad and my brother will haul it over and hook it onto the trailer hitch, while my sisters and I walk in rows up and down the campsite, searching out stray litter.

Always leave a campsite looking better than when you arrived, my dad says.

We know. Before we leave the lot will be furrowed with the parallel lines of a rake, our Japanese garden in the Michigan woods.

I am home and bored for two weeks, killing time writing my name and Gary's in curlicues and hearts. Then I go with my friend Robin and one of my favorite teachers and his wife to their cabin on a northern Michigan island.

I adore my teacher. He is like my father, except I know he'll never do anything that will make me feel bad.

The Murphys' cabin is of log, too, surrounded by the white of birches and the mirror expanse of a freshwater lake. There's a rowboat and a canoe, and a flagpole on a point of rock that juts into the water, where each morning we ceremoniously raise the American flag. At night Robin and I climb a ladder built into the wall of one of the bedrooms, up to our mattress on the floor of the loft above.

On the second day we are joined by the Murphys' son, Tom, a man in his twenties with his father's teasing manner

I've never met Tom, although I have heard that he has gone through a divorce, which makes him exotic. When we canoe, I splash him with my paddle. When we go on a hike, I wear my bikini top and my shortest shorts, and I giggle at everything he says.

Robin is disgusted. That night we climb the ladder to our bed while Tom tucks in to one of the bunks below.

Good night, Tom, I call down, snuggling into the covers on the ladder side of the bed, Robin on the other side with her back to me.

Good night, Janine, he says. Good night, Robin.

It sounds like something out of *The Waltons.*

I put myself to sleep by thinking about Gary, about our few kisses, about the thrill of holding hands, about the one letter I've received since I got home. I fall asleep happy. Hours later I wake up with Tom's lips just above mine, his finger in my vagina.

Shh . . . he whispers. Just lie back. It'll feel good.

I do, my eyes wide, my heart racing. It does feel good, but it feels yucky, too, like

53

something that shouldn't be happening, like something bad, something awful, something that is a sin. I push at his hand, but he puts his other hand over both of mine and holds them still. He is kneeling next to the bed, his hands under the covers, his eyes glassy.

What are you doing? Robin asks, and I turn my head toward her in shock.

Nothing, I say. I am stunned and humiliated.

Tom pulls his finger out of me, lets go of my hands and brings his own out from under the covers.

She looks at him and then at me. You're gross, she says.

I sit up. Tom backs away and retreats down the ladder as I stammer.

I didn't do anything, I say. When I woke up he was already doing it.

But she doesn't believe me. I don't even know if I believe me. And she's right. I'm gross.

The next morning we don't talk about it. We move through the flag-raising ritual, and then I ask Tom to wait a second while everyone else heads to breakfast.

You know that song, "Having My Baby"? I ask.

He nods. It's on every pop radio station

that summer.

What if that happens to us?

He just stares at me. Seriously? You're serious?

I nod, and he laughs and pats my shoulder. You'll be fine, he says.

But what about us? I ask. I mean, will we see each other?

He laughs again. You're, what, like thirteen?

I nod.

He shakes his head and walks away.

When I get home everything is normal. My mom meets me in the driveway and thanks the Murphys, then hugs me and tells me to throw my stinky laundry downstairs. Amy drags me inside, clamoring for me to watch her latest show. I sit on the couch and applaud as she twirls a fireplace broom in lieu of a cane while she shimmies in an old dance costume of mine, the crotch hanging to her knees and the fringe on the leotard twitching across her tiny bottom.

This time I don't tell.

CHAPTER 3

Growing up we live in four-bedroom houses, my parents in one room, my brother, the oldest, in another, and the sisters divided between the other two. Sometimes I room with Amy, but we are both slobs, so our room fractures into a chaos of missing shoes and lost homework and broken toys. More often I share with Jane, who deals with my slovenly ways and my tendency to borrow her clothes without permission by taping a line down the middle of the bedroom. The closet is on her half, so she marks off a balance beam–thin path to my clothes.

On Wednesday nights we go to catechism class, on Sundays we go to Mass. One day we are driving home from church in our olive green station wagon. Mom and Dad are in the front seat, and we're scattered in the back.

"What's masturbation?" one of us sisters ask.

There is a moment of silence from the front seat.

"Ask your brother," Dad says.

The conversation stops.

I alternate my catechism with *Of Mice and Men* and my world history book with Judy Blume's *Are You There God? It's Me, Margaret.* It's here I learn about menstruation and petting and breast buds. I talk too often in class, pound the drums in band, sing open-throated, with my hands by my side, in choir. One day after class I kiss Joe Parks out by the drinking fountain. Years later I will mention it to him and he will shrug. He'll have married five times by then.

In church I learned: Girls are seductresses,

starting with Eve, who got us all kicked out of the Garden of Eden by being weak, by taking a bite from the tree of knowledge, and — most important — by enticing poor, innocent Adam to do the same. Everything bad can be traced back to women, and the only way to make up for the lustiness of my gender is by acknowledging my guilt, carrying it, wearing it like a badge.

Especially when I am in my early teens and I lie back in the bathtub, the only place in the house where I can be alone, and let the water run *down there.* I don't know what's down there, and I don't have a name for what I'm doing, but I know it feels good, and that means it must be bad.

Still, I lock the bathroom door and pull out the first drawer on the vanity, which blocks the door so it can open only a few inches. Even if my dad or my sisters use a straightened paper clip or bobby pin to pop the lock, saying I'm hogging the bathroom, using all of the hot water, I have time to slide back up to an innocent sitting position before yelling an irritated, Do you mind? I'm taking a bath here. Jeez, can't anyone get any privacy?

Afterward I come out pruny and sheepish, guilty and relaxed.

In ninth grade I go home after school with

Ron, the new boy with the slow, sexy Oklahoma accent that makes me melt in social studies. His parents both work, so we have the house to ourselves, and we use it. Use his bed, mostly, where we grope and explore and roll around. We kiss and open our mouths and taste each other's tongues and run our hands over each other's bodies, for the first week over the clothes, and later just a little bit under, his hands tugging and untucking, sliding up under my shirt, over my training bra.

One day Mom takes me aside.

One of the other moms called me, she says. She says you're going home with Ron, when his parents aren't there. I told her it wasn't true. Is it?

I blush red and hot, guilty and itchy and blank faced. I snort.

Of course I'm not, I say, pursing my lips and shaking my head. I would never do anything like that.

I am the good girl, the one who stays in catechism classes on Wednesday nights while the other kids skip to smoke cigarettes or flirt in the parking lot. I listen intently to the priest, nod in agreement, do the readings between classes. I argue. I debate. I acquiesce. I wear a white dress for my confirmation, the monsignor giving me the traditional blessing, a slap across the face. I am startled and angry. He has no right. My father says he does.

My family fills a pew, my father proud in his leisure suit, my mother with her Jackie O dress, Steve in his brass-buttoned suit coat, Jane with her gymnast's posture, Pat with hair to her waist, Amy prepubescent and rail thin, her hair flopping forward in curls and ringlets that I envy. I smile at them as I return from the altar, unsure what I'm expected to feel, beyond the outrage at the monsignor's slap and wanting to get home for the cake. I try hard to look appropriately pious, but it's an act.

In high school Jane's and my bedroom has off-white walls, deep rose carpet, and curtains and bedspreads of swirling hot pink and orange and purple. We have a green lava lamp. We wear mood rings and bright blue eye shadow up to our eyebrows. We have a mirror on the back of the bedroom door, and we use it to practice our makeup, to try to do something — anything! — with our hair, and to see our butts in our flowered bell bottoms and the too-short skirts we wear even though they're not particularly flattering. The carpet next to the mirror is permanently stained from the waterproof blue mascara I spilled, a stain that grows with each attempt at cleaning. I tried water and Windex. Once I got out fingernail polish remover, but Jane stopped me. Weeks before she had been giving herself a manicure, sitting cross-legged on the floor in her acetate nightgown, when she spilled a few drops of polish remover. She screamed as the yellow gown shriveled, leaving a hole the size of a hamster.

I come home with top grades, edit the school's literary magazine, land a part in the school play.

You want a medal or a chest to pin it on? my dad asks.

The driver's ed teacher sends me home with orders to change a tire.

I want a note on my desk Monday that's signed by your dad, he says.

At home I hold out the note.

Sign this, will you?

After you change the tire, Dad says.

Oh come on! You have to be kidding.

I stomp. I complain. I call Mom.

You'll thank me someday, he says.

The hell I will, I think.

Why couldn't he just sign the damn thing like the other parents? I slouch and grumble and act weaker than I am so he will help me loosen the lug nuts.

Jump on it, he says, fitting the tire iron onto the nut.

I jump, then jump again, loosening the air-wrenched lug nuts. I drag out the spare, then use my knee to hoist the flat into the trunk.

This is stupid, I say.

You want to drive?

I glare at him, and change the tire.

After school Jane and I go to gymnastics practice, where I compete in the vault and uneven parallel bars, an event that leaves red and purple bruises on my hip bones and bloody ripped calluses on my hands, even though I procrastinate during practices by taping them elaborately.

After practices and meets we run the half mile from the gym to the parking lot, our bodies wet with sweat, our breath making clouds in the winter air, trying to get to Dad's car before he drives off, irritated and impatient at us for dilly-dallying in the locker room.

During gymnastics meets and swimming tournaments he is in the stands, yelling, cheering, always pushing me to do better. At home he pulls me onto his lap to go over my report card, one grade at a time.

Why a B? he asks. You're a Latus. You

should get A's.

His breath is on my face as he looks at me.

Hold still, he says. He tips my head and pushes my nose to the side. He lines up his fingernails on either side of a pimple and squeezes. Just a couple more, he says. When he is done my eyes water and my face looks like I have chicken pox. I argue and struggle. I am fifteen and I just want to get away.

On bridge club nights Dad hugs my mom's friends, his hands sliding down to their backsides. In party pictures his arms are draped around women, his palms hovering over their breasts. When Mom passes him in the kitchen he gives a proprietary squeeze to her ass. I feel always as if he's about to do the same to mine.

I'm leaving home the minute I turn eighteen, I yell for perhaps the dozenth time. I am fifteen and sixteen and seventeen, and I am storming out of yet another room. I am always storming out of rooms. Also, I slam doors. I stomp and storm, ripping a path through adolescence, trampling as often as I can on my mother, a woman who is working full time and then coming home to make dinner for seven, who spends her weekends sorting our laundry into piles based on owner and drawer, the socks and underwear in one pile, shirts in another, pants in another. She asks only that we carry them upstairs and put them away.

Still I storm at her.

I hate this family. I hate my life. I hate myself. Everyone hates me. I wish I was dead. You wish I was dead.

I never go so far as to wish *she* was dead.

My siblings hide or duck or stay out of the way. I am the thunderstorm perpetually ripping through the house.

For a while they send me to see a shrink, but he looks almost entirely like my father, so I don't talk to him. He makes me feel stupid, like I don't have real problems. And his eyebrows are so long you could braid them. I quit after a few weeks.

At dinner we spar, stabbing always with the most hurtful jabs, the cutdowns that will make the others laugh. Someone always gets hurt. Someone always cries.

You could iron clothes on that chest, Dad says.

You're getting a little chubby there, Dad says.

How'd you screw up this time? Dad says.

At night I ask my mother, Do you love me? Do you love me do you love me do you love me? Please say you love me, even though I don't deserve to be loved.

Behind their door I hear my parents muttering, sometimes yelling. About jobs, about money, about who's doing what around here and how a certain someone better step up or else.

When I am seventeen I meet Kenny, a blind date for the holiday dance, arranged by my friend Mary as a favor when I can't get a date in my own school. Kenny is a dream. He is attentive and funny, affectionate and handsome.

On New Year's Eve his mother sends us upstairs with a bottle of cheap champagne and her blessing. Kenny's twin-sized mattress is on the floor, a TV set up at the foot, stereo speakers on either side. We sit on the mattress and watch the ball drop, the soundtrack from *The Nutcracker* throbbing from the stereo as we grope and fumble and giggle and finally figure out how to put tab A in slot B, as we joke, and then move together, briefly, until he is lying by my side spent and I am staring at the first of hundreds of ceilings wondering, This was the big deal? This was the thing I was never to do or even think about?

I am happy, because this means Kenny loves me. I know that sex equals love. Know it in my bones. I learned it from my parents and from TV and from song lyrics and from the Church. I know that when you have sex with someone it is a bond. I know, too, that it is what I have to offer. If I am putting out, Kenny will stay with me and I will have value.

Kenny actually does love me, with the puppyish devotion of an eighteen-year-old. He says it's because I am incredible, amazing, but I think it's because I give him sex. I will think that and think that and think that. With man after man. I will think that each wants me only for sex, that sex is what I have to offer.

During my junior year in high school my mom takes an administrative job in the Detroit area, two hours away. She rents an efficiency apartment there and only comes home on the weekends. It is the first time she has had a place of her own, without the caw and clatter of a houseful of children. My father stays at home with us, sitting most afternoons at the kitchen table, wearing the robe Mom made, playing solitaire.

Their careers are on opposite trajectories; the more Mom makes, the less Dad works. Still Mom spends every weekend cooking, freezing lasagna and chili and chop suey in family-sized Tupperware, each with a masking tape label.

We bigger girls take turns thawing them out, or making dinner from the recipe cards and groceries she leaves. Amy's job is to set the table. On my day I take out the recipe for spaghetti.

At 4 p.m. take one of the packages marked ground beef from the freezer, it reads. Put it in the green frying pan with the burner set to medium. Scrape off the meat as it browns. Add one chopped onion and one chopped green pepper. Let cook for 10 minutes, stirring often. Add one can tomato paste and two cans tomato sauce, plus the contents of one spaghetti spice baggy. Stir. Turn to low and let simmer while you boil water for the spaghetti. Make sure you cover it or it will splatter all over the stove.

One weekend Jane and Pat and Amy and I go to Mom's for a sleepover, piling four-to-the-bed on the pull-out couch, terrified by the nightly news, with its talk of car jackings, muggings, and murders.

Our small town rarely makes the news, and then only for football scores and community fluff pieces about pageants and plays and the Fourth of July parade.

Are you sure you're safe? we ask Mom.
She laughs.
I'm fine, she says.

My brother works at the golf course all summer, mowing, maintaining the greens, cleaning golf carts. My older sister works at McDonald's, serving up burgers and fries, wearing a paper cap and a perky smile. They are both paying their own tuition and living expenses at college.

I save up by working three nights a week at the Meridian Four Theatres, the multiplex at the mall five miles from home, where I wear black polyester pants and a red-and-black shirt stained with coconut oil. My arms are marked with half-moon burns from flipping the silver cylinder of popping corn, my face is pimply from the grease. Sometimes I work the door and let Amy and her friends in on my family pass. On my break I mix a tall cup of Dr Pepper and Coke and orange soda and walk through the mall, hoping to be noticed by the cute boys who work in the record store, even though I know I'm too young and pimply and plump.

On the first day of school each of us girls dresses in culottes and knee-highs and the new shoes we get each fall — one pair for school and one for gym. We burst out the front door with our lunches and book bags, rushing for the bus. On the front porch Dad kisses each of us good-bye.

You kiss like a fish, like your mother, he says to Jane. I'll teach you the right way to kiss.

He leans in, plants his lips on Jane's and moves them intimately, the way you do with a lover. She faints, sliding out of his arms onto the concrete. I think I will barf.

After that I stay away from him. I tell my friends to stay away, too, but he still pulls them down onto his lap when they come around, so I don't have them visit. Instead we go out in their cars.

I share a Ford Fairlane, bought used and driven by Steve before he left for college, then by Jane and me. The front seat is no longer firmly bolted to the floor, so it flips backward if you push too hard on the clutch, and the manual steering takes two hands and a lot of determination.

It runs, though, until my friend Mary and I are rushing to beat curfew, and I take a corner too fast onto a dirt road, spin out, and barrel into a tree.

The tree is small, like a sapling, and we are both fine, although my face has bashed into the steering wheel and a lump is forming on my forehead. I am more worried about the car and the curfew and the world of shit I'm about to be in than I am about my injuries. We sit there in the silence and the dust.

Shit, I say. I'm gonna get killed.

We sit there in the dark, listening to the crickets and the owls and the slowing ticking of the engine.

Mary has no curfew. Her parents are cool. They don't pin her down with rules or mealtimes or church. They don't check her grades or ask about her homework. She's prettier and more popular than I am, too. And she has a cool big sister who has sex right in their parents' house.

For this rare moment, though, I'm grateful for my own family's rules, because I know someone will come looking for me. My dad will be angry and I'll be grounded for the rest of my natural life, but at least I won't be sitting here on the side of a dirt road in the dark.

My door makes a metal-on-metal screech as I open it. The grill is in pieces, the hood is accordioned, and one headlight aims at the treetops. Mary and I look at each other. We are screwed. It's dark and no one is going to pass by for hours, we just know it.

What should we do? Mary asks.

I look around. I can't see the lights from any house, and the road doesn't get much traffic.

I have no idea, I say. Maybe my dad will come looking for us.

And would that be a good thing or a bad thing? Mary asks.

I don't know how to answer. It would be good because I need my daddy right now, need someone to look at the car and hug me and tell me that everything will be okay, that he's glad I didn't get hurt, that we can fix the car, it's no big deal, that's why they call them accidents, right?

It would be bad, though, because he's not going to hug me and make sure I'm okay. He's going to rage about the car and about how I'm irresponsible and about how he should never have let me drive it and you can lay bets on one thing, young lady, you will not be driving again any time soon. No sirreeBob.

Good question, I say to Mary.

We sit on the trunk and wait.

It takes my dad less than half an hour to find us, and he is furious. He is grateful that no one was hurt, sure, but the fear he felt when I didn't get home on time has only amplified his anger over the missed curfew and the totaled car.

I'm sorry, I say.

We'll talk about it when we get home, he answers, followed by a tirade about irresponsibility and carelessness and driving like an idiot and do I think money grows on trees?

He has me get back into the car and try to back it up, but it can't even limp home.

Get out, he says, then gets in himself and drops it into gear. Still it won't move.

Leave it, he finally says. We'll deal with it in the morning.

Mary and I climb sheepishly into the backseat of Dad's station wagon. When we get home I stomp to my room.

Later that year I move downstairs to the basement. When Steve left for college my parents had given his room to Jane and set up a temporary room for him downstairs, with a bed and a square of carpet and curtains for privacy. That's where he stayed when he came home on school breaks and summer vacations, but he is rarely home now, so I move down there, putting as much space as I can between myself and my parents. At night Amy comes down and sits at the foot of my bed. She is twelve, I am seventeen.

I don't want you to live down here, she says. Everyone who moves down here leaves.

She has tears in her eyes.

I know, hon, I say. I know. And I'm sorry. But I have to.

She lies sideways across the bed, lanky and lean. I tangle my fingers in her curls.

Why do you want to stay down here, so far from me? she asks.

I don't know how to answer. Because I can't stand my parents, because I don't want to hear the tinkle of ice in their glasses, because the idea of staying near my dad makes me crazy, because every time he touches me I get the creepy crawlies. I don't say these things to Amy, though. Not all of them. I tell her that I hate my parents, but she knows that. I've been shouting it out loud for years. I tell her that I just need my space, that when she's my age she'll understand.

Night after night, she sprawls across my bed and we talk about her classmates and her classes and a movie she saw, about a boy she has a crush on who doesn't know she exists, about an argument with my boss and a friend who may be pregnant, about our sisters and our friends and whatever else comes to mind.

For a while Amy wears her hair in an Afro,

both as social protest — we both think integration is long overdue — and because her hair is so thick and full and curly that her other choice is tight ringlets. We talk about abortion and women's liberation and how stupid it is that *Charlie's Angels* can run in heels when we can barely walk. Still, at least they're wielding the guns and kicking ass instead of relying on some man.

She is mad at Dad for telling her — again — that she's bad at math, that she couldn't find her way out of a paper bag with a map.

Ignore him, I say. He says the same to all of us.

Except with me (I think but do not say) he's right. I am bad at math. The numbers don't line up, the facts don't stay memorized, I am stupid when it comes to numbers.

It is fall 1977, a few weeks before my eighteenth birthday. I am grounded. Again. But a group of my friends from work has parked in the lot next door to serenade me. They sit on the hood of the oldest boy's car. One is playing a guitar and they all are singing. I sit on the end of the front porch and call to them through the hedge. Thank you for this, I say. My parents are so mean.

Never mind that I am grounded for missing curfew, for driving like an idiot. My parents are wrong. They are unreasonable. The other kids agree.

We are laughing and singing. I see their faces drop before I hear the front door slap shut.

You kids get out of here, my father yells.

He is in his robe, which has blown open to reveal his underwear. I run past him, through the door and down to my room, making sure each door slams as loudly as possible. I will never be able to face these people again.

Later I storm up from my room for a screaming match with my mother. She is in the dark-paneled family room, the furniture in shades of gold and olive green. She is on the couch. Steve, who is home from college, is sprawled out on the floor. My father is in his recliner next to the fire. His cigar smells of Saturdays and football.

The minute I turn eighteen I'm leaving, I yell yet again.

You probably should stop saying that or you'll have to do it, Steve says. He is right. It is put up or shut up time.

Within days after turning eighteen I storm out the door for good.

I am halfway through my senior year of

high school. It is winter. I spend two nights with the Mormon family down the street. They are the strongest family I've ever seen. They love each other. I buy a Book of Mormon, read their tracts. I want to become Mormon.

I spend a few days with my former gym teacher, the woman who was Jane's Girl Scout troop leader, who showed me how to lace up her knee-high leather boots with one hand. I try to thank her by cooking a spaghetti dinner, but I burn the onions.

I am a failure, I say.

Everybody burns onions sometimes, she says.

I sleep on couches, in guest rooms, carrying my toothbrush and clothes to school in a plastic bag. My friends' parents tolerate my ranting, my rage. They feed me and give me rides, even as I tell family secrets.

Usually I leave campus at lunch and ride with my friends, Mary and Sandy and Debbie, down to McDonald's, where I eat a fried cherry pie and a chocolate shake. We aren't always prompt about getting back, and Mr. DuByne, my physics teacher, is prepared. Over the years he has posted a list of excuses students have given for being tardy — I missed my bus, my mom's car wouldn't start, I had to stay late at my last class, I was locked in my locker — so all I have to do as I slide into my seat is give a number.

Number 27, I say, and DuByne walks slowly to the list.

You got held up by a car accident? he reads.

I nod, and he smiles.

Not good enough, Latus.

He walks to his grade book and makes a mark.

Yeah, well, I think, you don't have a listing on there for "I had to work last night and then had to hitchhike in this morning," or "I'm so tired I think I have narcolepsy," or "It rained last night and some jerk drove through the puddle on the corner and doused me."

I don't say anything, because I don't want any more attention. I just want to be normal.

Every few days I fall asleep in his class, drowsy from long hours and a post-junk-food drop in blood sugar.

Latus, DuByne yells, wake up!

I jerk upright, a string of drool running from my notebook to my face. He shakes his head.

Stay after, he says.

When the bell rings I stand by his desk.

You need to straighten up, he says. I don't know what's going on with you, but your behavior is unacceptable.

I look down, afraid I'll cry.

Sorry, I mumble, I'll do better.

I make it into a bathroom stall before the tears come.

Later he stops me in the hall.

I hear you're having some problems, he says. I didn't know or I'd've gone easier on you.

That's okay, I say.

There is an awkward pause, but I don't say anything else.

You do need to stay awake, though.

I know.

Word gets around; Mr. McIntosh asks if I need anything, and the gym teacher asks if I'm okay.

It takes me a few weeks to find an apartment cheap enough to afford with my part-time jobs. My parents allow me to take my own furniture — a twin bed, a desk, some old pans and silverware. Friends come to help me carry things out. My mother cries. My dad whistles and acts like nothing is happening. I slam around. I am terrified.

Don't go, Amy says.

I have to, I say.

We lean into each other, hold on tight. We

are both crying.

Mom turns on Dad. The way you keep picking on Amy and Pat, she says, they'll move out, too.

I am going to share an apartment with a classmate from the other side of the tracks. I don't know why she is moving out, but her mother isn't mad. She gives us an old couch and a dinette set, and we move into a one-bedroom garden apartment, the view out the window of car tires and cat shit and strangers' feet. We buy a shower curtain, go to garage sales for cups and plates and bowls.

I take a second job selling shoes at Stride Rite, where I pretend to care about the development of children's feet. I don't know anything about fitting shoes, yet people are paying extra to have their precious children's feet measured by experts. I learn the company line, about how important it is to buy our expensive shoes so that the kids' feet will grow strong and healthy. It is the foot version of giving your child every advantage in life. Too often I am straddling my stool, learning forward to tie a hard-soled hightop on a toddler, and the kid kicks me in the head. The parents laugh. I don't think it's funny.

On my first day a co-worker sends me on

an errand. Shoot, she says, we got in too much inventory. Can you go to the other shoe stores and ask for a shelf stretcher? I head out, proud of my official duties. At the first store, the teenage boy laughs at me. I have been had.

My apartment is one town away from my school. I am out of district, so I go to the principal. I have moved out, I say. I cannot bear to live with my parents anymore, but I want to do the right thing and pay tuition if I have to. He looks at my jutted chin and responds respectfully, although I think he wants to laugh. Let me think about it, he says. The next day I'm called to the office. Since my parents pay taxes in the district, he says, he is only going to charge me a dollar. I feel weepy and proud. I pull my wallet out of my purse, the wallet that came with a gleaming-toothed photo of Tony Curtis, and fish out a dollar, lay it on his desk. I am an adult.

Some mornings Mary picks me up. Other days I walk or hitchhike the five miles. For dinner I eat Campbell's cream of tomato soup. I float popcorn in it to make it more filling. Night after night I eat it while I do my homework in my dim, cold basement apartment. The closest I come to hearing rain on the roof is the sink dripping, and the closest thing to thunder is the pounding of the bass of the stereo in the apartment upstairs.

On the first Sunday I go home to do my laundry and eat dinner. No, my dad says. If you're out, you're out. Either you're a part of this family or you're not, and if you're not, you don't get to just come here and eat and use the house. No.

I stomp out, slamming the door. Who does he think he is? How can he throw me out on the street? How can my mother let him?

Dad bans my brother and sisters from talking to me. Amy is in sixth grade, in a building half a mile away across open sports fields. Every day the bus stops and disgorges at the high school, then makes a big looping turn back to the junior high. One day Amy, who is spelling her name A-m-i-e now, in defiance of our parents, jumps off. She runs into the high school and shoves a rumpled paper bag into my favorite teacher's mailbox, then runs the half-mile path to her first class.

When I walk into AP English Mrs. Lee hands me the bag. Inside is an eight-inch-long fluorescent pink beanbag in the shape of lips. They're soft and fuzzy, made of velour. In marker she has written, "To Janine. I love you no matter where you are.

Amie." I picture her down in the basement, cutting with pinking sheers and sewing on the ancient Singer. I run to the bathroom where I can cry in private. I miss her so badly, and she was so brave to risk dropping them off. I sob. I am hungry. I am tired. I don't know if I can bear my banishment. I don't know if I can graduate.

Every day I work at at least one job. Every day I eat tomato soup with popcorn, or open-faced tuna sandwiches with cheese broiled on top.

Ride home? I ask Mary as we walk down the hall, lockers clanging around us.

Sure, she says. I think. We'll talk at lunch.

I lean my forehead against my locker and spin the combination. On top of my algebra book is an envelope.

I look around. It has been a long time since a boy put a note in my locker, and junior high since I got one from a girl, threatening vengeance or serving as liaison for some boy with a crush.

When I turn it over, though, I see my name written in my mother's perfect Peterson penmanship. I look around again. If Mom put it here it means she knows which locker is mine, and she bothered to sneak in and tuck the envelope through the vent. If she didn't, then she got a teacher to do it, which means I have an ally.

I stand there for a minute, the envelope unopened. I look down the hall toward Mary's locker, but she's gone. The whole hallway is emptying, in fact, as students are siphoned into classrooms. I'm going to be late for algebra if I don't hurry. But I can't wait.

I love you, the letter reads. You will always have a home when you need it.

I close my eyes and lean against the locker. When the tardy bell rings I jump, startled, then grab my book and run down the hall.

On weekends my roommate and I go out. The drinking age is briefly eighteen, so we are free to wander from bar to bar, unsupervised, without curfew.

One night we go downtown to a disco called the Green Door. We show our IDs to the bouncer and mince over to a booth, where we settle our purses and tug at the hems of our miniskirts, push back our hair, inspect each other's teeth for lipstick. The waitress brings us each a slim frosted glass — a Tom Collins for her, a Sloe Screw for me, just because it feels nasty to place the order. We take speculative, early-evening sips and look around.

There are prospects, but no one approaching yet, so together we take to the floor, shimmying and twirling, doing the bump, pretending that we don't know we're being watched, that we are in fact advertising our wares.

Look down, Beth yells.

I do, then look at her in panic. The black light is making my white bra shine through my dark sweater. I grab her hand and drag her toward the bathroom.

We debate our options. Braless is better, we decide, so I unhook it, pull one strap through a sleeve, the whole thing then produced like a magician's handkerchief through the other. I roll it into a tight ball and fold it into my fist, hiding it until we can get back to our table, where I will cram it into my purse, where men already are hovering, waiting to ask us to dance.

The song is Abba's "Dancing Queen" and Beth and I sing full voiced, young and sweet, barely seventeen. Or at least, closer to seventeen than the polyester-clad men jerking and shaking awkwardly, shuffling their feet step touch step touch in front of us. We shimmy low, shimmy high, not touching them but implying we might. Between dances we sip our drinks and suck on the cherries, the bar patrons' smoke swirling in an ever-lowering cloud. Soon we will disappear.

An hour later, or hours, I leave, sliding on the ice in my platform shoes, heading out to my Pinto. Beth is staying. She'll get a ride home later. She'll be fine, she assures me.

The Pinto, not always reliable, fires up. I pound the steering wheel to the beat of the radio, which is blasting against the equal blast of the heater. I turn the rearview mirror, sing into it. Nod my head to the beat. I do not see anyone behind me.

My parking spot at the apartment is open. I downshift, twirl the wheel with one finger, skid to a stop on the snow. I hop out, still singing, and skip down the stairs to my tireview apartment. I prop the screen door open with my hip as I unlock the door.

I feel the screen door lifted away and I turn, smiling, expecting Beth. It is a man. A polyestered man. Short, paunchy, losing his hair, smelling of smoke and bourbon. He reaches past me and shoves the door open. I don't know whether to run away or run into the apartment and slam the door. I think too much. He shoves me backward, and I trip over the threshold and fall on my butt.

There are words, but they don't register. He steps toward me and I crabwalk backward, until my neck is against the sharp Formica edge of our coffee table, a display table salvaged from the children's shoe store where I work. Round. A donut.

Get up, he says. I am paralyzed. He puts his loafer on my thigh, high on my inner thigh, and steps down. I cry out.

Get up, he says. You who think you're so cute. Get up.

I get up. He pushes me backward, hard. I fall onto the table, try to roll off, to scramble. He lunges for me, pins me. Bites me hard on the shoulder.

I am smothering under him, trying to scream. He grips my wrists, slams his knee up between my legs.

Take off your clothes, he says into my neck.

No, I say. No no no.

I struggle, and he presses harder into me, my back ripping against the hard edges of the table with every move.

He lets go of my wrist long enough to grab the front of my sweater and tear. It rips, and my chest is exposed. I start to cry.

Please, I say. Please no.

He pulls up my skirt, unzips his pants, yanks off my underpants. I am sobbing. My back is bleeding. I kick at him, claw with my hands. He takes a leg in each hand and pulls them wide apart, then plunges into me. Over and over, me crying and slapping at him, and then finally giving up. There is no point in fighting. Better to just lie still, get it over with.

He bellows, and finally the pounding stops. He pulls out, stands over me as he zips his pants.

I slide off the table and curl into a ball on the floor, between the table and our hand-me-down couch. I don't hear whatever he says, only watch with gratitude as he leaves.

It is perhaps an hour later when Beth comes home and finds me there, sobbing, spent, bleeding.

She stares, then comes to me and tries to gather me into her arms, even though I am naked and bleeding and she is only eighteen.

Is he gone? she asks. She doesn't ask who or how — that will come in the morning and the morning after and the days and weeks that we worry that he'll be back.

Instead she leads me to the tub and softly washes my back, then gently dabs at each stripped spot with the wand from the mer-thiolate, the pink acrid drops stinging so fiercely that I want to turn on her, take my anger and helplessness and horror out on her.

You look like you've gone up against a

cheese grater, she says. And the cheese grater won.

I smile as best I can.

We agree never to go to the Green Door again, to stick together if we go out, to take care of each other.

For weeks our eyes lock every time we hear the song, "She was a dancing queen, young and sweet, only seventeen."

It will be more than a decade before I tell anyone else.

CHAPTER 4

A few months later I graduate with honors and pride, and a certain amount of screw you. My parents throw an open house to celebrate, which my mother coordinates long distance, dashing home to assemble burgers and buns and chips, and to order a cake scrolled with icing that spells "Congratulations Janine!" I pose with a rotating constellation of grandparents, cousins, and siblings, smiling and proud in my mortar-board.

I feel awkward, though, teetering between guest and family member. When the time comes for the inevitable photo with my parents I force myself to smile, even though having my dad's hand squeezing my waist feels creepy.

When Amy's turn comes I put the mortar-board on her head and she beams, her bird legs in pretend ballerina poses, her curls ruffled by the wind. I grin in return. It feels good to have my baby sister look up to me.

Then I go home to my little apartment. Living on my own — so defiant and roman-tic at first — has already lost its charm, with high school over and the rest of my life looming. Plus, every time I walk into my apartment I pass the coffee table. One day I roll it up the steps and across the parking lot and to the Dumpster. When I drive past the next morning, it's gone.

We're selling the house, my mom tells me a few months later.

They're moving to Brighton, a bedroom town halfway between their jobs. Each of them will commute an hour in the morning and an hour at night, in opposite directions, but at least this way they'll be home together in the evenings rather than just on weekends. Pat will move into an apartment so she can finish high school with her class, and Amy will go to school in the new town.

I am a little bit envious of her fresh start — the chance to go through school as an individual and not as someone's younger sister. Amy is less excited.

I can imagine how she feels. When we moved when I was little, I always felt like I was on the outside of a scaffolding built of friendships and cliques and shared history. I'd win at Four Square and raise my hand too often in class, but my eagerness to belong got me beaten up on the playground. Now here Amy was doing it in high school. In high school in a new town with the flying-buttress supports of her siblings gone. I can only imagine.

Amy is thirteen and scrawny when she leaves. Soon, though, she billows into puberty, her breasts and hips swelling so quickly that Mom asks the doctor to check her for thyroid problems.

She and I have the same face, the same height, yet somehow she develops a matronly bosom and fleshed-out hips, while I have neither.

Eat less, I say.

You don't understand, she answers.

■ ■ ■ ■

I save my money for months and buy a green Dodge Dart with a bashed-in left rear quarter panel. It smells like baked dust, but it is clean and reliable, its bench seat wide and smooth. The family that sold it to me took my $500 and went out to dinner.

I name it Irma.

When its starter goes out at a 7-Eleven I have a friend take me to the junk yard to get another. I lie down in the parking lot with my garage sale wrenches and change it myself. I change flat tires by the side of the road, and walk miles carrying gas cans until I learn to budget my money and my fuel. I feel competent and like an idiot, like everything is too hard.

Things between Mom and Dad deteriorate. Dad lives at least part of the time in the family camper, which he has set up in the parking lot behind his office, within a few miles of my apartment. Mom and Amy are still in the house in Brighton. Mom is paying for it — it and everything else — and she's sick of it.

You make the house payments, she says to Dad. It's your house, too.

One day she comes home from work to find a notice tacked to the front door. It's signed by the sheriff. This house to be sold at auction. For nonpayment of mortgage.

Within months Mom and Amy move to an apartment in Southfield, a Detroit suburb with a school full of princesses with pert figures and expensive clothes. Amy doesn't fit in and Mom can do little to comfort her, pitching as she is between the scratch and claw and travel of her executive position and the relentlessness of being a single mother. Dad sues to keep Amy with him, saying Mom cares more about her career than she does about her children. Mom hires a lawyer. Dad represents himself. He thunders at the judge, jabs his finger toward Mom.

Mom wins.

I am mostly oblivious to the drama. I do well on the college entrance exams and get offers of full-ride scholarships all over the country. Each insists that all freshmen live in dorms, though, and I refuse. I have lived without supervision just long enough to chafe at the idea of dorm mothers or resident hall advisors or whatever they're called, so instead of sharing a bathroom and stories and notes and midnight gab sessions with girls my own age, I rent a tiny one-bedroom apartment and share my stories with my boyfriend of six months. I take a full load of classes at the community college and work full-time at a family restaurant, where my boyfriend and I joke about our nearly plastic wash-and-wear uniforms and compete to see who can carry more plates at a time.

We are just back from a date to the circus one night when the phone rings. It's my mom.

Your dad and I are getting a divorce, she says.

I am still holding my rabbit fur monkey-on-a-stick, and I bounce it as we talk.

You okay? I ask.

I want details. I want to know why and how they decided and whether there was a fight and how she got up the guts, but I don't ask.

Instead I say, It's about time.

She doesn't answer.

That summer Dad takes Amy to Switzerland on a trip he won in a contest put on by one of his insurance companies, for selling the most of a certain kind of policy. Amy is giddy with excitement. She's going to travel! See the world! Fly on airplanes and eat exotic foods and see things she's never seen! Never mind that Dad isn't paying any of Amy's living expenses and that he has forgotten or ignored nearly all of his children's birthdays and Christmases and milestones.

It is a week, she says, that changes her life. It is there she meets Dick, an insurance agent who lives in California. They write back and forth, first formally, then personally, then seductively.

Meanwhile I move to a dusty-smelling room with a clanking steam radiator in a boardinghouse of women at least ten years my senior. It is cheaper and closer to school. Every day and every night I come and go, occasionally warming something up in the kitchen, but mostly hiding out in my room in the interludes between work and school.

One day a woman is raped in a boardinghouse nearby. The victim reports it to the police and it makes the news. They don't identify her, they only say she is my age and lives in my neighborhood. My family calls in a panic.

Are you okay? they ask.

It wasn't me, I say.

I find their concern ironic and overdue. Still, I say nothing about what happened to me.

I work on the school newspaper, take journalism classes, study rocks and minerals and the geography of the United States, and plan my next move, which will be as far away as I can manage. I want to write — I know that. I have been writing since I was in the first grade. Beyond that, I have no plan. I don't know where to go or what I want to do with my writing or how I want to finish my education or how, most of all, I'm going to pay for it all. Yes, I have scholarships, but I still have to come up with rent and lights and heat and food. And I have to find a place to wash my waitressing uniform and I have to find a parking space on campus and I have to figure out what my teachers want and how I can eat enough and at the right times so my stomach doesn't growl in class or I don't fall asleep, my head down on the desk, my notes smeared with drool.

It's so cool that you have your own place, Amy says. I wish I did.

I barely talk with my classmates. They are like the ones in high school — calm and happy and confident. They have the right cars and the right clothes and the right answers.

I stick instead to the losers like me, the outcasts, the ones who are working as hard as they can. It eludes me that most people don't go to any kind of college, so for me to be a loser and a miscreant is a construct, a story I tell myself.

Regardless, I know I'm not okay. I know because I've been told over and over again, by my father mostly, that my hips are too wide, my chest too flat, my feet too big, my laugh too stupid. My dad was right; my body is only good for one thing. I prove him right over and over. With the photographer at the newspaper, the bartender at work. They sleep with me, so they must find something about me that's worthy. I secretly think it's because I'm smart. Or I think I'm smart. But then I think that people who aren't smart aren't smart enough to know that they're not smart, so maybe I'm not smart, although the teachers and the grades and the scholarships would suggest that I am. Still, I must not be, because here I am eating tomato soup and popcorn and living in a mildewed house far from my suburban roots with crotchety strangers and old maids and people who can't do better than to live in a ratty boardinghouse downtown.

When I can't stand it anymore I run to my grandparents' place, a bungalow in the crook of a blueberry farm. It is my sanctuary. I lie on the couch and even though I'm almost twenty, my mom's mom billows a turquoise cloud of a comforter over me and waits as it settles. I lie there listening to the nightly call of the cuckoo clock and the long moan of passing trains, my grandmother's hand softly stroking my hair for what feels like hours as I try to sleep. In the morning the silk quilt is puddled on the floor. I get up and pour a bowl of cornflakes and carry it out the back door. I top it with the juiciest of the blueberries, fresh from the field.

I sleep and eat and take comfort for two days and then climb back into my Pinto. Gramma slips an extra twenty dollars into my pocket when Grandpa isn't looking, and they both smile and wave until I can no longer see them in my rearview mirror.

I get another call from my mom. She has been headhunted, recruited away to a stupendous job, but it means she has to move to Atlanta, far far away, in the South, a part of the country we have held in contempt.

You going to get a drawl? I ask.

She laughs.

What does Amy think? I ask.

She's fine, Mom says.

Later I talk with Amy. She is grateful to get away from the Southfield snobs, but mad that Mom has unilaterally decided, without asking.

Kids don't get to vote, I say. Not even fifteen-year-olds.

But that only makes her madder. She feels powerless because she is.

At the new school Amy is surrounded by gum-cracking Southerners with wasp waists and big hair. She cannot ever fit in. She is the Yankee.

She joins the newspaper, compensating for her otherness with wit and irony, and secret journaling.

It is long distance, so Amy and I don't talk often. When we do, though, it is most often about writing and feeling lonely and how the popular kids make fun of her. She has two good friends. Robin is the daughter of a single mom who lives across the street. Kris is Amy's co-editor at the newspaper, who is shunned by the in crowd for being tall and skinny. Kris lives with her divorced father who travels as much as Mom, so she understands. Together they pull pranks and sneak cans of Budweiser and conspire about their parents.

One day Dick, the California insurance agent Amy met in Switzerland, flies to Atlanta. Amy meets him, and they head straight from the airport to a motel, where they kiss and fondle and play. Then he ties her hands and legs to the bed frame. It isn't until afterward that she tells him she was a virgin.

And then we started all over, she says. It was wonderful.

It was your first time and he tied you down?

He didn't know.

Still.

They stay in touch for a month or two. Then he fades away.

Meanwhile, I'm trying to figure out what I'm going to do after I finish my two years at the community college.

The smartest of my fellow students, a man with Einstein hair and one eye that drifts randomly, tells me that the Missouri School of Journalism is the best in the United States, so I apply and am accepted. Now I know where I'm going next. Halfway across the country, to the middle of nowhere.

But my lease in Michigan ends in July and my one in Missouri doesn't start until August, so I move to Atlanta to stay with Mom and Amy for a month. Each day I walk through the thick heat to my job at a bar frequented by underage drinkers and rugby teams. Each night Amy and I stay up late, talking still and again about boys and politics and how we each hate our hair.

She looks in the mirror, turns this way and that.

Do you think I'm fat? she asks.

I pause.

Do you? I ask.

I think I'm going to go on a diet.

Her eyes are worried, and I feel sad.

What about exercise? I say. It's more fun than dieting.

She looks at me and scowls.

For you, maybe.

I change the subject.

For the rest of my visit I try not to open chips or pop popcorn in front of Amy, and I try not to notice when she does. We both leave crusty dishes on the counter and wet towels on the floor. We drive Mom nuts.

Mom, meanwhile, is putting on a suit and carrying a briefcase, showing up each day for her corporate job. Sometimes in the evenings her boyfriend comes by. He is an ugly man whose hugs are like my dad's; too long and too tight, underlain with the sensation that he's copping a feel.

By the time I leave for Missouri we're all ready for me to go. I fly from Atlanta to St. Louis on an airliner, then from St. Louis to Columbia on a puddle jumper that follows Highway 70, straight and unbroken, and then banks so hard it feels like we will cartwheel. Out the window I see fields and a winding brown river. The fields go on and on. Whatever is growing in them is crinkling and curling around the edges.

It has been over one hundred degrees for more than twenty days now, I hear, and everything is desiccated. The grass is brittle, the leaves on the trees are thick and beige with dust. I beg a ride from a grad student who is being picked up by another grad student, who is driving a battered Ford. Buzzards circle over the car as we pass between exposed bluffs. It feels like the Wild West, and it smells like baked cedar, like my grandmother's attic in mid-August.

Where I am from there are pine trees, and the water is glacial and clear, the lake bottoms sandy. Here the evergreens are cedar and the water is river runoff, brown and thick and alarmingly scarce.

I have $500 in my bank account, no job and no friends.

The grad students drop me off at my boardinghouse and wave as they rattle away. The house looks like a slightly listing cake, vanilla on the bottom layer and chocolate on top. There are thirteen women living in thirteen bedrooms, with a shared kitchen and three baths. One wall in an upstairs bathroom doesn't meet the floor, so when the toilet overflows it drips down into the kitchen.

My room is in the front on the second floor. It is tiny and hot. Suffocatingly hot. My dresser and desk are against the wall on the left, but the bottom drawers don't open because they are flush against the edge of my twin bed. I must sit on the bed to use the desk, climb over the bed to get to my closet, move the bed to get anything out of the lower drawers, but there's nowhere to move the bed to, so those drawers are empty.

At night I lay sprawled, my window fan shoving the stifling air, the inside of my nose and the outside of my lips cracked from the heat and dryness.

The rent is $100 a month, plus my share of the utilities, which we will squabble over each time a bill arrives. The house manager, Lee Ann, lives in the best room downstairs. She has witchlike black hair and flea bites on her legs. She scares me. In a back bedroom is a girl from British Guiana. She watches the squirrels in the backyard and laughs. To her they are like monkeys.

I move in and then walk the streets asking everyone I see about a job. I am running out of money fast. The students aren't back, the town is dirty and dry and unbearably obsessively hot. I can think of nothing except how tired and suffocated I feel. I want to dive off a building, but the tallest — the Tiger Hotel — isn't big enough. Not if I want to die, which I do, because the heat is obsessively suffocatingly stiflingly overwhelmingly hot.

My dad calls. He has had his marriage annulled. After twenty-four years and six children. He is proud of himself.

Gosh, Dad, I say. Doesn't this make us illegitimate?

You're all little bastards anyway. He laughs.

Someone tells me the Heidelberg is hiring. It is a dark bar and restaurant straight across from the university, a hangout for future lawyers, journalists, and doctors, where the homemade soup of the day comes straight out of a can and the cheese for the nachos is so yellow it looks plastic. The walls are soaked in cigarette smoke and the tables are heavy and scarred, but it is air-conditioned and the money is good. I apply and get hired. Each of us waitresses can carry two or three pitchers in one hand and five or six mugs in the other. We are stalwart and sturdy, laughing off advances and drunken stupidity. On football Saturdays we are each assigned a busboy, who clears a path through the crowd like a lineman.

The waitresses become my friends, my lifeline in the new town. We sit at the bar after our shifts, nursing employee-discounted beers. A couple of times I go out with one of the cooks, a curly-haired man whose flirting makes work more fun. When customers ask me out, I tell them I'm dating someone, even though I'm mostly not.

Our boss lumbers around, herding us, evaluating us, but mostly just sitting at the bar with the regulars. One day he hands me a cigar tube.

In case you don't get any tonight, he says, smirking.

I look at him. It takes me until late in the evening to get the phallic joke.

My journalism classes are full of bow heads who know exactly what they want and how to get it. They also have trust funds. At least, I think they have trust funds. They have something, because they're always wearing new clothes and chanting sorority rush songs and having their nails done. They say things like, I'm going to have to call Daddy and get more money if we're going to the lake this weekend. And then they giggle.

I barely speak to them. Instead I dash to work or back to my tiny room to study. I keep myself apart, because I feel both inferior and superior. Inferior because I don't have their ease or their presumption or their money. Superior because I know how to pay utility bills and cook spaghetti and carry five plates of hot food up my arm, keeping my other hand free for a pitcher or two more plates, whatever the customers need. Being self-sufficient is better than being taken care of.

I don't realize that I am okay. Normal. Attractive. Because inside I am walking on marbles, unable to believe in solid footing, so that flailing and scrambling is the only option. I am never ever calm. Not inside. Never calm inside. I think again about diving off the Tiger, but then I think that if I do that I can never make my parents proud, never prove them wrong.

I take the school's weed-out class, the prerequisite you have to pass to get into any of the good classes, and it is grueling. I write deadline stories on a manual typewriter, pounding the keys and complaining loudly to the teacher that the assignments are unreasonable. They are too much, too hard. The equipment is obsolete. I get a C.

I don't get C's, I tell the professor.

You just did, she said. And you earned it.

I toggle between humiliation and outrage.

Look on the bright side, she continues. A C is average. Being average among some of the best journalism students in the country isn't such a bad thing.

I walk out along the long halls, out into the sunshine, muttering about dropping out of college. Instead I trudge across the street to work, where I lean on the bar and complain to Jan, a friend who has been waiting tables and going to grad school for most of a decade.

I'm going hiking on the Buffalo with a bunch of people next weekend, she says. Come with us.

The group will be led by some profs from the horticulture department.

I'm bringing Bill, a guy I met a few weeks ago, she says. You can bring someone, too.

Count me in, I say. I need a break from the smoke and the deadlines and the customers and professors who think I have nothing to do but step and fetch for them. And I can bring my friend, the cook.

The Buffalo River is gorgeous, surrounded by hidden canyons. We hike along bluff trails, high above the river, then work our way down crevasses to the water, where we skinny-dip and build sweat lodges that we sit in until we're slick with sweat. Then we roll out our sleeping bags to sleep under the stars.

Somewhere along the way I become enthralled by Bill, a kind and gentle man who has eyes that crinkle at the corners when he smiles. He thinks I am brilliant and funny, even though he's there with Jan, who is willowy and implausibly busty and blond. At the end of the trip we exchange phone numbers, and within days we are dating, walking hand-in-hand through the midnight streets to his job entering data for one of the big banks, and sleeping cupped against each other in my twin bed.

After a few months we move in together. I change my major to horticulture and spend my time playing in the soil, my days paced to the rotating seasons of poinsettias, petunias, and impatiens. In the evening I can tomatoes straight from our garden, and make pickles and bread and egg noodles. At night we pile into bed with our two dogs. We are euphoric.

One day my dad calls. He is coming through town and would like to visit. Bill has to work, but we agree that he will meet Dad and me later at the Heidelberg.

Relax, he says, and kisses me. I'll be there.

It'll be fine.

I don't think it will be fine, but I don't know how to explain it to Bill. My dad does not feel me up with his hands, but he does with his eyes. And he tells me I have sexy legs. The parts of me that aren't too wide or too flat or too big are sexy. And that's good, because that's what women are for, in my dad's mind.

I try to explain it to Bill, but it's too amorphous, too insidious.

I wave as he drives off to work, and then look around the house. What will Dad criticize first, my hair or the cleanliness of my place? I tidy the house and take a shower, then put on my baggiest jeans and a sweatshirt.

That evening I take Dad to the Heidelberg as planned.

How are you, girl? Jan asks as she comes to take our order. What are you doing here on your day off?

Slumming, I say. Jan, this is my dad. Dad, this is my friend Jan.

Pleasure meeting you, Dad says, running his eyes over her slim, busty body.

A pitcher of Bud, please, I say. And three glasses.

One for your imaginary friend? Jan asks.

Bill's joining us when he's done with

work, I say.

Jan has been nonchalant — even cheerful — about Bill splitting with her and coming to me. I guess when you look like her you don't worry that there won't be other options. I worry.

Which is not to say that there is anything wrong with Bill. He is motivated and smart and loving. If there's anything wrong with him it is that he is too steady, too good.

Wow, Jan says, smiling. Bringing him to meet the folks already! I'm impressed.

She's kidding, I say to Dad, as Jan walks to the bar.

Tell me about him, Dad says.

Well, he's from Illinois, studying to be a banker. . . .

Oooh, a rich kid, Dad says. Good plan!

He is really into music, I continue, and we have a good time together.

I'll bet you do, Dad says. Good-looking girl like you.

Jan comes back with our beer before I can come up with a response. As she reaches to set it on the table, Dad grabs her wrist and kisses up her arm from her hand to her elbow before she can yank it away.

Dad! I say. Then, I'm so sorry, Jan.

Jan wipes her arm on her apron and glares at Dad before she walks away.

What the hell are you doing?! I ask. I work here. She's my *friend!*

Oh, relax, Dad says. She expects stuff like that if she works in a place like this. Besides, she looks like a gal who can handle herself.

I stand up and stalk back to the kitchen to find Jan.

I am so sorry, I say.

Jan wraps her arms around me. No, she says. I'm sorry. He's not my dad.

I slump against her, grateful for the support. I am surprised and embarrassed to have to wipe tears from my eyes.

When I get back to the table my dad has poured beer for both of us, flagged down a passing busboy to clean up the puddle he has made, and downed half of his glass.

Tell me three words that mean small, he says.

What?

Three words, he repeats, that mean small.

I have no idea, I say. What three words mean small?

He pauses.

Is . . . , he says,

it . . .

in?

He smiles, pleased with himself. I am ashamed.

When Bill arrives I am relieved, even

though I'm afraid Dad will say something embarrassing. The men shake hands and Bill sits down. I slide over. I want to be as close as possible to this man, to his crinkled smile, his warm hands, his steady normality.

At home again I show Dad where he'll sleep, where he can find the bathroom and clean washcloths and towels. I show him the refrigerator and where Bill and I will be.

So you're sleeping with my daughter, he says to Bill.

Bill looks puzzled.

Come on, Dad, you know we live together, I say.

I just want to know if he knows what a gem he has.

He knows, Dad.

I push him toward his room, but he grabs me into a hug.

Good-night, sweetheart, he says. He tries to kiss me on the mouth but I crane my head away. Bill steps forward.

Good night, Dad, I say. I push against his chest and he lets go.

That night Bill lets me lie with my head on his chest. I can hear his heart.

I avoid seeing my father again for a couple of years. I opt out of my graduation ceremony. I don't want my family gathering to honor the occasion, in part because I don't want the hassle and in part because I am ashamed. I have failed at journalism and am hiding behind a meaningless degree in something I consider beneath my potential. I don't deserve a hoopla.

Still, Amy has a T-shirt made for me. It reads, You can lead a horticulture, but you can't make her think. The line is Dorothy Parker's, but the shirt is pure Amy. I'm not sure I think it's funny.

That summer Amy goes on vacation with Dad. She is sixteen and they're staying in the old family camper, traveling from a Parents Without Partners campout in Ohio, on out to the East Coast and back.

How was it? I ask after.

Fine, she says.

She is quiet for a beat.

Everybody thought I was his girlfriend.

Gross.

She laughs.

For a few years I run a small business, driving from hair salon to bank to clothing store in my green Volkswagen, watering and fertilizing and pruning plants. People in town know me as The Plant Lady. They wave as I putter by. Hey Plant Lady! they yell. I feel special.

Amy and Mom feel special, too, but for different reasons.

We did it, Amy says to me, giggling. She is seventeen and going into her senior year.

Did what?

Kris and I got Mom and John to meet.

Seriously?

Kris is Amy's friend from the high school newspaper. John is Kris's dad, and Amy likes him a lot, even though when she goes swimming at their apartment complex he won't let her have one of the daiquiris he makes for the neighbors.

Not without meeting your mom, he has said.

So I called Mom and I talked her into going to the Fantasy Island with us so they could meet, Amy says.

Fantasy Island is the video arcade where Amy works after school.

Mom hates video arcades.

I know, she says, but she went with us.

She played Frogger.

Mom played Frogger?

It was so cute! He put his arms around her to show her how to play.

Mom played a game? At a video arcade?

She did. And she giggled, Amy says, giggling. John gave us a ton of quarters. So many that they gave him a hat.

I am amused. She and Kris have pulled off a modern-day version of *The Parent Trap.* Good for you, I say. Good for Mom, too.

Mom takes John to concerts at Chastain Park, an outdoor amphitheater in Atlanta. Mom packs a picnic, John brings the wine. They go to baseball games and movies. They dance. He insists on driving and on carrying everything, and she lets him.

I meet him a few months later. He is lanky and laconic, charring chicken on the grill and dealing out family poker games in a Notre Dame hat, his cigarettes and beer close by. He looks at Mom with reverence, and Mom glows. When they hug they both sigh.

Mom is relaxed and happy, and Amy settles in, content for the first time with a father in her life. John has emphysema, though, and Mom knows that loving him is risky, that she is nearly guaranteed the pain of loss. She prays about it. She talks to her minister.

I'm going to take what I can get, she says. If I only get a few years with him, it's still better than not having him at all.

At Christmas John nestles a ring inside ever smaller boxes, like Russian nesting dolls. He reads a poem asking Mom to be his wife. Mom says yes, and Amy gains a live-in sister and a dad who teases and supervises and cheers her on. Years later he will deliver phone books door-to-door to help her buy books for college.

Mom and John hold a weeklong party to celebrate their marriage and to blend their families, and the kids fly in, from Montana and Missouri and New York and Michigan and Maine, converging on the Atlanta airport, where we have agreed to meet at the top of the big escalator.

I am giddy, telling my fellow passengers the news.

My family is at the top of this escalator, I say. I haven't seen them in a long time. I absolutely cannot wait.

Strangers smile and nod, infected with my excitement. They wish me well as I reach the top and walk forward into my family's embrace. When I get to John he hugs me, and I cry. His arms are safe.

Do you know what I mean? I ask Amy later.

Absolutely, she says.

Afterward I fly back to Missouri and my dogs and my plants. Bill and I do our version of homesteading — growing our own vegetables, raising rabbits for meat. We get three, and name them Breakfast, Lunch, and Dinner so I won't get attached, but it doesn't work. When the day comes to kill one of them I can't even watch, and I choke through every bite of the Crock-Pot-cooked meat. We let the rabbits go, let their cages warp in the weather, don't even bother to tear them down.

I call Amy and she laughs at me.

You killed Thumper, she says.

Thanks a lot.

Bill and I both go to school during the day. I intersperse my work hours with my classes. He works in the evening, sometimes well into the night. Too often I am asleep by the time he comes home, and eventually that takes its toll. We don't so much fight as agree — regretfully — to part. He takes one dog and I take the other. He gets the stereo and I get the TV. There isn't much to divvy up.

I rent a shotgun apartment in a house split into four units, where mice bowl in the oven with chunks of dog food. Occasionally I find one, dead, bloated, and stuck in the broiler pan. I keep a set of rubber gloves under the sink for their removal.

My neighbors are students, too, living like

I am on the barest of margins, working and studying and having a kaleidoscope of romances, gathering in the evening on our porches, where we drink beer and slap at mosquitoes.

I can't afford to make many long-distance calls, but sometimes I talk with Amy. She has a work-study job at an auto parts store, which cracks me up. I can imagine her there, sassy and flirtatious, teasing the professional mechanics and weekend grease monkeys, withholding their spark plugs and gaskets and air filters until they at least smile back.

There's a guy there, she says, and giggles. His name is Jim.

A few months later Amy graduates from high school and the family travels to Atlanta to celebrate. Jim is there. He is short and skinny, seven years older than Amy, with a bushy mustache and thick brown hair that he combs over the top in a puffy pompadour. Amy flirts with him, holds his hand, gazes at him adoringly.

Her plan is to move to Montana in the fall and enroll in a community college, but now that she's met Jim it's like ripping off a limb when she goes.

I love him, she tells me.

I can tell, I say.

Jim has no plans. He is proud to even have graduated from high school, and he makes the best money of his life working in the auto parts store.

He might get into his parents' business someday, Amy tells me.

Still, at Christmas he is the one with the sixty-dollar sweater for me, a sister-in-law-to-be. He is the one making the extravagant pot-matching bids in the family poker games and the big tipper who picks up the tab for everyone when we go out to eat.

It's ridiculous for him to buy me such an expensive gift, I tell Mom.

Just say thank you, she says.

Meanwhile, Amy beams. She is on the giving end, the one whose lover is the bestower.

See how much he loves me? her smile asks.

A few years later at a fancy restaurant he gets down on one knee.

Will you marry me? he asks.

She cries as he gives her a diamond the size of a garden pea, and she flaunts it, flashing it as a symbol of love and status and finally being accepted, being wanted, being enough.

Are you sure he's the right guy? I ask.

Why? she says. Don't you approve?

I don't approve or disapprove, I say. I just want to make sure you're sure.

He's wonderful, she says. I'm lucky to have him.

I don't see how she's all that lucky. She's twenty-three, funny and smart and pretty, even though she's overweight. He can't hold down a job and he still lives with his parents even though he's nearly thirty.

Then I kick myself. I have no right to make her feel like I don't trust her judgment. She is a grown-up. She doesn't need me to treat her like she can't make her own decisions.

I shut up and smile.

Her wedding is storybook lavish, her dress corseted and long-trained, her smile brilliant. She asks our stepfather, John, to walk her down the aisle.

Dad's going to be pissed, I say. You worried?

No, she says. John's been more of a dad to me than Dad has.

I nod.

At the reception the family lines up in two rows.

Amy laughs. Our family has been putting on skits and singing songs all her life, and this one is for her.

"I caught you, sir, having a look at her, as she went strolling by . . ." we sing. "Now didn't your heart . . . beat . . . boom da boom da boom? And didn't you sigh . . . a sigh?" We drop to one knee, Al Jolson style, to Amy's delighted laughter. Then we stand and step-kick as we sing the chorus, "Once in love, with Amy, always in love with Amy . . ."

She is radiant, her porcelain skin clear, her blue eyes bright. Her new husband is uneducated, but he has a job. He isn't as bright as Amy, but who is? I make fun of his big belt buckle and laugh at his Southern slurring. But I go away wishing I was as happy.

Afterward I talk with her often.

What's that noise? I ask.

He has three birds, she says. They stink.

She says it cheerfully, as if it's just one of those cute things newlyweds put up with.

What's with that? I ask.

It's part of the deal, she says. You know, marriage?

The implication is that she knows more than I. What she doesn't tell me is that the birds peck her, or that she is the one who cleans their cages and sweeps their thrown feathers and feed from the floor while her husband pours tumblers of bourbon and talks of grand plans.

■ ■ ■ ■

He bought me a puppy, she says, a year later. A cocker spaniel.

That's great, I say.

Its name is Pete.

Pete is our father's name, and seems an odd choice.

Its name is Pete? How'd that happen?

I don't know, Amy says. Jim named him.

Okay, I say.

Amy and her Peetums become inseparable. It is Pete who wiggles all over when Amy walks through the door, Pete who curls up next to her in bed, Pete who lavishes her with kisses and gifts of socks and squeaky toys and soggy kibble.

I visit a few times, although it's a hassle to fly all the way to Atlanta from Missouri. Their apartment is always a wreck — in part because Amy is naturally slovenly and in part because she is working full-time, bringing in the bulk of the household money. Jim has been fired from the auto parts store, so now he mostly sits and drinks.

Amy is getting bigger, too, and she has to heave herself up and out of the couch. In the evening we sit in front of a movie eating popcorn or potato chips with french onion dip or Oreos, while Jim sleeps. It is her nightly routine.

I've been walking, she tells me.

Great. Are you feeling better?

I'm no athlete myself, but compared to her I'm thin.

She laughs. I'm not all that consistent. Jim likes to keep me here with him.

Really?

He likes me this way, she says. Less competition.

Un huh.

Eventually she gets tired of sitting around bored, tired of working as a secretary, tired of having her greatest stimulation come from memorizing the casts and directors and plot lines of every motion picture ever released. She signs up for night classes at the local community college. She takes pre-geometry and gets an A. She takes geometry and gets an A. She takes pre-algebra and gets an A. She takes algebra.

I got an A! she tells me over the phone.

She is excited and proud.

I guess you're not so bad at math, eh? I ask.

She laughs. Years later she will tell me that Jim rages at her for studying, calls her uppity, tells her she thinks she's so smart.

Every once in a while he hits her, out of frustration and failure. Then he apologizes, and lavishes her the next day with love letters and attention, and dozens of roses sent to her office. The roses are charged to their joint credit card, the one she will have to pay. Those are the things she'll tell me later, but now she only tells me this:

I got flowers. They're beautiful.

How romantic, I say. I wish I had a man who sent me flowers.

CHAPTER 5

Eventually, the novelty of watering plants wears off, so I enroll in graduate school in journalism and take a job in the hospital pharmacy to cover expenses. This time I don't care about the bow heads or the overly confident future anchormen or my own self-pity. This time I am in up to my elbows, arguing and debating, highlighting my books and hammering away at the school computers.

Much of my time is spent in the law library, where the windows are high in the walls, above dark cases lined with matching spines, burgundy next to gray next to green. The lights are dim and two floors above, the air so still that dust motes hover, unmoving. I rub my forehead, fingertips hard against the ridge forming between my eyes.

The book part of grad school is a long, slow slog, a reminder that my brain is a swallow darting in and out, flitting from thing to thing, never holding a pattern. The project part, though, is great. I get to ask questions, play with words, nose into things that are none of my business. Those things make me happy. It is fifteen years post-Watergate but I still feel the glamour of Woodward and Bernstein. I am going to hold government officials accountable, hold their feet to the fire, make them answer to their bosses, the people, the ones who put them there. I am going to turn the system upside down, one rock at a time, and see what crawls out.

The school also has programs in Paris and London and New York City. I want Washington. There I would serve as a mini-Washington bureau for a far-flung newspaper, covering whatever is happening in the capital that has an impact on the paper's readers. So if I wrote for a paper in Pittsburgh, I'd cover manufacturing, and if it were in Florida I'd write about congressional action that affected the citrus crop. My byline would show up in some distant community while I got to live in the nation's capital.

For now, though, I work as a pharmacy technician in a hospital. Between post-op rushes and stocking the shelves and taking inventory and entering prescriptions into the computer I sit at the desk around the corner and study. I hide to avoid the parade of medical students, residents, and fellows, all of them certain of their superior intelligence. (Anyone smart enough to be a doctor becomes a doctor, one tells me.) They order the wrong drugs, we quietly suggest an alternative. They demand something stat — now! — and scowl as we explain that it will be several minutes, that there are others before them. Heart attacks, accident victims, people seizing and stroking and stopping. We appreciate their concern, but their orders — the high blood pressure medicine, the stool softener — will get there. Soon enough. Promise.

Every hour on the hour I do rounds. I pick

up orders and banter with nurses and doctors and med students, then return to my drug-lined room with its Mr. Ed–like half door to begin the cycle again.

A man named Michael banters back. We joke and flirt. Whenever he passes by he sticks his head in to say hello. From there he invites me to sit out on the terrace and have lunch, and from there come other lunches and then a beer and then a dinner and then sex and then we are dating.

Tonight I am staying at his house. Over the course of weeks my toothbrush and some of my clothes have migrated from my place to his, so I peel out of my school clothes and pull on jeans and a Mizzou sweatshirt before heading for the living room.

I love this house. The walls are real plaster and the ceilings are high. At night I cook him dinner and we eat by candlelight, quietly talking about our days. Michael has hung framed posters from wires hooked over the wainscoting, so it looks like an art gallery. One wall is devoted to an altar to his sound system, albums filed by genre, spines out, the Discwasher propped against the turntable. Putting on an album is a ritual. I don't touch them, but I've seen it often enough. First, he slides the album from the cover, touching only the edges. Then he tenderly runs the Discwasher over it in slow circles. He lowers the record onto the turntable, then settles the needle into the first groove. His taste ranges from jazz to classical to not-yet-discovered underground music that only he can recognize. My own musical taste runs toward Top 40, something I am trying to change. Ear candy, he had called it early on when my car radio blared when I turned the key. Now I turn the radio off before I get to his house, to hide my lack of sophistication.

I also make better coffee for him. I have been instructed. One morning I tried duplicating what I'd seen him do.

No no no, he'd said, coming up behind me and kissing my neck. Let me show you.

I had been raised on Maxwell House, good to the last drop. Not raised — I didn't drink coffee until I left home — but it was my standard, my image of what coffee should be. The silver percolator on the counter, my parents' breath, their adult craving every morning.

Hold on, I haven't had my coffee, they'd say, the five of us clamoring for sleepovers and rides to gymnastics and more sugar for our oatmeal.

I put water on to heat, then pull the bag

of coffee beans out of the freezer and measure a pot's worth into the grinder. The grinder is a Melitta, the pot is, too. The water has to be just right — not boiling, he has said, because that will burn the flavor.

Americans drink their coffee too hot, he has said.

After a few minutes I pour just enough water in the filtered funnel to dampen the grounds. I count off thirty seconds, then pour in the rest. Even without him here I do it the right way.

The house still smells acrid from last night, when I let the water go dry while steaming broccoli. It was the second time I'd done it, although I had forgotten the first.

What do we need to do to make sure you don't do this again? Michael asked, his head down so he was looking at me through his brows.

Waiting for the coffee I remember, and I think that I have to be more careful not to let the water burn dry. Also that maybe he could be the one who cooks once in a while.

Tonight we are meeting our friends at Booche's, a one-hundred-year-old bar redolent with cigarette smoke and grease that is a downtown institution. It's a Friday thing.

Whoever shows up shows up, although they all are from his circle, not mine, so I am the outsider. Being Michael's girlfriend gives me entree, but too often I don't get the jokes or the cultural references or the snippy comments about profs or people in their classes. Still, I'm looking forward to it. By evening's end our long table will be covered with empty beer bottles and our voices will be loud as we shout over each other or yell at the Cardinals game on the small TV mounted on the wall, next to the perpetually revolving model of the Budweiser Clydesdales.

I sip my coffee and think about the Debras, both of whom I think have designs on Michael. They work late together, lean into him as they laugh, touch his arm when they talk. Twice I've visited at work to find the first Debra rubbing his shoulders, his eyes closed and his head rolled forward, her face close to his hair.

I am assessing her as competition as Michael walks through the door.

Hey, there, he says.

I jump up and hug him, my whole body pressed against his, my face turned up for a slick, promising kiss.

What was that for? he asks.

Just happy you're here, I say.

We kiss more, me sliding my hands around his back and then down, holding him against me as I move, but he pulls away.

Let me get out of these clothes and we'll head down to Booche's, he says. What are you wearing?

I look down at myself. I am comfortable in my jeans and Mizzou sweatshirt, and we're only going to a pool hall. He looks at me for a long minute.

I change.

At Thanksgiving he takes me home to meet his parents. It is a lovely suburban home of crystal and mahogany and many, many rooms. It is in a neighborhood of lovely suburban homes, big-shouldered on small lots. We have stayed there once before, when his parents were out of town, sleeping and having sex in the bed his mother had made for him daily since he was a boy. I had tapped into the liquor cabinet, making fun of the clients who had given his dad the best scotch, the best bourbon.

You can either make fun of it or drink it, he said. Not both.

I drank.

This time, though, I am nervous. I doubt they'll like me. I am not fashionable. My hair is short. I am not studying to be a

132

teacher. Or a nurse. I am not an appropriate partner. Michael has warned me that they might not be happy that their boy is in love before he's becoming a success. Still, just roll with it, he says, squeezing my thigh. They'll love you once they get to know you.

I am not so sure. The one thing I know is that people most decidedly don't come to love me more once they know me. Once they know me they'll know that I'm not smart or nice or funny. I am an imposter. I am pretending to be confident, but I know I'm a failure and that I'll be a failure at anything I try. I will not know which fork to use, I will spill my water glass, I'll ask for a second glass of wine, I'll try to help in the kitchen and I'll burn something — a hole in the counter or the potatoes or the after-dinner coffee. Somehow I will screw up, I know that. And if I don't, then I'll sleep wrong, use the bathroom too many times, get up at night and wake someone, trip over the cat, make noise. Somehow, I know, I will humiliate myself. And him.

Stop worrying, he says. You'll do fine. Just remember to keep your voice down. And don't mention politics. Or religion.

Right. I'll just relax and be myself, no problem.

Michael's father is tall and deep-voiced,

his handshake strong, his eye contact steady. Michael's mother is slim and fashionable, her hair perfect, her eyes warm.

We're so glad to meet you, she says, giving me an A-frame hug, our arms around each other but nothing touching below shoulder level. She smells expensive.

Michael's dad ushers him into the study, a place of leather chairs and cut crystal decanters.

Brandy? his father asks.

They sit as Michael's mother leads me into the kitchen.

Do you want an apron, dear?

I don't do much — toss the salad, carry the rolls to the table — all the while answering questions.

Where are you from?

What does your father do?

What are you studying?

Do you want children?

Finally it is time. Candlelight glitters on china and silver, the tablecloth long and pristine, three forks at each plate, two glasses, one for water, one for wine.

She sends me in to gather up the men.

Dinner is ready, I say.

Michael stands and comes to me, raises his eyebrows. I nod. Okay so far.

134

In the dining room he pulls out my chair and I sit and spread my napkin in my lap. The turkey is on its platter in front of the patriarch, the potatoes in their silver bowl, the salad in cut crystal. I do not know etiquette. At home we would just serve ourselves from the closest bowl, then pass it along and take what comes next. I do not know if that's okay here. I wait and watch. As the guest, though, I'm expected to go first.

Shall we give thanks? the father asks.

We bow our heads as he rumbles through a prayer that includes gratitude for their guest. Michael's hand slides up my thigh under the tablecloth. We say "Amen" and raise our eyes. The father picks up the ivory-handled carving tools and surveys the bounty. Then he sets down the utensils. He plants his hands on either side of the platter and glowers the length of table.

Where the fuck are the yams?

I jerk backward. "Fuck" at the holiday table? Then I look. There are no yams. No little marshmallows, no brown sugar goo.

Goddamnit! he yells. You never do anything right!

He picks up the turkey and hurls it, platter, decorative sprigs of parsley, and all. It clears his wife's head and slides down the silk wallpaper. We are stunned to silence. After a beat she jumps up and bustles, scooping the bird back onto the platter with her hands. She lifts it and tries to stand, her hand making a greasy print on the wall, as her husband storms to his study and his scotch.

I close my mouth, which I only then realize has been hanging open. Michael taps my leg under the table and tilts his head. I raise my eyebrows. He jerks his head harder and squeezes my thigh. I raise my eyebrows higher. He hisses at me, Help her!

His mother has picked up the turkey. She is standing there with the bird sideways on the platter, the golden brown skin torn and the soft flesh exposed where it hit the wall. Her hands are slippery with grease and her eyes are wet with tears. She doesn't look at either of us before she turns and carries the bird into the kitchen.

The anger I grew up with simmered, it boiled and bubbled just under the surface. We knew it was there, knew it from the too-hard pinches and the public love pats that weren't quite gentle. We would ask at bedtime, Is it me? Am I a problem child? Mom would reassure us, but going to sleep I'd toss and put the pillow over my head and roll from side to side, sure I was ruining the family, that I was the problem.

Here, though, it is in the open. It is in the open and that is good. It is in the open and you can see it and you know what caused it and even if you don't agree with it, don't think it was worth the explosion, at least you know what it is and where it is and what brought it on.

I look at Michael. He will not get away with anything of the sort. Sure, he shoved me once and I tripped over the coffee table, and instead of helping me up he followed and crammed my face into the couch. And another time we were out hiking and he picked me up by the arm, leaving bruises that aligned exactly — if anyone had checked — with his fingertips. He had apologized, though, with tears in his eyes. Both times. And we had talked then about how he is sweet and smart and good, but he feels unloved, like he was never good enough, like a person who should be ashamed. I am going to love him enough to erase that message, though. I am going to love him and tell him he's beautiful and stroke his skin and convince him that he is handsome and worthy and good.

Right now, though, he is jerking his head and hissing Help her and I refuse. I refuse by burrowing my butt further into the chair. I refuse by not moving, by glaring back at him.

Finally he gets up and follows his father into the study. Now I am sitting on the white satin upholstered seat at the crystal and silver table by myself and it is awkward. So I stand up. But I don't know whether to follow him into the study or to go into the kitchen, where I hear quiet sobs. I know, actually. I know that I cannot go into the study. That I am a woman and women aren't allowed in the study with the brandy and the cigars. I know I should go into the kitchen and act chipper and pretend I don't notice, don't see. I know I should go into the kitchen and pretend so that she can have dignity. So I do.

Between us we pretty up the turkey with judicious placement and more parsley. We get the yams out of the oven. They are soft brown and crusty, warm and sweet and smelling of molasses. She puts on oven gloves and carries them to the trivet on the table. When she comes back she carries the potatoes, which she scoops into a glass bowl and reheats in the microwave. We use a spatula to get every spoonful back into the silver bowl, then carry it ceremoniously back to the table. Once again she tells me to go tell the men that dinner is served.

Everything is repeated. The chair is pulled out, the napkin is spread, the heads are bowed, the hand returns to my thigh, the blessing is said again. This time we look up. The father stands, takes the utensils in hand, carves the turkey. The meal passes with polite talk of the weather and Christmas plans and Michael's profs and my classes.

After dinner I lean to Michael.

Break tradition, I say. Help in the kitchen.

He looks at me. Doesn't reply. When we stand he heads for the study. I gather plates and take them to the sink.

When we leave it is in icy silence, not because he is appalled by his father's behavior, but because he is appalled by mine.

Later, I make Amy laugh at the image of the turkey grease sliding down the wallpaper. We envision the mother moving furniture to hide the stain. We pretend it is hilarious. I want it to be funny, so I stop the story there.

What I don't know until years later is that Amy understands, because Jim has gone into rages and thrown her textbooks off the balcony of their apartment and into the Dumpster below.

He's a pretty good shot, she says.
She is trying to make it funny, too.

CHAPTER 6

A month or so later Michael and I fly together to Colorado for a ski vacation. I have only flown a few times, and skied just once, in Michigan, on a hill called a mountain. Where we are going, though, the mountains are real. And so is my fear. Michael skis with confidence. Even though he was raised in the Midwest, it is clear that his family has spent some of its massed money on lessons and family ski vacations.

Michael is using interest from his trust fund to pay for this trip. I am grateful, but also angry at the inequalities in our realities. No matter what I say or do, he can't understand what it's like to scrabble for the money for rent and heat and food. Worse, he thinks he does understand.

I worked an entire summer once to pay my own way on an Outward Bound trip, he says.

I roll my eyes.

Big whoop, I say. Working a whole summer for a want, not a need, is not the same. There's no desperation there. No life or death. No crisis should you fail. If I miss a payment I'll be chattering in the dark, or worse, asking my family for help.

Don't be so melodramatic, he says. Your family would help.

I look at him like he's from the moon. Which family member does he think is going to step up? Two of my siblings are in college, another is less than a year out, and Mom is in no position to help. As for my dad, he wouldn't give me money even if he had it, which he doesn't.

I was raised to be self-sufficient. It is a virtue in our family. A virtue born of necessity, perhaps, but a proudly held virtue just the same.

You wouldn't understand, I say.

You're being melodramatic, he counters.

It is an argument that repeats itself endlessly, like a Möbius loop.

Perhaps I am being melodramatic, but I'm not comfortable being beholden, not comfortable with him tucking my plane ticket in the outer pocket of his carry-on, handling things as if I were feeble or incompetent.

I try to relax into it, to just feel lucky, maybe grateful.

On the plane he is sweet to me, giving me the window seat and holding my hand during takeoff and landing. In Denver he handles everything — the rental car, the navigation to our room, the ski rental. I follow and marvel. That night we have dinner, then fall into bed together, groping and seeking and straining. In the morning we ski.

I hate it. It is a stupid sport. Stupid and hard and I'll never get it and if I fall down again I'm going to scream or cry or bury my face in the snow and never come up. I am angry and cold and tired, aching from the unaccustomed demands on my muscles and the incessant iciness on my feet. Plus, he keeps telling me what to do. If he tells me again, if he gets his know-it-all face anywhere near mine I will cram it full of snow. He's not as good as he thinks he is, either. I watch other skiers and I watch him and his butt is too far back and his weight is too far forward and he is not graceful at all, so what business does he have telling me what to do?

By midafternoon we are no longer speaking, but I at least have learned to carve long, slow **S**'s down the slopes. Still, it's painful and cold and not fun enough to justify the effort or the expense.

Want to call it a day? he asks.

Yes, I say gratefully, thinking that if I do another run I'll break a leg or an arm or my back. He looks disappointed, so I suggest he make a few more runs without me.

I'll just wait in the lodge and watch, I say.

He skis off happily, and I pop out of my skis and trudge into the lodge, where I order a beer and fries — which I cannot afford — and then sit silently in the rough-hewn dimness, squinting at the brightness outside.

I am tired, and the warmth and the beer are making me drowsy. I want to go back to our room and sleep, but I don't want to let Michael down. I want him to have a blast, to remember this vacation fondly. I secretly hope that in ten years we'll look back on this vacation and laugh at our early selves, so rigid and determined.

That's what I'm thinking as I watch the skiers fly by. I'm looking for Michael's jacket, his blue ski cap. I want to be able to say I saw him, that he looked great out there.

But I don't see him. Not for a long time. I order a second beer and pull off my ski boots, rubbing my toes to restart my circulation. If he doesn't get here soon I'm going to have to pay my tab myself, and I don't have enough money. The waitress is already hovering. I think she's at the end of her shift and wanting everyone to pay up, like I did when I waited tables. She's not approaching, not saying anything, not handing me my bill, so I pretend to ignore her. It's not like I can pay her and set her free. Besides, Michael and I had agreed to meet right here in the lodge, so I have to stay.

I am finishing my second beer and picking through the last of the fries when he comes in, stomping his boots to knock off the snow.

The powder was great, he says, leaning in with a billow of fresh air to kiss me. Someday we'll have you out there jumping bumps.

I smile up at him, ever the good sport.

Sure, I say. Someday.

■ ■ ■ ■

Later that night we're in the room, dehydrated and groggy.

I wish I'd grown up taking things like this for granted, I say.

I am thinking about the cost of rental skis and lift tickets and restaurant meals and this room in a hotel.

Immediately I regret saying it. I sound ungrateful, like I'm whining or criticizing him somehow, calling him the poor little rich kid, an epithet he got often enough from classmates back in school. He hates it when anyone brings up his father's money. He thinks I am a snob because I don't recognize that he has worked just as hard as I have for the things in his life, and he gets irritated when I insinuate otherwise. We have had this argument before.

This time, though, he doesn't argue. Instead he stares at me for a long moment, then he reaches out and pinches the flesh on the back of my arm.

Do you like that? His eyes are fierce and locked on mine.

He twists the skin and my eyes fill. I stare back, defiant. I do not cry out, do not say uncle, and his anger flares. He puts a hand against my jaw and slams me against the wall. Then, with a look like he is about to cry, he drives his fist into my ribs.

The pain is explosive.

It knocks the wind out of me and I double over, holding my stomach.

After a moment I catch my breath. I straighten up and slap him. He hits me in the face, then again — one-two — in the ribs. I fall to the floor and he kicks me in the kidney. I reach up and grab at his groin. I want to go for the one thing that is a weakness, the one thing I can possibly hurt. But I miss. Instead my fingernails leave seeping claw marks down his thigh. For a split second he looks shocked, and then he smacks me across the face, and I am down, bleeding from the nose.

He stares, then drops to his knees as I flinch backward.

Oh, baby, he says.

He cradles my head against his chest and I try to push him away. It hurts.

He looks at my face.

I'll get ice, he says.

I curl into a **C** on the floor, holding a pillow to my stomach as armor. I can barely breathe.

He comes back with ice from the machine in the hall, which he wraps in a towel and places gently on my nose.

Sit up and tilt your head back, he says.

I do and blood runs down the back of my throat, the front of my shirt. I swallow. It tastes like rust, and the sharp edges of the ice cubes hurt my nose. I try to push them away, but he holds the ice with one hand and the back of my head with the other.

I'm so sorry, he says. I love you so much.

I am silent.

I love you so much, he says again. Why did you have to go and push my buttons? You know better.

I say nothing. I am breathing raggedly through my mouth, my head immobilized. I want to recoil from his hands, from the horrid ice on my throbbing, clogged nose.

Eventually I agree to stand up, and he helps me to the bed. I sit gingerly, flinching with every shift in weight, my ribs and nose screaming with each move.

He lies down next to me. Then he gets up. Then he lies back down. I do not look at him, do not speak. Every jolt of the bed makes me gasp. But quietly.

Lying on my back hurts, too. It makes me feel vulnerable. I am afraid to roll up on my side, though. I'm afraid to face him for fear he'll take it as encouragement, and afraid to turn my back for fear of what he'll stick into me. I touch my tongue to the corner of my mouth and taste the blood there. I can feel my eyes swelling shut, the lids getting heavy.

My heart is pounding, flooded as I am with adrenaline, yet I can neither fight nor flee. Every part of me is twitching. I am overdosing on my body's own drug, and I can't move, can't gasp out a simple plea for help.

Hours pass. My heart is clenched, my bowels roiling. I'm afraid I'm going to soil myself. I must not fall asleep. He is humming with tension. I cannot trust him now, not after what I have done, slapping him, scratching him in that most vulnerable of places.

He gets up again, the bed lurching painfully, and goes into the bathroom, flipping the switch and flooding the room with a temporary rectangle of light.

In the afterburn darkness I slide my hand slowly up my body to my ribs. Pressing my fingertips in, just barely, I wince in the night. This is going to leave a mark.

I want to leave, but he has my plane ticket. He has my plane ticket and all of the money we had planned to spend on this trip. I have about fifteen dollars in cash, and that won't buy me a place to stay, let alone a ticket home.

I want to sob, but I do not want to attract his attention. Instead I lie there silently, sliding my hand over my body, assessing the damage.

After a minute he comes out, and again the room is briefly bright. Then it is dark again, and he prowls between the bed and the TV stand, pacing, glaring, fussing with my covers, brushing his fingers across my cheek, kissing me gently. Apologizing.

I didn't want to do it, but you made me, he says. Why did you have to do it? Why couldn't you have just shut up? Why do you antagonize people? Why do you push my buttons?

I have no answers for him. I hear him telling me it's my fault and I don't have the energy to argue. It's my fault he beat me? I did know better. I could have chosen my words more carefully, could have just appreciated the free vacation, could have kept my mouth shut for once. But was anything I said worth a beating? I can't remember. I can't even remember what we were talking about. I can't remember and it doesn't matter, because whatever I said just gave him the excuse to do what he had wanted to do all along. I know that now. It was simmering underneath, ready to erupt, ever since . . . ever since what? I can't think when it started, only that I've known it was there for a long time, and that something like this — the combination of fatigue and alcohol and my big mouth — something like this would make him explode.

I feel myself sinking into the bed. I am tired and getting more tired by the moment. My energy is draining away. My thoughts are getting groggy. I want him to take care of me. I want him to go away. I want him to give me my plane ticket and a ride to the airport. I want him to die.

I know I can't risk falling asleep, not with him still angry, so I call to him. He sits gently on the side of the bed and runs his hand over my hair. I pull his face down to mine and kiss him carefully, my lips still tender and bleeding, then run my hand into his pants. He is already hard. I figured he would be. This has turned him on. I know that if I let him have what he wants he will go to sleep and I will be safe. I require only that he support his weight on his hands to protect what later a doctor says are broken ribs.

When he is done, he sleeps. I do not. Everything inside me is racing. I have diarrhea. I want to get up and use the bathroom, but I don't want to wake him. Instead I focus every nerve on holding still.

In the morning I have black eyes and bruises across my rib cage. I do not go out. He does, for groceries and bandages and gauze for my nose. When he comes back, he climbs into bed beside me. For three days I give him sex whenever he wants. It is tender and gentle, interrupting as it does his ministrations to me, his eagerness to bring me carryout, to plump my pillows and pull the blankets gently up over my body.

Sometimes when he is in the bathroom or out hunting and gathering I shudder at the realization that I am a woman who has been beaten. I shudder that I have been beaten and still I am giving the man who beat me access to my body. I shudder at my ability to act as if this is normal, it is okay, it is forgiven and forgotten, it was a mistake and he is sorry. At times I believe it.

We watch old movies and eat pizza in bed. He seems calm and peaceful, and I am grateful. I know it is the sex that keeps me safe.

After three days we fly home, him carrying my bags at the airport and answering the ticket agents' concerned looks with an easy lie.

She skied into a tree, he says, but she's fine. Aren't you, honey?

I nod.

On the plane he gathers blankets and pillows, and lifts my bag into the overhead compartment as I carefully maneuver into the window seat. He holds my hand as the plane taxis, and I let him, though I close my eyes and lean away from him, against the window.

I am finally going home.

As we rise into the sky the pressure builds in my swollen sinuses. My eyes feel like they're going to burst from my head, and my eardrums are pierced by something not quite sharp, like a paper clip.

I bring my hands to my face, but Michael pulls them away.

Your eustachian tubes are clogged, he says. Yawn. That'll clear them.

They're clogged because you punched me in the nose, I think. And I can't yawn because when I even breathe deeply it feels like there's a dagger in my lung.

Every time the plane changes pressure the pain builds again, until it's a screaming teapot in my head. I want to double over but I can't, not without gasping. Landing is miserable.

Landing and then rising from my seat and seeing the other passengers look at me and then quickly away. And they can only see my face.

Michael carries my bags into my apartment and then kisses me tenderly. I walk into the bathroom and look in the mirror.

My eye sockets are purple and black, from brow to cheekbone. I touch my nose. It is tender, but it doesn't bleed now unless I blow it.

I do not lift my shirt. I don't want to know more.

I don't know what to do. I need diagnosis and comfort. And confidentiality. If I go to the hospital the people there will look at me with pity and treat me forever after as a battered woman, whispering behind their hands that they don't want to be the one to suggest I deserved it, but you know how she can be sometimes. Or they'll say — to themselves and each other — that they never would have let it happen, never would have given him the opportunity, would have defended themselves or run away or somehow made it not possible for this man, this man who was known and loved, to beat them up.

Besides, it has been days since the injury, so there's nothing anyone at the hospital can do. And I don't want to get Michael in trouble. I was the one who started the fight, and then he was so gentle and apologetic afterward, in the room and on the plane.

Still, there are the bruises, the silent testimony, and they tempt me to tell, to stand up and announce to my boss and my friends and my co-workers, the beautiful nurses, the earnest med students, that I have been hit. I didn't ski into a tree, I'd say, and then I'd hold up my shirt so they could see the purple and blue and red that would eventually fade to yellow.

I was hit, I'd say, by one of you. By your colleague, your friend.

I know what they would think, though. They'd think I asked for it. Even the ones who think hitting is never justified would look at me and the thought will niggle, What did she do to deserve it? I know this. Women who are hit are to be pitied for being hit, but also looked at askance, as women who somehow asked for it, who maybe like it.

Lots of things happen between couples, and nobody needs to know. I don't need to air my dirty laundry. I don't need to tell.

I pace the living room. I have to talk to someone, so I call Amy.

How was your trip?

It was good, I say, twirling the phone's

cord around my finger, except I'm a crappy skier.

She laughs, and we talk about other things.

Hey, I finally say, he hit me.

He what?

He hit me. A couple of times. Pretty hard.

She is quiet. Then she says, Are you okay?

I don't think so, I say. I think my nose is broken. And maybe my ribs.

She gasps.

He hit you in the face?

Yeah.

That son of a bitch, she says. What are you going to do?

I don't know.

You broke up with him, didn't you?

No, I say. I mean, it wasn't all his fault.

Janine, she says, there is nothing you could have done to deserve this. Repeat after me, nothing.

She is my baby sister and I am ashamed that she is witness to my failure. I don't say anything. We are both quiet. Then she speaks.

Are you going to wait until he kills you?

I snort.

He's not going to kill me, I say. Good lord.

Okay, but I want you to see a doctor.

I'm fine, I say.

No you're not, she says. Call a doctor.

I don't want to get him in trouble.

You're kidding me, right?

I don't answer.

Look, call someone, she says. Call a friend. Call one of the residents you're always flirting with. Call someone.

Okay okay, I say.

And then call me back and tell me what they say.

I will.

Promise me, she says.

I promise.

Good. I love you.

I love you, too.

I hang up. She is right. I will break up with him. I will call him or write to him and tell him that it's over, that I want my clothes and my toothbrush and my house key back.

Or maybe I'll go over there while he's gone and pick up my stuff and leave a note.

You only get to hit me once, I'll write.

That's what I'll do. I'll get rid of him.

I nod my head, determined, and wait for euphoria and relief. That's what I expect to feel. Instead I get loneliness and fear, that I will forever be a battered woman, that he will return. That he won't. That I have no other options.

CHAPTER 7

The first thing I need is a doctor. I follow Amy's advice and page Kurt, one of the residents I joke around with at the hospital.

I need help, I say. I'm beaten up pretty bad.

He hit you?

He is shocked, even though I'd told him Michael and I were having hard times.

I'll be right over, he says.

I met Kurt a month or two earlier, when his residency rotation landed him on my floor. I razzed him about an order or about his tie or about flirting with one of the nurses — who knew how it began? — and it morphed into the two of us giggling at the pharmacy door and whispering together just outside patients' rooms.

He's married, you know, my co-worker Laura said.

I looked at her.

He isn't wearing a ring, I answered.

Like that means anything?

Good point, I said, leaning out of the pharmacy door to watch him walk away.

His wife's pregnant, too, Laura said.

I pulled my head back in and looked at her.

You're kidding, I said.

Nope, she answered.

That's not good, I said.

Still, I need him now. He is my friend, and he is qualified to tell me what to do. I give him directions, and then look around my apartment. There is dog hair on the floor, in tumbleweed-sized balls in the corners, on the sofas and chairs. Some mornings I wake up with it stuck to my ChapSticked lips.

I find a broom and start sweeping, but it

hurts, so I push the biggest piles under the couch and go to find the roller that will get at least some of the dog hair off the couch. I've cleared a reasonable-sized patch when he pulls up in front of the house.

He bounds up to the door. When I open it he gasps. He takes my face between his palms and turns it toward the afternoon light. He pinches the bridge of my nose between his fingers, and wiggles gently, and my eyes fill with tears. He wipes them away, running his thumbs over the dark bruising.

Your nose is broken, he says. He kisses it lightly.

He pulls me into a hug, and I rest gratefully against his chest.

I'm so sorry he did this to you, he murmurs. So sorry.

My ribs are hurt, too, I say.

He puts his hands on my shoulders and steps back.

Show me where, he says.

I point to my left chest, below my breast.

You mind? he asks, gesturing to my shirt.

I shake my head. He is being kind, and I am grateful.

He lifts my shirt and examines the bruising. Gingerly he presses with his fingers, watching my face as I wince.

They're broken, too, he says.

I cry, even though I'm trying to be brave.

It's okay, he says, pulling me back into his arms and smoothing my hair. It's going to be okay.

It feels wonderful there in his arms. Strong and just firm enough. I want to stay there. He wants me to stay there. We hold still for a long moment. Then I turn my face up and he kisses me. I kiss him, and feel my body swirl and flood with pleasure and arousal and gratitude. I want to connect with him through my lips. I want him to hold me and keep me safe and assure me that nothing like this will ever happen again, that I have paid the dues I'll have to pay, that from now on my life will be good. I want him to make me safe. I want him to erase the pain.

I pull away.

So what do I need to do?

Not much, he answers. Your nose is in alignment, so you don't have to do anything to it, and your ribs will hurt, but they'll heal on their own. Mostly you need to take ibuprofen or Tylenol and take it easy. He doesn't suggest I press charges.

I look at him for a long minute. The answer is unsatisfying, but it makes sense. I am surprised, but I agree with his silence, agree without words that to press charges would be unfair, since no one can know what really happened out there. It will be a case of he said/she said, and both of us would lose. Better by far to just heal and get on with life.

We hug one more time before he reluctantly leaves.

I know he will be back. I can feel it.

One thing about Kurt is he knows I am a battered woman and he wants me anyway. With anyone else I would have to start over, explain everything. With him I don't have to. I don't have to tell and I don't have to keep secrets, and I hate keeping secrets. What happened to me is too much to carry in silence.

Also he is handsome and smart, and he lights up as soon as he sees me. He lights up even though he knows the truth about me, that I can be ugly and I can make a mistake and I can make someone so mad that he beats me. Still his face lights up. I like that in a man.

I like it, but I know that if he really knew me, really knew the me of me, he wouldn't like me. But that's okay, because he's married and we can never be anything but what we are right now.

He's married, you know, Laura says again.

I know, I say this time.

His wife is pregnant, she says again.

I know, I say. But they're not really happy.

She shakes her head and walks out of the pharmacy.

But she doesn't know anything. She doesn't know the truth about us, that we have fallen in love. We are in love, even though he tells me he will never leave his wife and son, never leave the unborn baby.

I left Jim, Amy says.

You what?

I left him. I tried my best, but I can't do it anymore.

I'm so sorry. What happened?

Lots of things. He can't hold down a job. He's drinking again. I'm paying all the bills.

I want to jump in and tell her it's about time, that I never understood what she saw in him, but I hold myself quiet. I wait for her to say more.

Does he hit you?

Not very often, she says.

Oh, Amy . . .

I know I should keep my mouth shut, but I start in anyway.

I've never thought he was good enough for you, I say. You're so much smarter than he is. You make almost all of the money, you do all of the work around the house.

You're better off without him.

What I don't point out is that she pays all of the bills, buys the groceries, cooks the food, washes the dishes, feeds the birds, takes care of the dog, and takes the car in for maintenance. All while he sits on his ass sneaking sips of bourbon from bottles stashed under the couch.

He's worthless, I say. He's a weight, dragging you under. He doesn't have the balls to build himself up by actually doing something, so he's doing it by cutting you down. You don't need that. And you sure as hell don't deserve it.

I know, she says, crying quietly, but I'm still scared.

I know you are. I'm sorry. Remember how scared I was when I left Michael? You'll find someone better.

Will I?

Kurt will not leave his wife, he says again and again. And then it changes.

I can't leave until the baby is at least six months old, he says.

It's a little frightening that he has gone from never to soon. He will leave his wife and be with me. That's what he's saying. I'm thrilled. I am panicked. Do I want him? Now that there's the possibility of ever and always, is this the man I want? He's smart and handsome and affectionate and ambitious, and now he could be mine. He could be mine, but I wasn't looking at him for forever, and now he might be for forever, him and two kids and his wife, who would be his ex-wife and who would be angry, would hate me.

Plus, I would be someone who broke up a marriage. A homewrecker.

A month later Amy calls.

I moved back in, Amy says.

I think back to all the time we'd talked about what a shit Jim is and how much better off she'll be alone.

What inspired that?

He's changed. He loves me, and he's really trying. As long as he's trying, I want to try, too.

I wince. We talk about whether she's sure, whether this is the right thing, whether she's worried.

Only about one thing, she says.

What's that?

What you guys think, she says. She chokes up. I don't want to be the family fuckup.

Now I'm choking up, too. She has said things before that made me think she thought she was the loser, the one who hadn't finished college or gone into the high-visibility career, or married the man who made the big money.

You're not the family fuckup, I say.

I just want you guys to love me.

Don't you know? Don't you know, Amy, that you could leave Jim and go back to him a hundred times and we will still love you? We will always love you, no matter what.

We stay on the phone crying for a few more minutes. Then we both blow our noses and say good-bye.

For a couple of weeks I resist calling her. I am angry that she went back and embarrassed that I said such ugly things about her husband. She rarely calls me, either.

When his baby is six months old, Kurt moves out so we can be together. His children become mine, in an every-other-day sort of way. I learn to make pancakes shaped like hearts and shamrocks and Christmas trees, to dye milk green on St. Patrick's Day and talk baby talk while changing diapers. I rock and read bedtime stories and marvel over crayon masterpieces.

I am madly in love with him and with the children, and with whom I have become, a nurturer, a maker of a home. I have graduate school to make me feel smart and Kurt and the kids to make me feel loved.

Underlying my happiness, though, is guilt. I have ruined a family. I tell myself that Kurt wouldn't have been interested in me if the marriage was good, that everyone will be better off this way. I think of the ways his ex-wife let him down, of how Kurt and I are meant to be together. The rationalizations get me through the day.

One day we are shopping together at a department store.

You would look great in this, he says, holding up a simple cotton sundress. It is pale blue, with a tank top bodice and a full, below-the-knees skirt.

I couldn't wear that, I say. It's too sexy.

Oh, come on, he says. You're gorgeous. Quit being uptight.

I shake my head.

This is because of your dad, isn't it? he asks. Let go of that. Do it for me.

I shake my head again, less sure. Am I being a prude? Am I still hiding my body, protecting myself?

He buys it anyway, and within a week I give in to its silent taunt that I am being uptight, and its promise that in this I will be attractive. It will please Kurt, I know, so I put it on. It hugs me from chest to hip, and then flares. I put on flat sandals and look in the mirror. I do look good, although in this bra my nipples show just a little. When I come out of the bedroom my arms are crossed across my chest. He beams. At the grocery store I tug obsessively at the front, trying to pull it higher on my chest, even though it covers everything it needs to cover. Kurt holds my hand. He is proud.

It is a simple compromise, an effort by him to improve me, by me to please him. Like the daily weigh-ins, it doesn't seem like too much to ask. It is, after all, for my own good.

We are together a year and are so in love that I don't want to go to Washington. Or I do, but I am afraid to leave Kurt and our new life together.

I could just do a thesis, I tell my advisor, the same professor who gave me that first C.

You've been telling me for years that you're going to go to Washington, she says.

I know, but I'd have to leave Kurt and the kids.

She shakes her head. Writing a thesis will require a lot of time — maybe as much as another year, much of it spent in the stacks at the library doing things I loathe, eventually shaping statistics into what the professors call "new knowledge." And it wouldn't get me where I want to go, which is deep in a bustling newsroom, uncovering truths and forcing people to talk about things that are important.

Still, if I do a thesis I'll have a lot of time for the family. And Kurt would rather I stayed, of course. I could work at the pharmacy part-time, we'd live together and he would have his job and I'd have mine. The kids would spend half of their time with us, and I could write and research after they were in bed.

Going to Washington would toss me in with real journalists, real people who are making a difference. I picture myself being called on at a presidential press conference and being the one to ask the question that nails him, that gets him to tell the truth. Plus, going to Washington would give me a deadline, and I need deadlines. I don't want to wind up like some of my friends — just a thesis away from a master's degree, or ABD — all but dissertation — on a PhD. That's the point of deadlines; without them nothing gets written.

What should I do? I ask my advisor.

Go to Washington.

But I have kids here, I say.

They're not your kids, she says. Let their

dad take care of them. Besides, lots of students somehow manage, even though they're parents, and you'd regret it forever if you didn't go. Trust me on this.

I talk to Kurt.

I really want to go, I say. I've been looking forward to this for a long time, and I think I'd resent you if I give it up.

But we'd be apart, he says, pulling me into his arms. And you'd miss the kids.

I know, I say, but it's only for a little while.

He is silent, holding me.

Then he says, What if you meet someone else?

I scoff. I'm not going to be looking.

But what if you do?

I hold him tighter. I'm not going to meet anyone half as wonderful as you, I say.

Then why do you want to leave me?

I laugh.

I'm not leaving you. I'm going to Washington so I can get better at what I do. I have to do this in order to feel like a success, okay?

He is silent, still holding me.

I know what he's worried about. We started out as a lie, so it's hard for either of us to trust. That's okay, though. I understand. I would worry, too.

It takes a couple of weeks of discussion,

but finally I sign up to go. He flies with me to pick out a place, and then leaves, kissing me passionately and then tenderly at the airport and asking me again to promise.

Promise not to meet anyone else, he says.

I promise.

On the subway back to my apartment I feel light. Light and happy and free and scared and accomplished. I'm doing this thing. I may not do it well, but I'm doing it. Without help. I'm doing it on my own and I should feel proud.

I'm twenty-nine years old. I'm diving in and I'll just have to flail like hell so I don't go under. Eventually I'll swim.

At night the city sounds scare me: the sirens, the shouted laughter, the music from passing cars. When I flip on the light to use the bathroom, cockroaches scuttle. The first night I scream, although only briefly, and because I'm startled, not frightened. It's worse when one of the other tenants tells me about the rats in the basement laundry room. I've never even seen a rat.

When I have to wash clothing, I wear shoes and socks and long pants. I sleep with my arms and legs tightly tucked into the covers, even in the heat. If I wake up in the middle of the night with a hand or foot exposed I yank it back into the safety of my bed.

Gradually, though, I relax. It is beautiful in DC in the fall, the ginkgo trees lemon yellow, the air crisp. I walk along, kicking leaves, stepping on the curled ones that give a satisfying crunch like the potato chips I deny myself in order to remain a size 2. I walk the four blocks from the grocery store to my third-floor walkup, carrying a plastic grocery bag in each hand.

The air smells of leaves and falafel and roast lamb from neighborhood restaurants. I can't afford to eat at them, though. Not on the eight dollars a day that is my budget if I want to live off my savings and not get a job.

Once again I have sequestered myself, living alone in an efficiency apartment in Dupont Circle, a gentrified section of town where my room costs $550 a month, $50 more than Kurt is paying for a three-bedroom ranch home back in Missouri. It is a small price to pay for privacy. My classmates are in another section of the city, spending half as much to share sprawling houses, their food labeled in the refrigerator, their towels on designated racks, yet still they fight over who finished whose milk or used the last of the peanut butter.

But really I live alone, in the gay district and without a job for one reason: I must not meet a man. I will not work because if I do I might meet someone, and if I meet someone he will want to have sex with me. And if he wants to, I will become charmed and unable to resist, and then I will leave Kurt and his children and our life together, or our potential life together. I will succumb and he will be alone, after leaving his wife for me. That was the rationale behind getting the apartment here, of all places, although what we said was that it was safer, that any crime in my area was against gay men, not against single women.

It's tough to live within my budget, though. If it's not raining I ride my bike to my office. If it is or if I'm running late or just too tired to jockey with taxis and tourists and DC's potholes I take the Metro, but it costs $1.60, leaving $6.40 for groceries and beer and an occasional lunch of Thai noodles.

Once or twice I splurge and call Amy. Jim has lost his job selling pool tables in a store owned by his parents. Amy is paying the bills for both of them, so she understands being broke.

He's looking for work, she tells me. Something will break soon.

Un huh.

I learn later that he spends his days drunk, that she is trying to persuade him to check into a rehab center, that she is going to Al-Anon meetings.

Really, she says. Things are good.

Later I sit cross-legged on the floor, my typewriter in front of me, and write my daily letter to Kurt.

I wish you were here, *I write.* I think of you and the kids constantly. There are tons of free things to do, like go to the Smithsonians and the zoo. I ran into Ted Kennedy today. Literally. I was coming across the capitol steps — late, of course — and crashed into him. He was busy talking to someone else, so he didn't notice, so I didn't have to get all embarrassed. He looks more like a statue than like a man. His head is craggy and surrounded by this huge lion's mane of hair and he seemed really tall right then. Then I was in the Senate office building and I got caught in a group of men coming around a corner and one of them was Paul Simon. I didn't notice if he was wearing a bow tie, but other than that he looked just like he does in magazines.

174

It's all official now. I have my little press pass to hang around my neck on a chain, so I can get into the Senate and House press galleries and whatever important meetings I want to attend. It gives me free run of the Library of Congress, the National Medical Library at the NIH, and I don't know what else. I'm also a member of the National Press Club, and my office is in the National Press Building. The Club has a restaurant (which I can't afford), a bar, a great library, and a small gym. So far I've used the gym more than anything else.

The other night I was up there with Yvette and some other people and there were snipers on the roof of the Willard, which is across the street but from up there looks like it's right next door. The White House is only two blocks away, and the president was coming in by helicopter, so the place was surrounded. We decided that if anything fell off the table we should just freeze, rather than try to grab it, or else we'd get shot.

But you'll have heard all of this before you get this letter.

Hug the kids for me. Hug yourself.

I get up to check the sauce on the stove. My stepsister Kris and her soon-to-be-husband have recently moved in together, and I am benefiting from their duplicates. I am using their extra wok to sauté onions and garlic, to which I'll add basil and oregano and tomato sauce. I use another of their pans to boil water for spaghetti. When I'm done I'll store the leftovers in a pitcher that was meant no doubt for lemonade or Kool-Aid. Everything in my room is theirs. The twin bed, the coffeemaker, the Corelle plates, the blankets and sheets. All I brought from home were my clock radio and typewriter, my pillow and my clothes. The typewriter had been a gift from my mother and stepfather.

I want to ask something, I had said to Mom. I'll need a typewriter in journalism school, and I wonder if you could lend me $500 to buy a really good one.

From there I proposed a repayment schedule, making my case as calmly as I was able. Graduate school would be tough enough, but to do it without a typewriter at home would make it nearly impossible. I would have to go to the lab to do assignments, finding the time between classes and my full-time job.

Mom said she'd think about it, talk to John, and call back.

It was John who called. No, he said, and I

slumped. You can only have it if you accept it as a gift.

I cried.

So it was that typewriter I use now as I write my letter, scrimping every penny. I roll another sheet of paper into the machine and hit the shift lock key.

I — I type, then hit the return key.

WAS — return

GONNA

I rip the paper out with a satisfying zip, then cut it into the shape of a tombstone and tape it to the wall above my bed. It is a talisman, a reminder of my grandmother.

When I die, she had said to me, her petal-soft face inches from mine, I want you to engrave my tombstone with the words "I was gonna." And I want you to promise me that the same words won't go on yours.

I step back and admire my work. It reminds me that even though staying here, alone and broke, is hard, it is what I always wanted to do, what I said I wanted to do, what I promised myself I would do. If I had turned down this opportunity I would have resented it for years.

Remember that, I say to myself, crawling between the sheets early, since there's nothing better to do.

The next day when I talk to Kurt on the

phone I tell him all about the happy hour tacos and the snipers and some story Eriko told about there being no word for "feminist" in Japanese.

What does that tell you?

Was Scott there?

Sure, I say, hesitating. So were Bobbi and Darrell.

Scott is the only one of my fellow grad students who is male and heterosexual. He is also the one who inherited the list of happy hours from last semester's students, a list that maps out where we can get nachos or chicken wings or a pasta buffet for the price of a beer. I don't tell Kurt that, though, because it makes Scott sound fun, like someone I might spend time with. I also don't tell him that when Scott starts arguing about politics I turn and listen, or that sometimes he walks down to the park with Yvette and me and sits with us as we eat lunch.

Every time I talk with Kurt the question slides in — so, was Scott there? — and almost every time I lie, and then feel guilty about lying to the man I love, the man it looks like I might be making a life with. But then sometimes that changes and I feel indignant that the lying feels necessary.

One of my friends is a guy, okay? That's

what I should say. One of my friends is a guy and we're friends and I enjoy him, but we're not screwing, got it? He is my friend and I'm going to do stuff with him even though you get psycho whenever you think I might notice that there's another man on this planet. Stop. I'm in love with you. You have nothing to worry about. But I don't stand up and say it because it feels too risky, like it will make Kurt feel vulnerable, like what we have is fragile, and I don't want that for him. I want him to feel safe and loved, secure. Especially after all he has given up for me.

CHAPTER

After a semester in Washington I graduate with hoopla. I have moved into Kurt's house, where we have a futon couch and an orange plaid recliner, a Formica dinette table, and three beds. We have patched the hole in the hallway where Kurt put his fist through the wall after a fight with his ex-wife, and hung the children's masterpieces on the refrigerator. There are roses and balloons and vinegary champagne, coolers of Miller Lite and Budweiser, and a store-bought cake with a plastic mortarboard.

There is family everywhere. His family. My family. It is the first mixing of the tribes, and everyone is talking. Kurt is bursting with a secret, mingling and supervising, but also going to the front room over and over to look out the window. After a while he nods his head vigorously at the children, and they run to me, take my hands and hustle me with much giggling to the front hall.

Close your eyes, they say.

I hear a door open and people shushing.

Okay, open them.

My grandmother is there, flown in from California.

Congratulations, Kurt says, his face beaming with love and pride for the surprise he's arranged for me.

Amy and I rush to her. She is shorter now. Soft and plump and smelling of Estée Lauder Private Collection, her glasses hanging from a chain around her neck. I am Gramma's little Nee-nee, a derivative of my name that my stepchildren will adopt. Amy is her little Zsa Zsa, the wearer of all things spangly, the one who raided Gramma's negligee drawer every time we visited and then paraded around in as many flouncy gowns and necklaces as she could find. Even today she is flamboyant in reds and purples and blues, in a skirt she has made herself because nothing else fits.

Everyone is babbling, divvying up kids and cars and purses and Kleenex, when the phone rings. It's Dad.

I'm at the intersection of Stadium and Providence, he says. How do I get to your house?

I stop. We had kept the party a secret from him on purpose, so he wouldn't invade this celebration of much-delayed accomplishment with his sarcasm and his lewd jokes. I look around the room at the people looking at me.

My brain won't work fast enough and I am not strong enough to tell him to turn around and drive the nine hours back to Michigan. Could I say it? Could I say, Sorry, Dad, but you aren't invited? I can't. I can't because I can't then deal with how hurt he'll be, or how he'll come back at me with, I'm your father, or maybe, Are you really the type of person who would turn her own father away?

I can't figure out how he found out. I didn't tell him. Kurt didn't tell him. He always knows things. How does he always know things? I stall. I can't think of a good response, in part because there are too many people looking at me, but mostly because I don't have the guts to tell him to go away.

Maybe this time it'll be different. Maybe this time it'll be fine. Maybe I'm imagining things or he's changed and he won't grope anyone, won't try to pick up my friends, won't drink so much that his laugh gets even more booming, his jokes more biting.

I give him the directions.

When I hang up, the family asks me why.

I don't know, I say. I couldn't figure out what else to do.

Shit, I think I hear someone say.

I lean against Kurt.

Dad's coming, I say. He's here in town.

How'd he find out?

I have no idea.

We find out later that Dad had called Steve's office for something and the secretary had said, Oh, he's not here. He's at his sister's graduation in Missouri.

How are we going to keep him and Gramma apart? I ask.

Gramma is my mom's mom and she's done with Dad. She was polite when she had to be — serving us fish on Fridays and biting her tongue when he smoked his cigars in the house or put his feet on the furniture — but she doesn't like him and he doesn't like her and the farther apart they stay, the better.

The party deflates, or maybe it's just me, but I no longer feel delighted at my milling family, here to do me honor. I feel disappointed. I feel cautious, like I'm going to have to keep Kurt or a child or a piece of furniture between myself and my father. Even then he will get his mental tentacles on me and somehow sexualize even this day.

I look down at my clothes. I'm wearing a white silk blouse and a black skirt, a belt at my waist. It is modest, but he still will be able to see my legs.

Kurt takes my hand.

I'm here, he says. I bury my face in his shirt.

You okay? Amy asks.

No I'm not okay! I say. Why can't I just have my special day without him screwing it up? Why does he ruin everything?

Amy hugs me. She is here without Jim, who has lost yet another job. She is going to Al-Anon meetings alone, to find ways to cope with his drinking, and her language is sprinkled with talk of letting go, of letting God. She is eating potato chips as she speaks.

184

■ ■ ■ ■

Dad arrives with a salt-and-pepper beard and stale coffee breath.

Hello, honey, he says.

He kisses me on the mouth and squeezes me hard. I try to pull away and he holds on tighter.

I can't believe how long it took to get down here, he says.

Kurt steps closer and holds out his hand, forcing Dad to let me go.

How're you doing, Pete?

The two men shake. Then Kurt turns to me, wipes off my dad's kiss and plants one of his own.

The rest of the family is bustling about, herding each other out the door and into cars for the drive to the ceremony. I carry my gown on a hanger, its dry cleaner bag rustling, and duck into one of the cars. When we get to the arena I am relieved to be swept along with this mill of strangers, each of us proud to parade across the stage, anonymous in our caps and gowns but knowing that to at least a few people in the crowd we are the most important person there.

When I cross the stage I hear whooping

from a section high in the third tier of seats, and I raise my diploma in their direction. I feel good. Afterward we all go back to the house, where we pop beers and build sandwiches and slice off chunks of cake that leave our teeth blue from frosting. People pull out cameras, and I pose in various family configurations — Mom and John beaming, Steve staging a grip-and-grin, the children and my grandmother each in turn wearing my mortarboard, photos that say "some day" for the kids and "I wish" for Gramma.

When Dad walks in, the women leak from the room, excusing themselves to the backyard or the kitchen or the bathroom. Kurt's mother, the warmest of women, who cannot understand why everyone is abandoning Dad, makes nice. She stays and talks with him, laughing at his jokes. She is a pretty woman, newly divorced, with beautiful laugh lines. Later she tells us Dad invited her on a cruise.

I love you I love you I love you, I say to Kurt.

We spend our afternoons in bed, our mornings smiling over the children's heads. We are giddily, all-consumingly in love.

I have been back from Washington for six

months, and Kurt's divorce has finally gone through.

I don't want a diamond, I tell him. Diamonds have no personality. They just sparkle and get in the way. They show, what? That your man loves you? That he makes money? I don't want a diamond.

So one night at a restaurant he gives me a multistrand necklace of silver and asks if I'd consider being his wife.

Yes, I say. Absolutely.

I'll get you a ring later, he says.

I beam.

A month later we leave for a romantic weekend alone at Tan Tara, a resort at the Lake of the Ozarks. The lake is a dammed river, murky-bottomed and oily from the boaters who crowd it all summer, and on weekends into the fall. The resort is labyrinthine, built into the hills over time, the hotel rooms connected to the concourse and the bowling alley and the indoor shopping and the three restaurants and four bars and the photo studio where we pose in faux gangster gear. There is an ice rink and glass-walled racquetball courts, which we use even though afterward we fight viciously over techniques and strategies and who won. There are water views and pine trees and the squeals of children being tossed by parents in the pool.

I know from the beginning of the weekend that he is going to officially propose. I have talked with Amy about it — babbled, in fact — and she is waiting for the report. I anticipate how he'll ask. Will it be here? Will it be now? Then for dinner one night he shows up with an I-have-a-secret look on his face and a box-shaped bulge in his jacket pocket. He is not subtle at all, and I pretend not to notice. We have our salads, and then he reaches into his jacket pocket and puts the box on the table. It is a cube, at least three inches each way, much bigger than I expected. There is a moment of hush, of reverential anticipation, and then I unwrap it, loosening the ribbon, peeling off the paper, taking a deep breath and then opening the box.

It is a Mickey Mouse watch. A large-faced, vinyl-strapped Mickey Mouse watch. For a beat I am stunned, and then I burst into laughter that approaches tears. He has set me up, turned my anticipation against itself. I laugh until I cry, and he laughs with me, thrilled, I think, that his joke has worked. He takes my hand across the table, and I use the other to wipe away tears. It is that funny.

That was good, I say.

As I reach for him again he slips a ring into my hand, but because I'm not expecting it, it falls into the dish of olive oil, and the laughter starts again, until other diners turn to see what the noise is about and the waitress comes to see if everything is okay. The ring, an opal surrounded by tiny diamond chips, slides on easily.

I chose it because most of its beauty is on the inside, he says, so it reminded me of you.

My eyes fill with tears.

Will you marry me? he asks.

He is smiling directly into my eyes, and I am euphoric.

Yes, I say.

We are laughing and crying as I wipe the oil from my hand.

I tell the story to Amy later. She does not laugh. She is still with Jim, still struggling with her weight.

But you're beautiful on the outside, too, she says.

Thank you, but don't you get it? He thinks I'm even more beautiful on the inside than on the outside. Isn't that wonderful? It means I am enough.

We decide to marry quickly, with just one witness besides the children, in the living room of a minister I know. Our parents are all divorced and not everyone can make it on short notice, so we invite no one rather than risk someone feeling excluded. Instead we plan to redo our vows during a big party in the summer. We'll call that our wedding, too. That way we can celebrate our anniversary twice each year.

I spend my thirtieth birthday making my wedding dress, an off-white with a dropped waist and a lace knee-length skirt. It is simple but pretty.

I wish I had a little more up top, I joke.

Kurt wraps his arms around me and kisses my neck.

If it bothers you, he says, maybe someday we can do something about it.

I laugh. The very thought is ridiculous. Not in this lifetime, I say.

He squeezes me and smiles.

A few days before our wedding, the temperature plummets and the engine block on my Mazda pickup cracks. I still have to get to work each day and drive the kids to and from school and day care and get groceries and dog food and shoes and stickers and backpacks, and still bring dinner to Kurt at work. But it'll be fine, I'm sure.

Kurt gets mad, but not at me, and he doesn't stay mad for long. It's just that he's worried about the money, even though I'm working, too. I've been poor, so the idea doesn't scare me. Besides, we're getting married in a couple of days. What does a cracked engine block matter?

The next day it snows, small icy flakes that freeze on shrubs and roads and windshields.

Can I borrow your car?

He looks up from his desk. He just bought a new white Mazda 626, a solid, impressive four-door that we can't really afford.

What for?

Nothing, I say, smiling.

Nothing, eh?

Nothing important.

He looks at me.

I don't think you should be out on the roads in this, he says.

I'll be fine, I say. I learned to drive in Michigan, remember?

What I don't tell him is I plan to run up to the crafts store and buy a wedding doo-dad for the top of our cake. The kids and I baked it last night — cherry chip with butter frosting and sprinkles. I tried to make it look more formal by cutting away part of the top layer, but somehow it turned out shaped a lot like a Hershey's Kiss. It needs a plastic bride and groom, I think, to differentiate it from something I'd make for one of the kids' birthdays.

He shakes his head and smiles.

Sure, he says. But be careful.

I take the stairs two at a time, happy with my errand. I buckle my seat belt, back out of the driveway, and creep up our street, sliding a little at the stop sign. Our street is slick, but I'm sure the main roads will be cleared and cindered. A few other cars are out, and if other people don't drive like idiots I'll be fine.

I turn left onto the main road and let my speed climb to twenty. At this rate it'll take half an hour to get to the store, but the stereo is on and the day is sparkling white and I'm happy. I'm getting married in two days. I'm going to have a man who loves me forever and ever and ever. We're going to have adventures and make memories and raise the children and be everything I have ever dreamt of being.

Other drivers are fishtailing, but the big car holds tight to the road. I am singing as I tap the brakes. The car in front of me pulls slowly into the intersection. I have most of a block to stop, and I am confident. The wheels, though, don't grip and the car turns sideways. I steer into the slide, just like I learned in driver's ed, and the car swivels, so now I am sliding toward the intersection driver's side first. I correct, and the car straightens.

I'm tapping the brakes but they won't catch. There's no way I'll stop before the stop sign, I can see that. But the intersection is clear, so if I can just keep from bouncing right or left up onto one of the curbs, I'll be fine.

The cross street is a boulevard, so I will cross one lane that goes left to right and one that goes right to left. Both are clear, though, so I'm okay, even though I am tapping the brakes and steering into the swerves. I'm going to be fine.

And then a car enters the intersection from the left and I'm aimed right at it, me, the driver, my side. I can't miss it. I know that, even as I crank the wheel with one hand and cover my face with the other.

When the spinning stops I am up on the median, facing back the way I came, my front bumper jammed against a fire hydrant. My hands are white on the wheel and my heart is hammering, but there's no blood. I take a deep breath and look up.

Sliding through the intersection, aimed right at me, is a dump truck full of cinders. It's ironic, really, that it would be a dump truck full of cinders. That's what I think in what I think is my last moment, but the truck slides by, lurches up another curb and stops ten feet shy of a day care center.

I breathe.

The car I hit or that hit me is crumpled, my car is crumpled, the cinder truck is grinding its gears to back off the day care center's lawn, but I am okay. I am okay.

The noise outside and in stops, and I open the door. A police car slides through the intersection and stops, and traffic again starts to move. A neighbor pulls up next to me as I bend to inspect the damage.

You okay?

I nod.

I'm fine, I say. Although the car's not.

I see that. Want me to go get Kurt?

Would you? That would be great.

I am shaky and weepingly grateful that I have someone who cares, someone who will come and hold me and stroke my hair and tell me it's okay, that accidents happen, that he's just glad no one got hurt.

I am leaning against the car when Kurt is dropped off by the neighbor.

What the hell did you do? he yells. This is a brand-new car! We can't afford this!

I'm sorry, I say.

You said you could drive through this. What the hell did you do?

Kurt, I say, the cinder truck slid through,

too. So did the cop car.

It doesn't matter. I was going too fast. I wasn't paying attention. I saw the other car and didn't stop. I am a complete and utter fuckup. If he had been driving he would not have slid. Everything would be fine now. His car wouldn't be crumpled, we wouldn't be looking at hundreds of dollars in repairs and a hammering on our insurance premium, and we sure as hell wouldn't be standing on a street corner in the snow screaming about what a fucking idiot one of us is.

I cry, and then I get mad — at myself. If I hadn't told the neighbor I was fine, Kurt would have come up first with concern for whether I was okay. I'm sure of it. When he first heard he must have been scared, even if the neighbor had rushed to tell him that the only damage was to the car. That's what this is, a reaction to the adrenaline, to the fear that I was hurt.

Surely that's what it is. It continues into the night. The accusing, the finger jabbing. I barely sleep.

The next day he sends me roses.

I'm sorry, the card reads, in the florist's handwriting. Let's get married tomorrow.

CHAPTER 9

If it bothers you, he says, I'll pay for plastic surgery.

We have been married for three months and are lying in bed, the springtime sounds of birds and traffic drifting in through the open window. I look down at my chest. It's true that I am barely an A cup.

Does it bother you that I'm flat? I ask.

He brushes the back of his hand over one

of my nipples. It's a sensation I love.

No, he says. I don't mind. But I think it bothers you.

I lie back and think about it. I wish I wasn't flat, sure, but surgery? And then what? Parade around with big breasts as if I'd grown them myself? I would feel fake.

Then again, real breasts are just fat, so there's no point in being proud of them. Still, it would be surgery. And surgery hurts.

I gather my breasts into my hands and push them up to create cleavage. I'm thirty and fading away. The workouts and weigh-ins are making me flatter, but I don't care. At least I don't think I care.

It bothers him, though, I know. Of course he loves me just the way I am, but he'd like it better if I had bigger breasts. Or maybe I'm the one who wants them. Or maybe I want them because he wants them, because it would please him.

Would you do it if it were you?

Oh, yeah, he says. If it bothered me as much as it bothers you I would.

Later that day I look in the mirror. My butt is firm and my stomach is flat from hours in the gym. I call Amy, but I hide my question deep in the conversation.

I'm feeling fat, I say.

Amy snorts. Right, she says. What are you,

up an ounce?

She has listened to me obsess before.

Very funny, I say, although she's probably right. If I spend an extra ten minutes on the step machine later I can burn it off.

I saw a bumper sticker the other day that reminded me of you, she says.

What'd it say?

Work out, eat smart, die with a great-looking body. You're still dead.

Now I snort.

Funny, I say. Hey, I'm thinking about getting breast implants.

She is quiet for a minute.

Seriously?

Amy has had pendulous breasts since high school. We have talked before about whether a breast reduction would make it easier for her to exercise, easier for her to find clothes. As it is, bras dig into her shoulders and the weight of her breasts pulls her forward, making it hard to walk and impossible to jog.

Kurt and I were talking about it, I say. I'm thinking about it — just so I look better in my clothes.

Un huh, she says.

There is a pause.

Is this something you really want to do? It doesn't sound like you.

I know, I say, but it might be fun to have a chest for once.

What happened to, Women shouldn't be judged by their looks?

I know, I say. But sometimes women are judged by their looks, and we both know it.

I wince as I say it. Amy has gained at least twenty pounds in the past year. Jim has gone back to drinking, and eating gives Amy something to do in the evening. That and watching movies.

Okay, she says. Remember, though, sometimes busty people look fat. Even when they're not.

True. And I'm short, so I'm going to be like that joke of Gramma's.

Which one?

Something like, I've reached the bureau years: my chest has fallen into my drawers.

Amy laughs. Her chest fell into her drawers long ago.

I'm not going to let them add much, I say.

Un huh.

I get off the phone and look in the mirror again. My breasts are small, that's true, but it doesn't matter. What matters is that the parts that have to do with self-discipline look as good as determination and deprivation can make them.

I'm fine the way I am.

■ ■ ■ ■

That night in bed he says, Are you still thinking about implants?

I wasn't, I say.

He pulls me toward him.

It's just that I know it bothers you, he says.

Of course it bothers me, I say, but it would be vain to go through surgery. Besides, it would send the wrong message to women, that you can be slim and have big breasts. All they need is another reason to feel inadequate.

Being small-breasted isn't inadequate, he says.

It shouldn't be, but try telling that to all of the girls who grew up with Barbie, I say. Or centerfolds. Or pornography.

Oh, here comes the feminist rant again, he says.

I'm not ranting. And what's wrong with being a feminist?

Nothing, he says, rolling away.

What's the matter with you? I ask, sitting up.

Nothing, he says. Look, if you don't want to have sex, just say so. You don't have to pick a fight.

I punch my pillow and roll onto my own

side. Did I pick a fight? I hate this. I was perfectly calm and happy and now he's mad at me. I hate it when he's mad at me. Especially when I can't figure out what I did wrong. I wasn't even talking about getting implants, wasn't even thinking about it. And now I'm accused of being on a feminist rant? I hold tight to my side of the bed. I am not going to roll over to him, not going to try to get him to forgive me. Forgive me for what? I haven't done anything.

But he's hurt and mad, I can tell. And he loves me. He loves me just the way I am. He just wants me to feel proud of my body, and he knows that being small-breasted bugs me. It does bug me. It has always bugged me, ever since I was a teenager and Dad made jokes about me being flat as a board. But does it bother me enough to go through surgery? Yikes. There'd be a knife and blood and anesthesia and people wondering why all of a sudden I'm busty. It would be painful and embarrassing, and it would say that breast size matters.

I flip onto my back and run my hands over my breasts. What was that saying from high school? More than a handful is a waste. Or was that more than a mouthful? I roll toward Kurt and stroke his back. There is nothing he wouldn't do for me, I know. If we were in reverse positions, he'd have it done if I wanted, just so I would be happy. He has told me that.

I spoon up against his back, but he shrugs me off.

Fine, I think, and roll back to my own side.

During the night he must forgive me, because I wake up with his arms around me. Gingerly I ease out of bed, careful not to wake him. I shuffle into the bathroom, my feet tender from yesterday's aerobics class, and spend long minutes on the toilet before pulling the scales out of the bathroom closet. I step on slowly, shifting my weight in hopes of getting the reading down by half a pound. One hundred and thirteen point five, it reads. Twenty-two percent body fat.

I step off.

While I wait for the electronic numbers to clear I look out the window, down the sloped half acre to the lake. The yard looks lush, although from here I can see plumes of grass in one of the flower beds. I look up, at the mirrors that reflect my naked body from every angle, and scowl. For some reason I cannot get rid of that two-inch patch of cellulite high on my left thigh. I press it smooth with my fingers, but it comes back. There is no corresponding bulge on the right, which makes no sense. I turn to a different mirror, but it is still there. I suck in my stomach and flex my arms. Not bad, if not for that cellulite. I know Kurt would love me more if I were perfect.

I look back at the scale. The numbers have cleared, so I step back on. One hundred and thirteen point five pounds, 22 percent body fat. If I run the dogs and make it to the noon aerobics class, I should be okay.

What is it today? he says from behind me.

I start.

I thought you were asleep.

What is it?

I tell him the numbers.

Not bad, he says. I thought the way we pigged out last night they'd be higher.

I know, I say, laughing. That was quite a meal.

What's yours?

He steps on the scale.

Up one, he says. We can work out extra.

I was on my way there now, I say, and he smiles.

He climbs back into bed as I pull on shorts and a jog bra.

See you in a bit, I say, leaning over to kiss him.

Have fun, he says, then he reaches up and strokes the front of my top.

You know, he says, I can see why you'd like to go up a size or two.

I swat his hand away.

At the gym I jump on the step machine, open my book and focus. I want to burn 350 calories in half an hour, but that's hard to do at my weight. From here I'll go to lift weights. Kurt and I don't like flabby arms.

In the locker room afterward I see a topless woman with beautiful breasts. What size are those? I ask her.

They're B's, she says. I'm thinking about getting them fixed.

Why would you get them fixed? They're perfect.

You think so? She tilts her head and looks at them in the mirror. She is just out of the tanning bed, so they are toasted brown, the areas around her nipples an even chestnut.

I'd like to be a C, I think, she says.

I'd like to be a full B, I think. That would give me enough to fill out my clothes, and maybe make my husband happy.

She laughs.

I'm single, she says. Maybe if I had bigger boobs . . .

Do you ever think men will value us for our brains?

She looks at me, deadpan, and lets the

silence lengthen, as if she's thinking.

No, she says. And we laugh.

A few weeks later our families pour into the house for our wedding celebration. Technically we are already married — back in December to get the tax break, with only the children and one close friend as witnesses. But this is the one I intend to count. Our families will be here and we'll say the vows we wrote ourselves, about honoring and cherishing, about inspiring and supporting and being wildly in love forever.

There are tears, there is bad poetry, there is a party with catered food and candlelight and people doing the bump and the locomotion on a dance floor under a tent in the backyard. We crowd the floor for "We are Family." Jane picks up her daughter, I pick up my stepdaughter. Amy is there without Jim, who has stayed behind in Atlanta. She looks relaxed and happy as we all whirl around the tent's center pole.

Then Steve calls for attention. The siblings and stepsiblings and spouses line up. There is a clearing of throats and a rattling of paper, and then they begin to sing a song about how Kurt and I met, set to the tune of "Doo Wah Diddy Diddy."

Kurt puts his arm around me. He is laughing, too. By the end of the song my family is again down on one knee, arms spread wide, Broadway style. This tradition that looks so familiar to me, is as exotic to Kurt as an African tribal chant.

We applaud mightily, give hugs all around, and break into clusters to laugh about which mastermind came up with which line.

Later I am slow dancing with Kurt. I am wearing an above-the-knee summer dress, ankle socks, and white Keds. I look more like a gym teacher than a bride as I raise up on my toes and move into my husband's arms.

Dad comes up behind me. I feel his prickly beard on my neck before I hear his voice.

God, you have sexy legs, he says.

Kurt spins me away.

Six months later the doctor is asking me to take off my clothing from the waist up so he can evaluate my breasts. My face is red-hot with embarrassment, to have this man who does not care about me see my inadequate chest, to have him assess me clinically, and diagnose me, eventually, as having hypomastia — abnormally small breasts. When I read it on the pre-op papers I feel defensive.

My breasts are not abnormal; they're just small.

We chose this doctor because he had been trained at the same hospital that trained my husband, but he has set up practice two hours away, so it will be easier for us to remain anonymous, as if no one will know.

He is going to cut around the edges of my areolas, stretch the skin, insert what look and feel like circular Ziplocs full of silicone. There will be pain and swelling and bleeding and discomfort from the stretching. He assures me it will pass.

Will you have to cath me? I ask. I hate the idea of doctors snaking a tube up my urethra. It makes me clamp down just thinking about it.

No, the doctor says. We'll be done in a couple of hours, so we shouldn't need to.

I am relieved.

Will I be able to sleep on my stomach?

The doctor looks baffled.

Well, yea, he says. Of course. You won't even notice them after a while.

I nod.

Will I be able to breast-feed?

Both Kurt and the doctor look at me, startled.

If I got pregnant, I mean.

There is a pause.

Are you pregnant now?

No, of course not. But if I were.

Yes. Your odds wouldn't be any worse than any other mother's.

I nod. Kurt squeezes my hand. We have decided not to have children because we don't want his kids to feel like stepchildren. Still, I'm just checking. In case we change our minds.

You're going to need a bra to go home in, the doctor says.

Okay, I say. How do we know what size?

Initially you'll probably be a large C, he says. I tell most patients to just buy something inexpensive, and then when the swelling goes down and you're comfortable, you can shop for something more permanent.

I sign on the dotted line. Two weeks later, Kurt and I are trolling the lingerie section at the local Montgomery Ward.

May I help you? The saleswoman has lipstick on her teeth.

Um . . . no, I say. We're fine.

She glances at my chest and then at the bra in my hand.

Are you shopping for yourself? she asks, and I nod. Your size, darling, is over here, she says, guiding me to the racks of barely-there and training bras and bras so stiff with padding they stand out by themselves.

Thanks, I say, pretending to look and hardly holding back my giggles.

Kurt stands by my side, studiously looking at options. As soon as the saleslady's back is turned, we sneak back over to the C section.

This one? he asks.

I laugh.

Ohmygod, they're huge! I say. Let's buy a couple and see which one works.

The sales clerk reappears and clucks disapprovingly, but I stand tall and jut out my chest.

We'll take these, I say, handing them to her.

Fine, she says.

We lurch out of the store trying to contain our laughter. We barely make it to the car.

That night I toss around. I have never had surgery. I don't know what to expect, don't know how to behave. I hope I don't do anything embarrassing, like talk too much under anesthesia or wet the sheets or shit myself. I hope I don't puke. I hate puking.

In the morning I sit in the same-day surgery center in my backside-exposing gown, a cafeteria-lady net over my hair, my finger clipped into a pulse-oximeter with an ET-like glowing tip.

I kiss Kurt good-bye and drift off on a

current of drugs. It feels good to let go. I see flowers and fireworks. I hear music and laughter. I feel safe and loved.

The surgery should take four hours but takes seven because the doctor's scalpel nicks my left lung, which collapses, flat and worthless, the bubbles bloody. The doctor cuts a slit in my skin and inserts a tube between my ribs, into the punctured lung. It sucks in air and reinflates. We all start breathing normally.

The surgery takes so long that he does, in fact, insert a catheter. When I come to I am angry at this broken promise, this invasion of my privates, but I am so disoriented by the narcotics that I can barely stand without toppling over.

I raise my hands to my chest. It is enormous. Heavy and throbbing, a bludgeoning wound. The nurses help me into a wheelchair and Kurt steers me out of the place, even though each turn makes me want to puke up the sips of 7-Up they let me have in the recovery room.

We're staying in a hotel next door so we can get to the hospital quickly if there's an emergency. On the way there I tell Kurt I am having cravings.

For what? he asks.

Fudge Stripes and Cheetos, I say.

He mock vomits, then says he'll be happy to get them, right after he helps me into bed in our room.

When we get there I am woozy, and I lie back gratefully, then jerk upright. The pain is white hot as the weight of the shifting implants stretch the nerves. The doctor had warned me about it. He had told me it would be worse when I forced the implants around in the now-disconnected pocket between my ribs and my pectoral muscles, which I would have to do if I wanted them to move "naturally." The pain sears, and it takes courage every time I try to move.

Kurt props me up with pillows — two behind my back and one on my lap, to support my new breasts. Then he leaves to get my snacks.

I call Amy.

They're done, I say.

How do you feel?

Like shit, I say. I'm woozy and gross and my chest hurts like holy hell. How are you?

She laughs.

Compared to you I'm great.

How are you compared to someone else?

She laughs again.

I'm fine, she says. A little bummed. Jim lost his job again, and we had our usual fight last night about him getting a new one. But other than that, things are good.

I wish I could be there for her, listen to the details, help her figure out what to do, but I am dozing off as she speaks.

I'm sorry, Amy, I say. Truly. I'm fading, though.

I can tell, she says. Go to sleep. I'll call Mom and tell her all's well.

Thanks. Love you.

Love you, too.

I lie back against the pillows. Why did I let this happen? I chose this pain? I'm an idiot. I'm going to look silly. People are going to know. They're going to know I'm vain. They're going to know that I am so insecure that I need big breasts to feel complete.

I am obsessing when Kurt comes back through the door.

Can we look at them? he asks.

The doctor says we have to wait until tomorrow, I say.

Just a peek, he says. What harm can it do?

I look at him.

I feel like crap, I say. I just want to hold still.

He sits on the side of the bed and gently strokes the front of my shirt.

Wow, he says.

I am having trouble being a good sport. I

am nauseated, sore, and exhausted. I want to sleep, but I can't get comfortable.

Just one peek, he says. Come on.

He is smiling his beautiful boyish smile, his eyes sparkling at the fun of this thing.

I shake my head at the futility of resisting such a handsome man. I inch my legs over the side of the bed, my chest and arms screaming with each move, and shuffle to the mirror over the dresser, where I raise my arms childlike so he can unwrap the yards and yards of Ace bandage.

I wince as he reaches around and around me, afraid he'll bump me, afraid and excited about what I'll see. When he stops I see myself swollen and distorted under a layer of blood-crusted gauze, which he removes like unwrapping a mummy.

He peels it away and I gasp. My breasts are taut and round and huge. Also purple and maroon and green. The swelling and the bruising are overwhelming, as are the black stitches in tufts around my nipples. I am silent. There is no other response. Kurt, however, reaches around from behind me and cups one breast in each hand.

Wow, he says.

He squeezes each one gently, and I wince.

Bend forward a little, he says, and I do.

He rubs himself against my backside, and

I close my eyes. I can't stand what I'm seeing, but I'm glad I don't repulse him.

Okay, rewrap me, I say. I want a cookie.

In a minute, he says, watching in the mirror as his hands roam over my black-and-blue flesh.

In truth I feel a little less pain when he cups them and supports their weight, so I let him. I let him, too, because I love him.

I was so scared, he says now, wrapping his arms around me and pressing his cheek against my back. It took so much longer than it was supposed to, and I was so afraid I was going to lose you.

I support my weight on the bureau while he leans against my back. After a moment he stands and holds my hips, sliding himself against me.

You know . . . he says, and meets my eyes in the mirror.

You have to be kidding, I say.

I'd be gentle.

I look at him in the mirror. He hates rejection, I know. Hates it like a wound. And what harm would be done?

Very very gentle, I say.

He smiles.

Afterward I sit and watch TV for half an hour, but my legs are twitchy.

I have to walk, I say.

He helps me up and holds my hand as I walk gingerly down the stale hallway to the fresh air. The hotel we're in is on a ridge next to a dam, the land dropping sharply on either side. Looking down makes me vertiginous. I grip his arm and try not to topple. Each step is painful, but also dizzying. The world is swirling around me.

I've had enough, I say, and he guides me back to the room.

Ugh, I say. I feel like shit.

He helps me onto the bed and then goes into the bathroom and returns with a cool washcloth, which he puts on my forehead.

Thank you, I say, sighing.

He sits on the bed next to me and strokes my hair. Gently he lays his head down on my belly and runs a hand over my swollen front.

You have to get off, I say, pushing against him. My stomach muscles feel tender. Everything on me feels tender.

I roll onto my side — slowly — and he moves around behind me and cradles up against me.

This is going to be fun, he says, reaching around and putting a palm on my breast. I can't feel it, though, through the layers and layers of bandage. At least, that's what I presume.

The truth is that I have lost the feeling in that breast. There's a 10 percent chance of that happening in any augmentation, the surgeon had said. I had assumed I would be lucky. I'm always one of the lucky ones, right? But not this time.

It bothers me though that my chest — the space closest to my heart, the place I define as the seat of my love — has lost its feeling. When I hug I do not feel the skin on skin. If I have a child, I will not feel her nurse. I try not to care. I had been warned.

What I never expected is that the doctor detached my pectoral muscles from my sternum and now whenever my pecs are used — to pick up a child, to open a jar, to row a canoe or kayak — my breasts leap toward my armpits. It is alarming. Even at rest they are a palm's width apart. Between the two problems I am limited in what I can wear. This thing we did for vanity has turned out ugly.

Years later I object to him fondling my dead breast.

I can't feel it, you know, I say, and if you play with it it just reminds me.

This isn't all about you, you know, he says. Sometimes I don't like to worry about whether I'm on the right one. Besides, I can feel it.

I try to argue with his logic, but he has a point. He can feel it and enjoy it and the fact that I can't doesn't matter. That's just me being pissy about what I lost in order to be attractive. I need to just let it go.

CHAPTER 10

In the spring the carnival comes to town,
the greasy, half-toothed carnies setting up
the Tilt-a-Whirl and Himalyan Express and
Zipper on the mall's asphalt parking lot,
then turning their stubby hands onto the
kids, leaving grease and tobacco smudges
on springtime dresses as they lift the littlest
into seats.

The children chatter and scream, clamoring for cotton candy and fried dough and kettle corn, while the parents groan at the price, each ride three dollars per kid, parents extra.

We are there every year, Mikey and Claire bursting with end-of-school-year excitement, running through sawdust, screaming their pleas over the barkers and the clatter of machinery and the metallic blare of over-amped music.

I can barely keep up, dressed as I am in my little pink sweater and white miniskirt, my spike heels catching on the snaking cables.

The carnies, of course, look. They whistle. They stroke me with their eyes.

I hate it. I feel as smudged and handled as the children's dresses, only dirtier. I feel, somehow, their breath, the stink from their unbrushed teeth. I hold my husband's hand, seeking safety.

The other women look appalled, and then they look away. Always away.

Don't worry about it, my husband says. They're just jealous.

The same thing happens at horse races and hardware stores, where we can always get help, sometimes more than we need, the aproned employees approaching every time we pause.

Can I help you find something? they ask.

The Saturday husbands in their baggy jeans and flannel shirts stare intently at the tape measures and right angles and detachable bits, glancing up and then away, their wives and girlfriends glaring.

Don't worry about it, my husband says. They're just jealous.

It's hard to make friends, between the clothing and my husband's anxiety every time we prepare for guests, his drumbeat of disapproval of my friends.

Don't hang out with her, he says, she hates men. What do you need those people for, anyway? Aren't we enough?

I cancel lunches, turn down invitations, show up for the school Halloween party in a Catwoman costume so provocative it makes the teacher blanch.

Holy cow! she says. That's too sexy for school.

I am humiliated, and she quickly comforts me.

I'm just jealous, she says. If I had your body, I'd wear something like that, too. Really.

I feel a little better, although still awkward, teetering as I am between what I think is right and proper and appropriate and my husband's opinion that the other mothers' costumes — the mummies and witches and fully covered gypsies I like so much — are signs of a woman giving up, and I must never, ever give up.

In the basement of our home we have a room with a mirrored wall. I practice my aerobics choreography there under a Nike poster. "There is no finish line," it reads. I like it, and then I don't. Why is there no finish line? Why must I always be better?

At night when we go out I tart myself up in the high heels and tight skirts. One night I come home and go immediately into my closet and strip out of my stiff public clothes. I pull on my baggy flannel pants and an old sweatshirt that says "California," purchased years earlier during a visit to my grandmother. I wear it nearly daily, and it is broken in to just the right level of comfort, so soft and warm and safe that I wrap myself into it and then wrap my arms around myself, sighing.

Kurt comes to the door.

Well, that's not even subtle, he says, and walks away.

I chase after him.

What? What did I do?

He looks at my clothes.

Could you be less sexy?

I look down. I am comfortable, but not

sexy. I apparently can't be both.

I wrap my arms around him from behind, but he uses two fingers on each hand to lift them away, as if they were distasteful.

Don't even try, he says.

I go to sleep unhappy.

CHAPTER 11

I'm leaving him, Amy says.

Good for you, I say. I am cautious, though. I don't want to say much. Other times when she's left him I've said he was a loser and an asshole. Then they got back together and her calls were fewer, the talk strained.

I don't want to be alone, she says.

I know. I understand that. I cannot imagine being alone. But I also can't imagine being married to a manipulative, controlling man who is trying to suppress me.

Take the leap, I say.

I'm scared.

You can do it. You can do anything.

She sniffs.

You can do it, I repeat.

I don't want to be alone, she says again.

I know. It's scary.

Who else is going to love me?

I love you.

She laughs. You have to love me, you're my sister.

Yes, but I would love you anyway, I say. You're lovable.

She cries.

I know I am, she says.

You really are. You're beautiful and witty and smart and funny. You attract people.

She cries more, then sniffles.

I know, she says. I can do this.

I get off the phone, but I'm not sure she can do this. Or rather, I'm sure, but I'm scared for her. She lived at home until she got married. She has never been on her own, never believed she could pay all of the bills or do all of the ticky-tacky inherent in having a home, even though she's been do-ing it all along. Still, she has had the delu-sion of support. A man in her bed, another name on her checking account.

I don't know it yet, but leaving a marriage is a hurtling leap through space, with brief euphoria and then the realization that you are suspended, an instant away from failing in some dramatic way, in an emotional and financial explosion. A splattering on the rocks.

In the morning I drive to the sporting goods store, the one that puts kids' names on the backs of their Little League jerseys and engraves the plaques on Good Sportsmanship trophies, and ask the salesman to show me their medals. I want to make Amy a talisman, something that will remind her always that she is strong and brave.

The salesman shows me faux-bronze discs with raised figures of runners breaking the winning tape, of soccer players going after the ball, of men and women and girls and boys shooting basketballs or swinging bats. I consider my options. None seems right. Then at the bottom of the display case I find it, a depiction of Winged Victory, triumphant and brave, her arms raised to the sky.

That's the one, I say.

Next I pick out a two-inch metal rectangle. I have it engraved with one word: Courage.

I drive home thinking about Amy, wishing

she had lived on her own between Mom's house and Jim's, so she'd have more confidence in herself. I can't imagine why she has stayed with him as long as she has.

I snort. He had been fired by his own parents from a job selling pool tables and supplies. I laugh again, feeling light that she is finally breaking free. No more begging, pleading, and dragging his passed-out ass to bed at night. No more cleaning up vomit. No more being shoved or punched or called fat.

I feel giddy, even though it isn't about me.

She hadn't said much, but when she did she'd always make an excuse.

He was drunk, she'd say.

He's just frustrated about money. I love him. I don't want to be alone.

I shake my head, remembering. I think she was afraid of being alone. I can relate to the loneliness, but I'm not afraid of doing for myself, although it might be harder now that I've grown used to plush. Still, I know how to provide food and shelter and how to take out the trash. I have plugged radiator leaks, changed filters and spark plugs, rummaged through salvage yards.

Right after I got my license I went to court to defend myself against a ticket for running a red light in a boulevard intersection.

Dad drove me to the city's office of road design, where I picked up the intersection's blueprint. He drove me to the driveway where the officer had been parked and helped me take photos of the cop's line of vision. He drove me to the highway department to pick up timing records for the light.

I walked into court with the rolled plans tucked under my arm, the photos and timing records in a folder. My father came with me, although I stepped through the swinging gate in the bar alone. My father sat in the front row of the gallery, leaning forward to coach me.

She's doing fine, the judge told him. Sit down and be quiet.

I felt triumphant. More so when I won.

I wonder if Amy ever had that kind of victory?

On the way home Dad and I hooted and cheered and reenacted everything I'd said.

You see, he said, it's good to stand up for yourself.

I wonder if he ever told Amy that. I doubt it.

When I get home I use the glue gun Amy gave me to mount both the medal and the Courage plaque on a piece of black velvet. It looks good. I slide it into a frame and glue on a green felt backing. Over that I glue a piece of paper that reads, "Like the Cowardly Lion, you had the courage all along. You just needed the medal to prove it to yourself."

My father's voice echoes.

Do you want a medal or a chest to pin it on?

For a minute I am pissed.

I show the plaque to Kurt, who looks up from his computer and smiles.

She's going to love it, he says.

I think she will.

He looks back to his computer, but I don't move. He looks back up, his eyebrows raised. I am smiling at him, proud of myself.

Finally he says, Did you do any work today?

Not yet, I say.

Don't you have something due?

I do, but I thought this was more important.

He looks pointedly back at his own computer.

Well, some of us don't have that luxury, he says.

I get the message. I go to another room, wrap my creation in bubble wrap, slide it into a box, and address it to Amy. Then I sit down at my desk and work.

When I am done I go down to Kurt's office.

Let's go to Booche's, I say. I want to shoot some pool.

He is balancing our checkbook, his finger sliding down the list of transactions, his eyes shifting between the paper and the computer screen. For a moment he doesn't respond. Then he looks up.

Okay, he says. Give me a couple of minutes.

I go back upstairs and pull on jeans and a T-shirt. When he comes up he pulls me down on the bed.

You know, he says between kisses, that little black skirt?

I laugh.

That would be cute tonight.

People's heads swivel as we walk into Booche's, but they always do. Whenever the door opens people look up to greet friends, or to scold the one who lets in the cold. Kurt and I stop at the bar for two beers and a rack of balls. I lean against the table as Kurt breaks. When I lean over to take my shot my underwear is exposed, so I try bending my knees instead, shooting awkwardly, my high heels throwing off my balance.

Relax, Kurt says. You look great.

There are men at the next table. I see them looking at me, nudging each other and aligning themselves to look down my shirt or up my skirt. One drops his cue behind me, then bends to pick it up as I take a shot.

Their laughter is loud.

A few days later the phone rings. It is Amy. She is crying and laughing simultaneously.

This is great, she says.

I thought you'd like it.

And I do have courage, she says. You're right. Thank you for reminding me.

By the time we get off the phone we are both laughing, though my eyes are wet. I want so much for her to succeed.

So does everyone else. She has to move to a less expensive apartment, so Mom and John drive up to help pack. Other family members and friends carry boxes. I don't go. She is in Atlanta and I am in Missouri. I have kids. I have a husband. They need me.

My housewarming present to her is a box full of the little stuff — a screwdriver and a lightbulb and a roll of toilet paper, some candles and bubble bath and a refrigerator magnet — along with a gift certificate to a discount store.

This is for all the little stuff you need in a

new place, I write on the card. I sign it with my name and Kurt's. I hope it makes her feel loved.

I don't tell her that Kurt and I are going through a rough spot.

Part of the problem is that I am buried under work, trying to chug along like the Little Engine That Could and hoping that I don't stop.

So are you being a bitch because you have too much work, Kurt asks, or because you don't have any work and you'll never have any work and you're going to die alone and in poverty?

I try to laugh.

In a few days we're taking the kids on a family vacation, so I'm finishing two stories and a newsletter, plus planning the whole trip and packing everyone's everything and making arrangements for the dog and using up the food in the refrigerator and stopping the mail and the newspaper and asking a neighbor to water the garden.

Kurt is working at a frantic pace, too, the price extracted by the hospital for the one-week break. This is, of course, my fault. It is my fault that he works so much, my fault that he has to send money to his ex-wife, my fault that I don't understand the stresses of his job. Most of all, it is my fault that I don't recognize how damn much he does for this family.

Just two days ago he hung tennis balls from ropes in the garage so that when either of us pulled our cars forward to park we could stop in the precise spot, leaving room for the lawn mower and the wagons and the bikes. But then I got home with my stupid car with its stupid antenna that doesn't retract and which promptly got tangled in the rope, making him yell Stop! Stop!, lest my antenna snap off entirely, and then he untangled it and motioned for me to back out slo-o-owly so he could slap the ladder in place, climb up and undo all of his hard work. Do I realize what a pain in the ass that was?

Then yesterday he actually drove my car, which was a real hardship for him, since the air conditioner is broken and you have to crank an actual handle to open the windows. He took it to the insurance agent to get approval for a replacement for the cracked windshield, then up to the Honda dealer to see about getting a dog-chewed seat belt repaired. He's going to get the tires aligned and the air conditioner fixed, too, he says. Gosh, it's only been broken half the summer.

That was yesterday, and the stress level

has escalated, so I already am irritated when I get into my car. I turn the key. The stereo blares. I lurch for the knob. It's a big lurch, too, because he's left my seat all the way back, practically in the backseat, so far back that I can't even find the pedals with my feet. I yank the seat latch and jerk forward, grab for the radio, and sit there for a moment in the silence. I want to march back inside and scream at him. Instead I back out slo-o-wly. Because I know that he's going to say I have no right to complain. I know it because I've heard it before. He's the one making the money around here. If it weren't for his hours, we wouldn't survive. Wouldn't survive. You understand? And there you are bitching about how much you have to do. If you don't like it, go live on your own for a year. See how you do. See if I'm waiting when you come back.

I can hear it in a loop in my head. Over and over.

All I'm asking is that he leave my car the way it was when he got in. As a courtesy. A simple courtesy that says I am thinking about you, I care that your nerves shoot out of your skin when the radio blares. If I were cool and young and hip like he is, I would like the music loud. If I were successful I'd have a car like his, with a radio that reduces

233

to a "nominal volume" when you turn off the key. So it's not his fault if he forgets to adjust it on primitive cars like mine in which you have to actually turn a knob to turn on the lights, say, or turn off the radio.

Man, am I pissed.

I look down at my arm. This morning he punched me in the stomach. It was the first time in years, and it wasn't hard, but enough that I fell backward onto the floor. Now I've got a rash on my arm where it scraped the counter and a developing bruise on my butt. I was shocked, although it had happened before.

Afterward he had looked at me lying there on the floor and said, Okay, Miss Drama Queen. Have it your way.

And then he'd left the room.

No apology. Of course no apology.

So now I am frantic and laden and screamingly sad and angry. Inside I am crying.

I drive to the grocery store, where I smile at neighbors weaving up and down the aisles.

Gorgeous weather, isn't it? I say to one.

Fine, I say to another. How are you?

When I get home I call Amy. We talk about her new place, about her dog, about my stepkids. I am careful to sound happy. I don't want to drag her down.

Plus, she's so buoyant with her new life that I feel happier just from talking to her.

It's all a question of attitude, I think. I see these women who paste a cheery veneer over their crappy marriages and I shake my head. I avoid them. If I didn't I'd have to ask them, Can't you see he's treating you like a dog? Don't you know you're screwing up your kids by acting like everything's fine? Do you want them to think that this is what a good marriage looks like?

When I was at home as a teenager I could tell that something was always roiling just under the surface. It was like walking on smoked glass over something awful, like rushing water or lava or snakes. You're on it and it's fine, but it's glass and it could crack, and you'd drop into that something awful and be sucked down. And even if it doesn't crack, you can feel those snakes, that danger, vibrating the surface of things. So you make it across as fast as you can, to the safety of your bedroom or school or the neighbors'.

I remember that, and how if I brought it up I was reassured, Oh, no, honey. Things are fine. Everything is fine. Your dad and I are just having a bad day.

I'm never going to paste a veneer over

mine. That wouldn't be right.

I spend the day baking bread and sewing a dress for my stepdaughter. At dinner I serve meatloaf and baked potatoes and green beans, a family tradition. I ask the kids about their days as I butter potatoes, cut up meat, and pour more milk. They are happy and animated. I smile at Kurt over their heads. He smiles back and I feel it again, the flooding, engulfing love. This is the man I have chosen, the man who makes my heart skitter, who holds my history and my dreams. If we can remember to embrace each other, we'll be okay. We'll be fine.

That night I light candles around the bath. I turn on quiet music and stand in the doorway in a negligee. After all, he has been working odd, sleep-disrupting shifts, and I know that makes him frantic. And we do have money troubles. I need to work harder so he can worry less. It is not all my fault, but I can make it better.

CHAPTER 12

I flip off the radio and the lights and jump out of my car, still singing.

It has taken a plane and a two-hour drive to get home from my business meeting in New York, and now my garage door opener isn't working. I wrestle my suitcase out of the back and wheel it to the front door. The motion detector light comes on, but the door is locked.

Hello, hello, I call, pushing repeatedly on the doorbell. It makes a cheerful ding dong ding dong ding dong in the house. I shift from foot to foot, doing the I-drank-too-much-soda-and-I-have-to-pee dance as I hear the thunder of the children running across the hardwood. Claire gets there first and struggles with the lock while her brother tries to hip check her aside. Finally, they get it open.

You're home! they yell. I open my arms and Claire rushes in. She is wearing a bright green full-length skirt I made for her dress-up collection and a wedding veil. What did you bring us?

I laugh.

Hello. Welcome home. We love you. How was your trip?

Yeah yeah yeah, Mikey says, but what'd you bring us?

I reach out and pull him into the hug. Help me bring my bag in and we'll see.

My nearly tall stepson reaches for the suitcase and yanks it up over the threshold, and both kids fall on it, wrestling for the zipper.

You better hope it's nothing fragile, I say.

I hear Kurt round the corner.

What the hell are you doing? he asks.

The kids freeze, and I swallow hard.

Hi, honey, I say, turning.

What are you doing? How come you didn't come in through the garage?

I step between him and the kids.

My garage door opener didn't work, I say. I must have programmed it wrong.

I look at the kids, their eyes wide and mouths open, then back at their father, who steps closer. I cross my arms over my chest.

Fine, he says. That's fine. You ruin everything, so why not this?

My lips start to shake and I step back, almost tripping over the kids.

You just take off and leave us and then I try to do something nice for you and you ruin it, he says, stepping forward again.

What the hell are you talking about? I ask. I just walked in the door.

Right, you just walk in the door after doing God knows what in New York and you don't even notice all I've done for you.

I look around. The house looks great, I say, quashing any impulse to ask why he should get points for doing the little chores that go unnoticed when I do them every day.

Do I smell manicotti?

Nice try, he says, but too little too late.

I glance at the kids, who have crept behind me.

What? I demand. What is it this time?

He steps closer, his breath hitting me in the face, and tears fill my eyes. He clenches his teeth.

Why don't you go back out, he hisses, get in your stupid car, and try your damn garage door opener again?

I step backward over my suitcase, gathering the kids to my sides as I do.

Good idea, I say. Let's start over. Kids, come with me.

No, Kurt says. No, we are not doing this your way. The kids stay in here with me, since they're part of what's left of the surprise.

I look each child in the eye, offering silent reassurance. Without turning my back on my husband, I step out the door and around the corner, out of sight. Only then do I let myself cry, big gulping sounds that start somewhere deeper than my chest. What have I done? Why have I screwed up? He is obviously trying to do something nice, and I have blown it.

I slide into my car, close my eyes, and grip the steering wheel. Damn it! Damn it! Damn it! I say, pounding my head against the wheel until I misaim and hit the horn. Oh shit. The garage door opens and Kurt bends double and ducks out.

We were coming, he says. Quit it with the damn horn.

He ducks back in and the door rattles back down. I stare. Now what am I supposed to do? I flip down the visor and check my makeup. Two hours earlier I had stopped in the airport bathroom to pretty up for him. Now my mascara is smeared. I wet my fingers, run them under my eyes, and then snort. My friends always ask if I am afraid to go to New York. Hell, no. I am afraid to come home.

The garage door rumbles open and I start my car. Wafting in front of me is a white bedsheet painted with an enormous red heart. We love you, Nene! is painted across the top. The edges are festooned with multicolored handprints and signatures, and my children are standing at attention in front of their masterpiece. I gasp. They must have worked on it for days. I can understand now why Kurt is so upset.

I honk my horn as applause. The kids jump up and down and clap.

Oh you guys, it's beautiful! I say as I open my car door. You must have worked so hard!

I hug the children and smile at Kurt over their heads. Thank you, I mouth. He smiles, steps forward and gathers everyone in a family hug. I love you, he says, then kisses me, the kids looking up from the safe harbor of our arms. I lean into his embrace, relieved that whatever has happened is behind us, but puzzled, too. The garage door hadn't opened, so I had come in the front door. No matter how much I twist and turn the scenario, I can't make myself deserve his hissing anger. Still, it's over now.

Dinner is indeed manicotti, and the children are thrilled with the geegaws and souvenirs they find in my bag.

What about Daddy's gift? Claire asks.

Daddy'll get his later, I say, smiling at him.

Oh, I'll bet, he mutters.

Ruffling his hair, I say, What, hon?

I said, Kurt enunciates, Oh. I'll. Bet.

I frown and pull my hand away. What's that supposed to mean?

It means I'm sure you brought me something, he says. The question is, who you got it from.

I narrow my eyes at him then turn brightly to the kids.

Tell you what, guys, I say. I'll do dishes. You made me dinner and cleaned the house and made me my beautiful sign, so you've earned an hour of TV.

The kids scrape their chairs back and tumble down the stairs. I can hear them channel surfing, and then the ominous theme music of a gruesome cop show they normally aren't allowed to watch.

I consider hollering down to correct them, but in a brief moment of clarity I realize there is nothing in the show that will be more damaging than what they'll likely witness between us.

Chapter 13

Amy's divorce is perfunctory. He gets the birds, she gets the dog, he gets the couch, she gets the bed. They divvy up the over-laden credit cards. He'll pay these, she'll pay those. The marriage lasted five years, only a few of them good.

Woo-hoo! she says, when the paperwork goes through.

You're a brave woman, I say.

She hesitates.

I'm not so sure about that, she says.

Well, you are.

We have to see someone, I say to Kurt. Otherwise we won't make it.

We're fine, he says. We're smarter than any therapist. We can figure it out on our own.

I turn away.

Weeks later, after yet another night-long fight, I say it again.

We have to see someone. I can't do this.

The third or the fourth or the fifth time I say it, screaming, crying, slamming doors, he relents.

So now the marriage counselor leans forward, her hands pressed between her knees.

You love each other, right?

I look into his eyes, which are moist, like mine.

Of course, I say.

He nods.

Then show it, the therapist says. Go home and find ways to make each other feel precious. We sigh, our eyes still locked. I have yelled, I have cursed, I have cried. I am purged.

We walk out of her office holding hands.

We kiss in the parking lot. It is going to be okay.

Later that week Kurt comes up behind me in the kitchen. I am dressed for my aerobics class, but I'm mixing up a batch of bread to rise while I'm gone.

Don't plan anything for this weekend, okay?

Why? I ask.

Just don't, he says. I have something in mind.

I am intrigued, but as much as I pester and wheedle and tickle he won't tell. On Friday, though, he comes into my office with a sly grin on his face.

Come this way, he says.

He leads me to our bedroom and tells me to sit. Then he walks around the bed and crawls across it behind me.

Don't look, he says.

I laugh. He is in a playful mood, so this should be fun.

I hear him open and close a drawer. I feel the whisper of silk as he slides a scarf across my face before tying it over my eyes. I reach up to touch it, but he holds my hands.

We're going for a little drive, he says. And I want you to keep the blindfold on.

I nod, and he takes my hand, pulling me to stand. I shuffle my feet as we walk, feeling my way from our bedroom, down the hall, through the laundry room and into the garage. I hear him open the car door, then feel him guide me into the passenger seat.

The thunk of the closing door is solid, and I wait with nothing but the tick of the engine until I hear him open the other door and slide in.

He turns on the radio and tells me to lean back and relax, enjoy the ride. I feel us back out of the garage and turn down the drive-way, then turn right onto our street and left onto the connector. I can follow our path through sound and shadow and familiarity.

Do you have any idea where we are? he asks.

We're on Nifong now, I say. We just passed McDonald's. I can smell it.

He laughs. Then he takes an unexpected right turn, then a left, then slows for a speed bump. I don't know where we are anymore. I sit back and feel the alternating sun and shade, and the slight rise and fall of the highway south of town. I don't tell him that I once again know where we are. It is better to relax and enjoy, so I lose myself in the music and the leather seat and the vibration from the tires.

Every once in a while he tells me of a pass-ing car and how the passengers' heads swivel at the woman in the blindfold. When I hear that we're passing someone, I scratch and claw at the window as if I'm being kidnapped.

Stop that! he says, laughing. There are going to be 911 calls all up and down this highway.

I am laughing, too, and that makes me realize that I need to use a bathroom.

I have to pee, I say. We have to stop.

Hmm, he says. I hadn't thought of that possibility.

He drives on, giving me a blow-by-blow of potential bathrooms. There is the quickmart, but he'd have to go into the ladies' room with me, and he thinks it's a multiseater. There's a rest area, but that would be just as bad. Finally he finds a rundown gas station on the side of the road, the kind with outside restrooms that you can't get into without a key from the attendant, and the key is as always attached to a nightstick or a ruler or something else to keep you from pocketing it and walking mindlessly away.

We stop and I wait until he opens my door, then I take his arm and let him lead me into the Lysol-smelling unisex bathroom.

I can take it from here, I say, after he

opens the door and leads me to the toilet.

Don't take off your blindfold, he says.

I won't, I say, although it doesn't feel or sound or smell like a place that will be easily picked out of a lineup of a million other gas station restrooms.

When I'm finished I call to him and he comes back in and guides me to the sink, where I wash my hands and out of habit glance up at myself in the mirror, except all I can see is the inside of the scarf.

The whole experience strikes me as hilarious, and I am laughing as he guides me back to the car. That's good, too, as it turns out, because Kurt tells me there is a couple crouched in their car right outside the restroom, and from their posture it's clear that they have been writing down our license plate number. We fall into the car laughing.

An hour of dozing and listening to music and talking about nothing later and I feel the car slow, feel the breeze as he opens his window. I hear nothing, though, beyond the calls of birds and the whine of jet skis. We are near water, that's all I know.

Within minutes the car stops again and Kurt comes around and opens the car door.

Stand up, he says, his hand gentle under my arm. I stand carefully, and he guides me away from the door, then closes it. I feel his arm around my back, then his mouth against my breast as he bends to put the other arm behind my knees. He picks me up and carries me, blindfolded still, down a wooden walkway and into what feels like shade.

He sets me down and stands behind me, kissing along my neck before sliding off my blindfold. Pines frame a view of the state's big tourist lake, sparkling blue, the whine of jet skis and motorboats muffled by the trees. We are standing on a wooden deck behind an A-frame cabin, its clones scattered among the trees on either side. He unlocks the door and we go in, falling on the bed and groping at each other's clothes. Much later I feel him slide out of bed.

I'm going to go bring the stuff in from the car, he whispers, and kisses my cheek. He tucks the covers up around my neck and down around my body, knowing I'll be annoyed by a draft. I am smiling as I doze off.

Later we sit on the deck and have a drink as we watch the sun set.

Wait here, he says, and goes inside. After a few minutes, he calls me in. There on the bed are a red bustier, black thigh-high stockings, stilettos, and a slim-fitting red dress.

I'll be out here, he says, trailing a hand across my ass as he leaves the room.

I sit on the side of the bed and sigh, and then flop backward onto the still-messy bed. We are at a family resort. It would be fine for me to show up for dinner in something loose and comfortable, something that allows me to move without thinking about whether I'll fall off my heels or reveal a garter.

Just walking up the wooden walkway in those shoes will be hard, I think. Please don't let me sprain an ankle.

I stand up and peel out of the shorts and T-shirt I wore on the road. The bustier is tight, the stays running counter to my ribs, the underwires digging into my armpits. I tug at it, lift my breasts up and settle them into the cups, tug the bottom edge over my hips. The lace edges cut into my flesh.

The stockings, though, feel like silken luxury as I slide them over my legs, up my thighs. I smooth them out, point my toes, admire the line they give to my calf. I twist stiffly to hook the garters in the back. I feel like a cross between a prostitute and my grandmother, in girdle and stockings long before the invention of pantyhose. It seems odd that men find this archaic wire and bone exoskeleton attractive.

I step into the dress and pull it up over the bustier, then turn to look in the mirror. I am bulging out in front, Barbie-like. Implausible.

I slide my feet into the heels and walk out to the living room, where he is standing with his back to me. He turns slowly and smiles, making me forget about the wires jabbing into my ribs.

God, you're sexy, he says.

At the restaurant people stare. They look up from their chicken cordon bleu and marbled Midwestern steaks, the women with some blend of ridicule and fear. The men with lust and what I believe is a wish that their own wives were babes. That's what Kurt tells me, anyway.

They're just jealous, he says. They wish they had what we have.

I am not so sure. I sit stiffly, embarrassed, feeling like a whore.

Kurt's eyes, though, are enough. In his view I glow. It is worth looking different, worth trying later to bowl without bending at the waist — it is, again, a family resort — worth dancing in mincing steps, doing little more than wriggle when we go to the resort's nightclub, dancing on pencil-thin heels to "The Lady in Red" as Kurt gazes on, adoringly.

When Kurt goes to the bathroom I take off my shoes and rub my feet, relieved. I drop my shoes under the table, ready to let loose and allow the music to invade my body, to dance freely, or as freely as I can within the confines of my dress. I want to put my arms out and spin like a child under the sprinkled light of the disco ball. I stand next to the table and sway, my head tilted back. Kurt comes up behind me, slides his hands around my strictured waist, and kisses my neck.

Put your shoes back on so we can dance, he says between kisses.

I'll just dance in my stockings, I say.

The kisses stop.

That's fine, he says.

I turn toward him and put my arms around his neck, raise my mouth for a kiss.

If you don't want to have sex, you can just say so, he says.

I pull back.

What?

Nothing, he says. Why don't we just go?

I want to dance more.

I've had enough, he says. Let's just go.

He takes my hand. I pull away and gather up my shoes and purse. He stands still, looking at me.

What?

Are you just going to walk through the whole resort barefoot?

I stare at him. Then I bend and put on my shoes.

I totter through the resort, ankles wobbling and toes pinched.

Days later I call Amy.

The problem with being on a pedestal, I say, is that if you try to move, you'll fall.

What happened?

I'm quiet.

Just trust me on this, I say.

Un huh.

We are losing Dave, Kurt's co-worker and friend, who is dying slowly of lung cancer, brought on by decades of unrepentant smoking and quickened by the chemotherapy that has bruised the backs of his hands and robbed him of his thick white hair. Dave has five children by two wives. His relationship with the older ones is troubled. Now he is on his deathbed, so I rush two hours to the airport in St. Louis to pick up the sons from his first marriage who have agreed to visit.

I am late, and I run through the airport, panting, sobbing, so desperately not wanting to fail. I find them, I drive them — speeding — to the hospital. They are there for their father's final hours.

At the funeral Kurt and I are seated in the front row, a place of honor, for those closest to Dave and his family.

Lori, the head nurse at the hospital where Dave worked, steps to the microphone. She begins her eulogy, strong and eloquent.

I'm sure Dave is smiling now, she says, happy to see that Janine is wearing such a short skirt.

I am stunned. Humiliated. I don't know what to do. I sit, back straight, hands clasped, ankles crossed. Kurt reaches over and squeezes my thigh, below where my skirt barely covers the garters to my stockings. He smiles. I think he is proud. I try to be proud, too. Mostly I'm nauseous. I see myself — briefly — through someone else's eyes, and I am ashamed.

They're just jealous, Kurt tells me later. They all wish they looked like you.

I sit silent.

Things in Dave's family change from deathbed polite to their natural state of animosity. The sons from the first marriage want to take Dave's golf clubs, his pool table, the ancestral pictures on the walls. It is my job to intervene, to negotiate, to placate. I talk to the widow, talk to the sons.

The eldest of them makes threats, throws punches.

Two days after the funeral I am alone with the eldest son, the single one with the wild hair, and he kisses me.

I feel guilty. I feel excited. I feel scared. I cannot tell Kurt. Years later, I do.

Why? he asks.

I don't know, I say. I didn't mean to. I didn't initiate it.

He looks at me with tears in his eyes.

I trusted you, he says.

I have no answer.

A year later, Jim dies. He has lost another job. He has been evicted from his apartment. He is in his midthirties and once again living with his parents, and it is there that he dies. Of an eroded esophagus brought on by his years of drinking.

I'm going to his funeral, Amy says.

Is that going to be okay?

I think so, she says. His sister hates me, but the others said I could come.

Afterward she tells me all was as predicted. The sister was chilly. An aunt thanked her.

If it weren't for you he wouldn't have lived this long, the aunt said.

That's good, I say when she tells me.

It was okay.

I can't imagine walking into that funeral home, knowing some people will hate you. Or they might. "Might" is almost as bad as "will." It's scary.

Amy, though, is feeling strong. She's sharing her apartment with Lisa, a roommate who has become her best friend. She has been promoted at her job. She's taking classes at the community college. She is still struggling with her weight, but she sounds good.

A couple of months later Amy tells me that Jim had not been paying on their credit cards, the ones that are still in both of their names. She cries.

What do you mean they're in both of your names?

He took some and I took some. He didn't pay his.

But didn't you close them out during the divorce?

We didn't have the money to pay them off.

Couldn't you just roll the debt into a new card?

We didn't, okay? And now it's too late.

She owes more than fifteen thousand dollars. Plus back taxes, although she eventually gets out of those. She is earning twenty-four thousand dollars as a secretary. It will take her years to dig out of debt.

We are at Warren Dunes State Park, on the southwest edge of Michigan, where the sand piles twenty stories into the sky. Some of the family has gathered for the Fourth of July holiday, and Amy and I drove immediately here, to the lake we love.

As soon as we park Amy heads straight for the water. Now we stand shin-deep in the waves, wriggling our toes deeper into the sand.

Look at those girls, I say, nodding toward three high schoolers walking together and giggling. They're beautiful, and they probably don't even know it. They're probably obsessing about a zit or their hair or some other flaw. Too bad they can't relax and enjoy their beauty.

Amy looks at them.

Don't be too flattering, she said. They just called me a fucking whale.

I am shocked. Shocked and hurt. And defensive. I want to confront the girls, to chew them out, appeal to their humanity, make them look beyond the fat to the person. I want to claw them.

I sputter something about them being little bitches.

Don't be getting all righteous, Amy says.

Remember the pig family?

I stop and look at her. The Pig Family. The family in our childhood church, all heavy, all with flat faces and big nostrils. We used to point at them and giggle, make oinking sounds until Mom separated us and made one of us go to the back, to a different pew, where we still would barely contain our giggles.

The Pig Family.

I am silenced.

Jim is out of the picture, but Amy's weight keeps getting worse. I want to ask what it's like, why she doesn't try. I am weighing in every day. Over and over. Before breakfast, during the starving hour before lunch, at bedtime. Hoping always to be better, to be more perfect. She doesn't weigh herself at all. She doesn't seem to care.

Once she had asked for advice.

Don't eat sugar cereal, I told her.

I have to, she said. When I get the other kind I put on more sugar. Even when I get the sugar kind I put sugar on it.

It is true. She sugars Froot Loops and Frosted Flakes. She eats potato chips and hand-sized pieces of cake. She does it without thinking. Walking, sitting. Eating. Always eating.

I don't. I deny myself the things I want, referring to things as NWC — not worth the calories. It is code between Kurt and me. This candy or cake or main dish has more calories than it's worth. I throw half a candy bar away before I take the first bite. The last bite is the one I savor, the one everyone savors, so it doesn't matter how many there are between the first and the last. The first I taste, the last I taste. The ones between are just chewing.

My junk food is beer.

At night when I offer one to Amy she says, I'd rather have chocolate. Alcohol isn't worth the calories.

I'm thinking about all of these things as we walk, slowly, looking for shells, looking at the pretty people. I hold in my stomach, compare myself — always unfavorably — with other women. Women fifteen years my junior, women so young they're barely women. I am lean for my age, but to me that is an insult. I want to be lean, to be perfect, compared to *anyone.* I want Kurt to be proud. But I know about my cellulite. I know it is glaring in the sun. I hold my stomach in tighter.

CHAPTER 14

Hi, honey, he says. I struggle up through the cotton batting of anesthesia swaddling my brain. I wince at the light and the noise as he leans in to kiss me. His breath is heavy with the smell of chocolate. Chocolate. I struggle to roll away, weighted by the oven-warmed blankets they'd piled on to stop my chattering, the jerking freezing shuddering of coming out of surgery. I barely make it to my side before I vomit, clear liquid and stringy yellow bile pooling in the crescent-shaped bowl proffered by the nurse.

I roll back and close my eyes, drifting back into the silence.

Minutes or hours later I rise slowly. My body is inert, but I open my eyes as my mind swims hazily out of the fog. Kurt is in a chair next to the bed, a rose in his hand, his eyes closed, and his head resting against my side. My other leg is encased in a brace that runs from my ankle to within an inch of my crotch.

The surgeon has just repaired a ligament I tore on a ski trip half a year earlier, on a run that was late-in-the-day icy. It was our third day on the slopes and I was exhausted, both from the skiing and the single-digit cold. Midway through a turn my left ski veered. I heard the pop before I felt the pain, and then I was lying in the snow yelling to the lift overhead for someone to please please please call the ski patrol. The cold seeped through my ski pants, the thin kind, since the warm ones like Kurt wore made me look short and fat. I had packed a pair much like his, but while we waited at the shop to rent our skis, he had found a hot little pair of black leggings that made me look sleek.

I can't imagine they're warm, I said.

You'll be fine, he'd answered. I'll keep you warm.

How he planned to keep me warm while skiing I didn't know, but we bought them anyway, and when I lay in the snow they did nothing to protect me.

The ski patrol swished into view, evaluated my knee, and strapped me onto a sled. Then one grabbed the sled handles rickshaw style and took off down the mountain, me on my back, straitjacketed by blankets, him zigging and zagging and toeing in to cut our speed, which still overwhelmed me in my helpless head-down position. Kurt threw on his skis and tried to keep up.

At the first aid shed the paramedic ripped the scissors up the seam of my new ski pants, and out came the knee, already the size of a grapefruit.

Good job, the patrol guy said.

Thanks, I said. And it was my last run of the day.

Yeah, he said. These things always happen on the last run.

They do? I asked, then realized I had fallen for a stupid ski patrol joke.

Six months later I have finally convinced myself and my husband that I deserve surgery. For weeks I have complained about the pain, the swelling, the slipping, the feeling that my upper leg is going to slide off the lower, dropping me again in a crumpled heap, but Kurt said I was being melodramatic.

I thought you were tough, he said. You've been teaching aerobics on it, forgodsake. It can't be that bad.

Completely severed anterior cruciate ligament, the surgeon says.

A clean snap, his assistant agrees.

No wonder I felt unstable.

The nurse gives me sips of 7-Up.

I'm sorry about the chocolate, Kurt says. I got scared and snarfed down a Snickers.

It's okay, I say, giving him a hazy smile. Sorry I barfed on you.

He laughs. I'm just glad you're alive.

A few hours later I am enthroned on my bed, my leg stiff and elevated, my head swimming from the residual anesthesia and the pain pills. I am too queasy to eat, too tired even to sit in front of the TV, too bleary to read.

Thank you for being so sweet to me today, I say.

He sits gently on the side of the bed.

I'm glad I could, he says.

He lays his head on my chest and I clumsily pat his hair.

I was so afraid I would lose you, he says.

I pat at him absently. The nerve block that made my leg numb is wearing off and my knee is coming awake. My stomach feels unstable. One wrong smell and I am afraid I'll hurl again.

He kisses my neck, nuzzles in, his mouth moving in familiar soft bites and kisses, sucking and seeking, moving toward my mouth.

I'm just so glad you're alive, he murmurs again.

His lips meet mine, and I feel his tongue slip between my lips. Slowly he shifts his weight until he is lying next to me, his hands sliding up under my shirt.

Careful, I say.

I'll be careful.

His mouth covers mine, finds my neck, my breasts, everything except my immobilized leg.

Please, let's not, I say.

I'm just so grateful you're alive, he says between kisses.

My leg throbs.

I really could use a pain pill, I say.

He continues to kiss me, but I push at him.

I want a pain pill, I say. My leg is screaming at me.

He slowly stands, walks into the bathroom, comes back with a glass of water and a Vicodin, which I take gratefully.

Thank you, I say, and lie back against the pills, gingerly positioning my leg.

What if we prop pillows around your leg? he asks.

He is serious.

He strokes my face, runs his hands down my body, kisses me.

The pain pill makes me woozy and tired. His hands make me feel desired. I succumb, even though my head swirls and my body sinks deeper into the bed.

It only hurts when he bumps my immobilizer or when his weight heavy on top of me changes my leg's angle on the pillows, or when his moves jerk my body.

Afterward I hobble to the bathroom on my crutches. I splash cold water on my face, then look in the mirror. My skin is colorless, my lips chapped and dry and split at the corners from the hours under anesthesia. I am worn and drawn, a husk of myself. How could he make love to someone who looks like this? And then in a rush I realize, he loves me *even when* I look like this. I am weepy with gratitude.

He loves me so much that the very idea of

losing me, unlikely as it was during a simple orthopedic surgery, has made him crazy, made him pace the hospital corridors, raid the candy machines, lie in the recovery room clutching me, half asleep.

Another man might have left me alone to sleep, propping me up with pillows and bringing me 7-Up and saltines, leaving me alone so I could rest. But we're not like that. We're not boring. We have passion. We need each other, and sometimes that need is physical.

I am lucky to have a man want me so much.

When I am once again off the crutches I fly to Mom's house in Atlanta, a Toto-like basket over my arm. I am taking a pumpkin pie to my stepfather. He has lung cancer, and we won't have him for much longer. We kids rotate in and do what we can. I clean the patio furniture. Steve and Amy plant begonias, Steve's in a precise six-inch-by-six-inch grid, Amy's clumped randomly. When Mom sees them she laughs. Their personalities are laid out in her flower bed.

I am there to support Mom, and to perhaps say good-bye to John. But I also talk to Amy.

You okay?

She slides down on the couch and leans against me, as if I were the bigger of us two.

Not really, she says.

She is staying strong for Mom, who is staying strong for John, but she is devastated to be losing this man who for eleven years has been her best version of a father. She leans against me and cries.

I'm going to miss him so much, she says.

I know.

I will, too, but for Amy it's worse.

Mom calls. She and John have been saving money for a trip to Australia. It has been their dream.

Should we go? She is asking me, but mostly she is asking Kurt, the doctor.

Go, we tell them. There are doctors in Australia, too.

They start making plans. One morning, though, John wakes Mom up. Instead of Australia, let's bring all of the kids in for a week, he says. Like we did when we got married.

You sure? Mom asks.

There's nothing I'd rather spend my money on, he says.

We all fly in, this time to Florida, where we stay at a multihouse compound with a pool and a boat and plenty of bedrooms. On the first day we play in the pool and eat to excess and play cards until the kids are cranky. The second and third days are the same. Makeup disappears. Everyone turns brown. Kids climb onto the laps of aunts, hold the hands of uncles. We are a family, settled in.

One day, clouds roll in and fat drops fall. The kids flop onto sofas and chairs. There's nothing to do, they whine.

Play cards, we say, looking up from our books. Play games.

It is raining so hard you can barely see the railing to the deck.

Kris's husband, Michael, opens the door and steps through.

Come on out, he says. The water's fine.

No way, I say.

The adults all laugh at him, warm and dry on our side of the glass. Amy looks around, then saunters out into the rain. She dances in a circle, laughing, her hands raised to the sky.

Come on, you guys. Quit being wienies.

I smile at her, but I don't move. The kids, though, run out. They cavort and slide and catch rain on their tongues. Amy is joyous, in the midst of her family. It is here that she feels loved.

CHAPTER 15

Why do people talk about walking on eggshells? No one ever walks on eggshells. You couldn't walk on eggshells. It's dumb. It's impossible.

Through the phone I hear Amy laugh.

She is doing well. She has been promoted twice, so now she's an administrative assistant to some executive. She seems happy.

And we're talking about walking on eggshells because . . . ?

One of my friends said I sounded like I was walking on eggshells, I say, which is stupid.

She laughs again.

Come on, she says. Tell.

I don't want to tell. I do want to tell. I want to tell her that I am scared, that every day I know I'm going to make him angry. I don't know when or how, but I will. And then he'll storm out and I'll worry about losing him, obsess about the fight, try to figure out what I did and how and why and how to never ever do it again. Every day is like this. I am wound tighter than the ball of rubber bands at the core of an old golf ball. Peel off the protective cover and I will snap and explode, the shrapnel flying.

I don't tell her, though, because to tell is embarrassing. To tell means she'll look at me and wonder why I don't get out, why I don't leave, why I put up with that kind of crap.

I don't want to get out, I want to fix things. I want the good part, the sweet part, the part that puts a gentle hand on my shoulder, that makes love gently, lovingly. I want the part that lets me spoon up against his back when I have cramps, that talks about me with pride, that listens as I obsess about my work.

But that's not all. Not if I'm honest. I also want the drama, the part that makes my heart race, that makes me want to rip his clothes off in the middle of the kitchen. I want the thrill of hearing the garage door rumble, of racing down the stairs so I can throw my arms around his neck as soon as he walks through the door.

What I don't want is the anger.

I also don't want to be alone. I think about it sometimes, what it would be like to date, to try to find someone who will love me. But I have flaws. Wrinkles and scars and quirks. I hate cologne. I can't hold a conversation over music. I have bad moods, a weak knee. I can't find my way around. Give me directions and I'll make it, but I won't remember how to get back.

Kurt knows all of this, and he loves me anyway. No one else will.

Still, I could survive alone. I have marketable skills, a graduate degree. I supported myself for all those years before we married, and I could do it again. Kurt pays our bills now — because he earns more and because he gets a thrill out of balancing everything to the penny. But I could. I know how.

Instead I write in the morning and spend

the rest of the day doing the cooking and the laundry and the setting up of appointments, the carpools and the grocery shopping and the planning and prep work for birthdays and holidays and family visits.

And only losers are alone. It's an ugly thing to admit — especially after cheerleading Amy about how being alone is fine! it's great! it's liberating! — but there is nothing in me that thinks it would be okay to be alone, that I am enough alone, that being alone doesn't scream, "Nobody wants me!"

Also, being alone is lonely. It means relying on myself. It means no one caring whether my plane lands safely and on time or if I'm tired of my job or the president or the state of the world, or that my bunion aches.

That's another of my flaws. I have a bunion that throbs when I wear heels. It throbs and I walk stiffly. It looks bad for me to hobble, so I don't. I walk normally, but only with effort, only with a decision not to totter or scowl, even though my foot throbs and my back aches from compensating for the tilted pelvis and the weight, the too-tilted weight, on the ball of my feet, on my bunion.

After a drink or two, sometimes I complain, but that makes him mad.

Other women walk on them, he says. Look in the magazines. Look on TV. You're just complaining because you're a feminist.

I can't argue with that. I am a feminist. I believe women are just as important as men, and that we shouldn't let ourselves be objectified.

I think that it's obscene that women's work goes uncompensated. That the things we do for love mean we don't earn money, and that money equals value. Friends argue with me, saying it's not true, but in our society it is. We attribute importance, worth, social status to the people who earn the most. They are the best people, the ones the gods have favored.

We are those people. We have the big house and the cars and the sparkling jewels. Our life looks perfect.

We fly into Fort Lauderdale, rent a red convertible and drive north, past the high-rise condominiums and the T-shirt-laden boardwalks and the big-shouldered hotels.

Within a half hour we roll into the tiny tourist town of Lauderdale by the Sea, with its seafood restaurants and fishing pier and ice cream shop and stores selling seashell magnets and doorstops and paperweights, along with scanty dresses and bikinis and strappy sandals, sunscreen and pails and dried starfish and fudge, and its main road dividing around a statue of swooping gulls.

Look at that, Kurt says, grinning as we pass a cluster of men and boys playing pickup basketball on the court at the city park.

We roll on.

There it is, I say.

The Little Inn by the Sea. Deep coral pink, the lobby three stories tall, dominated by an ever-trickling fountain, its brightly cushioned furniture bracketed by racks of humidity-curled paperbacks and magazines. The smell of the morning's waffles lingers.

It is shaped like a horseshoe with its ends toward the beach. In the hollow, protected from the wind, gaudy bougainvillea and palms and Christmas lights surround an achingly blue pool.

The owners are German and French, two of each, their English lilted and rolled.

On the roof is an area for topless sunbathing, they say, their European amusement evident over American's prudishness.

Kurt looks at me eagerly, and I smile.

We fall into a rhythm of coffee and a morning run and then a book poolside for me while he sleeps, and then rum for me as I sit propped against a tree in the evening watching him play basketball.

Try this on, he says.

He holds up a black thong bikini.

I shake my head, laughing.

No way, I say.

Come on, he wheedles, laughing with me. It'll be fun.

We are in one of the dozens of tourist shops that line the beachfront. Each is staffed with toffee-eyed Pakistanis with coffee-with-cream skin, one of whom swoops up on me between the racks.

You want to try those on?

I hold out my selections, which spill from my hand like strands of spaghetti in red and purple and black, and she unlocks the door to a plywood changing cubicle, the light-bulb straight above, the mirror only a foot away.

I strip to my underwear and pull on the first suit. The bottom is a Brazilian cut, three or four inches wide, exposing more flesh than it covers. I turn to see my back-side in the mirror, and it doesn't make me happy.

Let me see it, Kurt says.

Just a second, I say.

I tuck the edges of my underwear into the

bottoms, which leaves lumps and the occasional glimpse of white, and plump my breasts into the cups. I open the door a crack.

Kurt?

I'm right here.

Stick your head in here.

There is a rustle, and he appears. His eyes glitter.

I like that one, he says.

I turn and look at the mirror. My cellulite is glaring in this light, but I know that if I lie out in the sun (or follow Kurt's example and spend time in the tanning bed before trips) it will look better. The top, though, has wires. And I hate wires. I hate the way they feel and I hate the way they look, like I'm going to erupt out of the top.

I shake my head. He shrugs.

Try on the black one.

I roll my eyes at him and he leaves.

The next suit has more of a bottom and no wires, but the top is so skimpy that my breasts look half a mile apart, a great plain between them.

Kurt?

Just open the door, he says.

I'd rather not, I say. Stick your head in.

I open the door a crack, then turn to look at myself in the mirror. There is a rustle, then Kurt opens the door and he and the willowy Pakistani eye me.

It looks good on you, the salesgirl says.

Kurt beams.

It really does.

I want to cover my chest with my hands, but I also want to have him look at me like that, like he can barely keep his hands off me. I would do anything for this man. I shake my head, but I am laughing.

Try on the black one, he says.

I try on everything but, and expose myself over and over to him and the salesgirl, who is hovering to make sure the rich white tourists don't walk out with a bathing suit under their clothes. There is a purple one I like.

It looks good on you, the salesgirl says.

Let's get this one, I say.

Try on the black one, he says.

Can we get the purple one if I do?

Try on the black one.

There's nothing else, so I do.

Open the door, Kurt says.

Stick your head in, I answer. I am turning to see my backside in the mirror. It's not a look I like. I am thirty-five years old and should not be in a thong. It doesn't matter if they're stylish or if they're all the rage, doesn't matter that in Europe I'd wear one without thinking twice, this is the United

States and the only people who wear them are flaunting, inviting, enticing.

Kurt peeks through a crack, and then opens the door all the way.

Turn around, he says.

I turn.

Wow, he says.

It looks good on you, the salesgirl says again.

She is bored by this middle-aged sexuality, standing vigil only so we don't steal, telling customers what they want to hear. I look from her to Kurt, who is looking at me with a compelling combination of love and lust.

You are gorgeous, he says.

I stick out my tongue and pull shut the door.

My vote is for the purple one, I say, when I come back out.

Oh, let's get the black one, too, he says.

He smiles at me, his eyes twinkling. There is a promise there. We buy both.

At the next store I try on sundresses. Swooping batiks, clinging rayons, elasticized dresses so short you can almost see my underpants.

I like this one, I say, twirling in a loose A-line dress with spaghetti straps.

I am being wild and free, trying to rise to

the occasion. Instead we buy a pair of platform sandals and a skin-tight sundress that he says brings out the blue in my eyes.

Back at the hotel he hands me the dress and shoes and black bathing suit. I go into the bathroom and put on the suit. I look in the mirror. It's flattering up top, with just enough lift to make me look normal, like these are my natural breasts. The high cut of the bottoms makes my legs look long, too, but when I turn so I can see the back I cringe. Doesn't he see the dimples? God. I tug on the dress on and go back out into the room.

You are so sexy, he says, pulling me toward him.

I pull the thong out of my crack.

This is ridiculous, I say.

Why is it ridiculous?

Because I'm not going out in public in this.

Why not? And you look beautiful. You work hard to look so beautiful. You should show it off.

Besides, we don't know anyone here, he says, and I like it.

I'm flattered that he wants me so much. Besides, in the room like this, when it's just us, this is okay. The clothes turn him on, and that makes me feel desirable, so in a way the clothes turn me on, too. They turn me on even while they make me feel like a piece of raw meat in front of a cartoon wolf who is drooling, a knife in one hand and a fork in the other. I shift from foot to foot.

Take off the dress.

I do.

I take a deep breath and start to kick off the sandals.

Leave them on, he says.

Let's go to the beach, I say later.

I pull out the purple bathing suit and rip off the tags.

Not that one, he says. The muscles in his back shift as he leans over and picks the thong off the floor.

You have to be kidding, I say.

Come on, he says. You're being uptight. You told me you'd go on vacation and just have fun with me.

I don't think having my butt hang out in public will be fun, I say, although I laugh.

It's a beautiful butt, he says. You'll look wonderful.

He holds his hand out. I don't take the suit. He moves his hand closer. I relent.

When we get to the beach I sit on my towel, still in my shorts.

Want to go for a walk? he asks.

I look up at him. Christ. He reaches his hand down and I stand. He waits.

Aren't you going to take off your shorts?

I sigh, unzip them, and work them down my legs, feeling the sun and the wind and what feels like a thousand eyes on my ass.

We start down the beach. I look straight ahead or out at the water while Kurt looks around, comparing us to the people we pass.

I see a woman coming toward us.

Do I look better than that? I ask.

Much better, he says.

What about her?

What is she, fifteen?

So I don't look better than her, and that stings.

Are people staring at me? I ask.

He looks around.

I hope so, he says, a look of pride and possession on his face.

He falls back a few steps. I try to walk with dignity, knowing he's publicly ogling me.

Please don't do that, I say.

I'm just looking, he says. Don't you like it that I like your body?

He comes up next to me and smiles, and I move toward him. He is the most sexually compelling man I have ever met. It is as if he has his own field of gravity, and if I so much as get near I am pulled in. He's exuding it now, consciously or unconsciously, and even though I feel humiliated to be walking around like this, I want him to want me.

He folds me in his arms and holds me, his hands running softly over my back until they slide down to my exposed white flesh, and then he pulls me against him, pelvis to pelvis.

Children chase waves or run by with buckets. An old man glances at us and then away. A woman glares.

Stop, I say. Let me go.

What, he says, can't a man hug his wife?

I try to tell Amy about it, but it's delicate. Over the past few years she has ballooned up to about two hundred and fifty pounds, and it's hard for her to find clothes.

It was embarrassing, I say. I couldn't believe I was doing it.

Why did you?

I don't know. I think it was because he wanted it so much, you know? And it made me feel sexy to have him want me like that.

You're sexy anyway, she says.

Thanks, but you're my sister.

She laughs.

I wouldn't do it, she says, then chuckles.

Not in public, anyway.

I am silent.

What I don't get is why he wants me to look that way.

Men are like that, she says. They're visual. I don't know whether it's biological or cultural, but they are.

Besides, she continues, you've got a hot bod.

I laugh, but I still wish being sexy in private was enough.

Guess what, she says. I'm going to massage therapy school.

You're what?

Even though Amy has been taking classes at the community college, she doesn't have a degree.

I've been getting massages from this sexy Latino — he comes to my house — and I've decided it's what I want to do.

I groan inwardly at the thought of Amy leaning over a massage table. I know parts of her body will have to be touching parts of the other person's body. There's just no way her weight won't get in the way. And as I remember things, her hands are small and delicate.

He comes to your house?

Once a month. He brings his table and gives me long, gorgeous massages. Finally last week I got him to kiss me.

Your massage therapist kissed you? Isn't that against the rules?

It took some persuading, but yeah. And it was good, too.

Okay.

I am embarrassed for her, imagining the scenario.

It's good money, it makes people happy, it's fun. I'm starting school next month.

Wow. Cool.

I don't know what else to say. If this is what she wants to do, more power to her. Still, I can't imagine her wrestling a big table into and out of a car, or lugging it up the stairs to someone's house. I can't imagine her having the physical strength. She'd be good at the mental part, though. She can be serene and giving, calm and centered.

When she graduates she invites us all to the celebration.

You guys going to wear caps and gowns, or just walk across the stage naked?

Very funny, she says. You coming?

Of course I'm coming. I wouldn't miss it.

We fly to Atlanta and drive to the massage therapy school, where Amy stands on a dais with seven or eight other graduates in a space the size of a hotel conference room. Family and friends are scattered among the folding chairs facing the stage. As each name is called, the director of the school makes a small speech about their strengths and idiosyncrasies. People applaud politely.

Then he calls Amy's name, and we stand, a whole cheering row. She comes to the microphone laughing.

That, she says, beaming, is my family.

A year later I am again trying on bathing suits. I hate trying on bathing suits. I know no woman who does not hate trying on bathing suits. As usual, the lighting is from directly above and every rumple is magnified.

And forget the chest. God. It looks so awful. A grown man could flatten his palm between my breasts. It's insane. If I so much as move my arms my breasts jerk and jump and deform themselves, even though it's been six years since the implant surgery and I've modified my chest presses at the gym. I keep expecting the muscles to grow flaccid from disuse, but they don't.

I hate buying clothes to cover my chest. I hate wearing clothes that expose it. I hate feeling like people are being polite when they don't stare.

I sigh. The bathing suits Kurt wants me to wear reveal the wide expanse of skin over bone. There is no fat, no muscle. You can see the bone. I prefer ones you don't have to pull out of your crack or yank up in front. Ones you can wear without thinking about them. Ever.

My swimsuit isn't for me, though. It's for Kurt.

I hate this, I say to him when I rejoin him outside the dressing room.

Why?

I just hate how fake my breasts look.

He sighs. We've been over this territory.

Do you think there's something anyone can do to fix them?

We could find out, he says.

This time I do research. I need someone who's good, who comes recommended, although I don't check into anyone within a hundred miles.

This time the surgeon listens patiently to my complaint.

Okay, he says. Let me see.

I feel like weeping as I open my hospital gown. He and his nurse look at my breasts critically, stepping around me to view them from each side, sizing them up.

Okay, now show me what you mean when you say they leap out to the side.

I look at Kurt, who nods.

I want to cry, but I put my palms together and press one against the other. My breasts do what they do, which is to jump, stretched and peaked like meringue, toward my armpits.

The doctor blinks.

Wow, he says.

His nurse turns away and busies herself with something on the counter.

Okay, the doctor says. Man.

He scratches his head.

I haven't seen anything like it, he says. Do you mind if I take some pictures?

I shake my head, tears now standing in my eyes.

His nurse hands him a Polaroid camera.

Press your hands together again like that, he says.

The camera flashes. It is humiliating, like I'm in a police lineup, except without a head.

He takes several and then tells me to go ahead and get dressed. We'll talk in his office.

There's only so much I can do, the doctor says. I can use an injection to kill the nerves that feed those muscles, which will probably work, but you won't be able to use them for anything. Your other muscles will probably compensate, but you would be significantly weaker. Or I can go in and try to detach the pectoral muscles from the skin. I can't guarantee I can do that, because somehow they were not reattached to your sternum, and now I don't see how that could be done. Another option is to just put in larger implants and see if they'll fill in that space.

I look at Kurt. I don't like any of the options. Already I am a full C cup, which looks ridiculous on my small frame.

Can you go in and try to detach the muscles?

I can try.

I'd rather do that than have you make them larger.

I understand that.

I nod.

We set up the surgery for a few weeks later, at a same-day surgery center three hours from home.

I lie in the bed, my head elevated, my body draped in the faded blue hospital gown, my mind relaxed with whatever they slipped into my IV to soothe my anxiety. Kurt stands by my side, holding the hand opposite the one with the needle.

We need you to sign this, someone says. It's a form authorizing the doctor to perform the surgery.

The nurse holds the clipboard in front of me.

The form is too long to read. The print is too small.

What does it say?

It's a form that gives the doctor permission to do the surgery, the nurse says.

I trust this surgeon. He is reassuring and calm. He only wants what's best for me.

I sign.

When I come to in the recovery room my chest is bandaged and Kurt is once again hovering.

What happened?

I look down. He is holding my hand. My chest is heavy. Too heavy to breathe. Like my lungs are full of concrete.

He got a few of the muscles detached, Kurt says.

Did that fix it?

I drift off without hearing his answer.

When I wake up again he is still there, still holding my hand.

I am woozy, although not as nauseous as I was after the last surgery.

Did that fix it?

He smiles. His eyes crinkle around the edges. He is happy to see me.

He brushes the hair back from my forehead.

The best thing was to just do bigger implants, he says. Fill in the space.

I drift away.

When I open my eyes again he is still there.

He made them bigger?

He nods, smiling.

I try to sit up. My chest is leaden. It pulls on my skin, on my ribs, my collarbones. My chest throbs and burns. It sits like a weight.

I need to clear my lungs, but I'm afraid to cough. I will pull out stitches, make myself explode. I clear my throat instead, but even that hurts. I smile.

I hate this part, I say.

He ruffles my hair.

I know, he says.

He kisses me. My mouth tastes sludgy. I turn my head away.

Sorry, I say.

Once again we stay in a hotel overnight. Once again there is an unveiling. Once again I recoil from the swelling, the ridiculousness of my bulbous chest. Only this time it heals quickly.

Within weeks I am back in the gym, teaching aerobics, self-conscious in front of the mirror and my students, making up some bullshit excuse about my absence, hoping no one asks why I'm bulging out of my tops.

You ruin everything. Every time I try to do something nice for you, you wreck it.

The veins are sticking out in his neck. We are in his office. It is a week after my birthday, and getting close to Christmas. I have picked up a receipt from his painfully tidy desk. It is for Wilson's, which is the name of our gym.

We put our membership on the card? I ask.

He manages our money, and I don't know if we pay our gym dues annually or through a bank draft or through our credit cards. I was mostly just curious, but now he is screaming at me.

I try to get you something nice for Christmas and you screw it up! he yells. Then he lowers his voice. Just forget it. We can just forget about Christmas.

But I didn't see anything, I protest. Just the name, okay?

It is not okay. He is furious, and I don't know why. I know I ruined something. I just don't know what it is.

It will be Christmas morning before I open the box from Wilson's, the leather company, to find a butter-soft leather jacket.

To replace that ugly bomber, he says. The bomber was a graduation gift from my siblings. It is baggy and comfortable, although even I know it makes me look short and fat. The new jacket is sleek. It follows my lines. It makes me look shapely and slim.

He scowls at me when I try it on. Too bad you ruined the surprise, he says. I duck my head. He tries to do special things for me and I screw them up.

CHAPTER 16

What do you think about having a baby?

The kids are thirteen and eleven, and their focus is more on their friends than on us.

Kurt runs his fingertips down the side of my face.

One thing we've always done wonderfully together is parent, he says.

The truth is our marriage is floundering. We snipe. We bait. We turn away. We are losing our connection. A baby would bind us.

We talk about it for weeks. One day I love the idea. The next I am paralyzed by the thought of never having a day to myself. Right now we only have the kids every other week, so we have plenty of time to ourselves. We travel. We read. We have afternoon sex. If we have a baby, those things will disappear. Still, we have been parents since the day we became a couple. It defines us. It is who we are, and now the kids are nearly grown.

Let's do it, I say. Let's have our own.

I call Amy.

I'm going to have a baby, I say.

What?

We're going to try, I mean.

Wow, she says. Are you sure?

Of course not, I say. Who ever is?

For more than a year we try, by ourselves and with an infertility doctor. Every day at three in the afternoon I open vials and line them up on the counter. I draw saline up into a syringe, then squirt it into a vial of powder. I crane in front of the mirror until I can see my backside, then stick the needle deep into the muscles of my butt.

I spend hours in waiting rooms, long

minutes in stirrups. I dash to the clinic with containers of sperm, then return hours later to have it injected into my uterus. The doctors draw blood, they shoot dye into my fallopian tubes. They operate to remove fibroids. Kurt and I have sex. Mechanically and on a schedule. We try to pretend it's fun.

I am bereft every time I see blood on the toilet paper.

One day my friend Vickie calls.

Would you guys consider adoption?

I don't know, I say. Let me ask Kurt.

I cover the phone.

Honey, would we consider adoption?

Sure, Kurt says.

Sure, I say to Vickie.

She squeals.

She has a friend who does private adoptions, and there's a baby who may be available soon. In the next few hours I gather photos and write an adoption portfolio. We send it to the birth parents. There are blood tests, criminal background checks, home visits.

Are you being a bitch because of the medications, Kurt asks, or is this just you at baseline?

I'm not a bitch, I say. I stomp away and slam the door. The next day I talk with a friend who had gone through infertility treatments.

I was such a raving bitch! she says. I'm surprised my marriage survived.

Two months later the attorney calls.

Congratulations, she says. You're a mother.

I scream.

That December I turn forty, yet my children and husband are silent. The kids wiggle with anticipation, but they don't bring me breakfast in bed or homemade cards or tape-heavy gifts, as is the tradition.

I know that something is up, though, because there are whispers and giggles behind carefully closed doors.

At dinnertime we get in the car.

Where do you want to eat?

Hmm . . . I say.

The children are dressed up, and the clothes laid out for me were special occasion: short skirt, thigh-high hose, a lacy sweater. Kurt opens the car door for me and strokes my leg as I climb in.

How about the Pasta Factory, Claire says.

Hmmm . . . I say. If you guys want Italian, how about the Olive Garden? I like their salads.

Kurt glares at me. I have given the wrong answer.

How about the Pasta Factory? he says. You always love the Pasta Factory.

But I like the salad at Olive Garden, and the kids love the meatballs.

The kids are quiet for a beat, and then start chanting for the Pasta Factory.

I look at Kurt. He is scowling. I am supposed to choose the Pasta Factory, although I don't know why.

On the other hand, I say, the Pasta Factory has better eggplant parmesan . . . I pause, let the suspense build. Okay, I say, let's go the Pasta Factory.

The children cheer.

We drive along singing to Christmas music. Colored lights are strung across Broadway, the fronts of stores are outlined with white lights and decorated with wreaths and Christmas trees and dioramas of Santa's workshop. I sit back and close my eyes.

It is a small downtown, recently revitalized after a slump during the '80s, when President Reagan came to visit and the business association had to hang bunting and set up pavilions and bleachers to hide the Out of Business signs that lined the streets. Now the owners have conceded most of the retail to the mall and replaced it with coffee shops and ethnic restaurants and an independent movie theater. The place bustles, but that means there isn't a parking place anywhere near the restaurant, so Kurt drops the kids and me at the door and drives off to park. I carry the baby, Sarah, and Claire hurries ahead. She is whispering to the hostess when I arrive. They both turn and try to hide their smiles as they look at me.

Right this way, the hostess says.

I settle the baby in a high chair and clip the harness, then slide into a booth and chat with the kids while we wait for Kurt. The hostess hands out menus. Mikey opens his, then slaps it shut and looks guilty. I pretend not to notice. Kurt walks up, smelling of fresh winter air, and Mikey opens his menu and gives him a peek.

The hostess gave me the wrong one, he whispers loudly enough that I can hear.

Well, that's it! Kurt says. He snatches the menu from Mikey and slaps it down in front of me. Here, he says, this one was supposed to be yours.

Mikey slides down in his seat and Claire starts to cry.

I paste a smile on my face. My mother-in-law used to do the same thing, smile when the honest response would be to sob, or fight back, and I hated it. I swore I'd never do the same.

Early in the marriage I had said, Your

mom is screwing you up. She acts like everything is happy happy all of the time, and it's not. How are you supposed to believe your own perceptions if someone is always papering over the truth with a pretty lie?

But now I am acting just like her, pretending to be happy when inside I am frightened.

I open the menu. Under the "specials of the day" clip is an itinerary. Australia, Fiji. Leaving in three days.

I am surprised. I try to compose my face. Sarah is eight months old. How can I pack adequately for her? How can I get ready for the eight people who will arrive less than twenty-four hours after our scheduled return date, to stay through the Christmas holidays? I can't. There's no way. Then I think, lighten up. Those things will take care of themselves. Be excited. Enjoy.

I look up and smile. Wow! I say. Holy cow!

You hate it, he says. We may as well not even go now.

No, it's wonderful, I say. I'm just trying to figure out how to leave in a few days, that's all.

That's what you're thinking? Most women would be thrilled at a trip like this, and you're obsessing over how you can pack? You just can't be happy.

The kids are crying.

The waitress comes up, acting like she doesn't see the kids' tear-streaked faces.

What can I get for you tonight? she asks.

I look down at my menu. Eggplant parmesan, I say, and a tiny bowl of spaghetti for the baby.

The rest of the family orders. When the waitress goes away we look down at our hands, toy with our silverware, comment on the antique-looking fans, do anything but look at each other.

The children give me their gifts and I make overjoyed sounds, even though I know the kids and I are barely keeping ourselves from weeping.

I want to lay my head on the table and close my eyes. Instead I cajole the kids into cheerfulness. We tell jokes, we laugh, we look happy. I ask them, What was the best part of your day? I do not ask them about the worst, even though that is our tradition, because I don't think we need to be reminded. If they had a worse moment than the ones at the table, I don't want to know.

My husband joins in the façade, but I can feel him seething, feel the anger underneath. When our eyes meet I can tell that he is furious.

The waitress comes to clear our dishes,

and Kurt gives her some kind of signal. The children wriggle expectantly. She walks away and returns moments later with a lighted birthday cake. The children and Kurt begin to sing, "Happy Birthday to You . . ."

I look at Kurt, tears in my eyes. He had baked the cake at a friend's house and then spirited it here, getting the manager to let him hide it in the walk-in. He had given up his day to make my evening special, and I had ruined it.

Three days later we leave for Australia, where Sarah spends the nights wide awake, bouncing and laughing, wanting to play, and the days draped in our arms, heavy and sweaty, as we negotiate the holiday mobs. We are itchy and irritable, thrown off our own sleep patterns and bickering about who should have to stay awake and play with her.

By the time we get to Fiji she has adjusted, and she is her usual happy self. During meals the islanders take her out of her high chair. They tuck hibiscus blossoms behind her ears and dance with her to the ukulele quartets.

Days after we get home I am still on Fiji time, slogging through my Christmas preparations and napping randomly, trying to reacclimate.

What do you think this is?

Amy tips her head to the side and taps a lump on her neck. I put my fingers on it. It is the size of a Ping-Pong ball.

It is Christmas, and most of the family has come to Missouri to celebrate.

I don't know, I say. Do you have a cold?

She shakes her head.

Kurt wears his doctor face as he presses the lump.

I'd get this checked out, he says. It's probably nothing, but it's worth having it looked at.

During poker games I see her pressing it, a distracted look on her face, although she laughs triumphantly and throws down her cards when she wins. She and Sarah build towers out of stacking cups, then laugh together as they knock them down. She whispers and giggles with Claire and Jenelle, her teenage nieces. She sings lustily to Christmas carols, and commandeers Kurt's recliner, where she sits, smiling and fingering the lump on her neck.

It is the first time all of Mom's children have been together for Christmas in twenty-three years, in part because Jane lives in Montana and rarely makes it back, and then only in the summer. This year, though, she has come, and she has brought her two children. Our gift to our mom is going to be a family portrait, so the two youngest are assigned to draw a stick figure picture of the family: five adult children, four spouses, and six grandchildren. They glue beads on for eyes, mount the picture in a frame and wrap it up.

It is a family tradition to make symbols of gifts that can't be wrapped, a tradition heightened between Kurt and me. One year I wrapped an ornament of a skiing Santa to symbolize a ski trip. Another year he made a hand-sized cheval mirror out of popsicle sticks and aluminum foil, letting me pick the real one out for myself.

Mom cries when she opens the picture, and we laugh. Mom always cries. At Christmas. At weddings and graduations. At parades.

What we don't realize at the time is that this will be our last family portrait.

One night I interrupt the poker game to propose a new family tradition.

Let's all write out predictions for the upcoming year. Then next year we can open them and see which ones we got right.

I bring out a pad of paper and a handful of pens.

"Mom and Amy will both find romance this year," Amy writes. "Claire and Jenelle will remain close friends and *share secrets!*"

At the end of Amy's visit I hug her.

Let me know what you find out about the lump, I say.

Of course, she says. She smiles. It's probably nothing.

Within a few weeks she has the biopsy results. It is not nothing. It is cancer.

What? I say into the phone.

Cancer, she says again.

What kind of cancer?

Hodgkin's disease, she says. It's a cancer of the lymph system.

Wow.

It's the best kind, she says. There's an 80 percent cure rate.

I try to think what to say. In the spring Amy got her associate's degree, summa cum laude. Everything about her life is on an upward trajectory. Now this.

That's good. I guess.

It's better than most, she says. Her voice doesn't even shake.

You don't have to be so brave.

She laughs.

I'm not, she says. I'm faking it.

A few days later she meets with the oncologist, who tells her she must immediately begin chemotherapy. We'll do two rounds, she says, then use radiation if necessary.

Aren't there any other options? Amy asks.

No, the doctor says. You'll start in three days, and you'll follow this regimen.

I'm not ready, Amy says. I want a second opinion.

The doctor gets huffy.

She treated me like I was an idiot, Amy tells me over the phone. But it's my body.

She finds a new doctor, who recommends a different course of treatment: Radiation five days a week for six weeks.

Amy signs on.

Within a week she has slim blue x's tattooed onto her neck and shoulder, the treasure chest X for the beam of cell-killing and life-saving radiation. Dig here, the tattoos say, but tiny. Subtle. Like concentration camp tattoos, something that will mark her always as a survivor.

I love you, she says.

She calls each of us and tells us again.

I know, I say. I know. I love you, too.

I am crying when I get off the phone, even though I know it's Hodgkin's and she'll probably survive. Still, she is my baby sister, and she has cancer.

She calls Dad, too, after a seven-year silence.

Hi, she says. It's Amy. I have cancer.

They meet at a campground, she and Dad and his wife. One weekend to catch up, just in case.

It was good, she tells me. I wouldn't want to do it often, but I'm glad I let go of all of that.

I know what "all of that" means.

At least, I think I do.

The rest of us rotate in, Mom driving again and again from her home five hours away, staying overnight on a mattress on the floor as her daughter moans and fades, getting weaker, her thick curls clogging the bathtub drain. Her siblings, too, take turns.

When it is mine I fly down and sit reading stale magazines as they shoot beams into her neck. Then I take her home and settle her on the couch while I bake bread in the machine I plan to leave behind.

The bread's yeasty smell masks the stink of the carpet, which smells like old dog and long-spilled milk.

I try to cook foods enticing enough to get past the grated rawness of Amy's mouth and throat.

This is one way to lose weight, she tells me.

I kind of liked it better when you were on Weight Watchers, I say. She laughs.

No shit, she says.

She pulls a handful of hair from the back of her head.

You need to get the landlords to change the carpet and paint this place, I tell her.

I know, she says, but they might charge me.

Get serious, I say. You've lived here four years. If you'd moved, they'd have changed it three times by now. Call them.

I will, she says, I will. Except Pete's not doing so well, and I don't want him peeing on new carpet.

I drop it. Bake my bread. Make spaghetti and meatballs. She manages to swallow a few as we sit in the dark watching *Love, Valor, Compassion!* a movie about eight gay men gathered together for a week on an estate. Two of the men are twins, one of whom is being cared for ever-so-gently by his lover as he dies of AIDS.

God, I love this movie! she says.

It's like a gay *Big Chill,* I say. I love it how they use that one actor to portray both twins.

I wonder how they did that, she says.

Weren't they both in a couple of scenes together?

She picks up the remote and rewinds through scene after scene. They're together a few times, but we only see the back of one of the actor's heads.

Clever, I say.

I love how much he's loved, she says.

I reach for her hand.

After three days I fly home, grateful for my husband and kids. I could not bear to be alone.

After a week I send Amy a card.

Congratulations to the graduate! it reads. Inside I write, Here's to the end of round one. The cancer doesn't have a chance.

Later that week I am at the gym, spent, sore, invigorated. In the locker room I chat with another woman.

I'm going to the one place in the world where I can be myself, I say, smiling fully, unself-conscious.

Oh, home? she asks.

Her answer surprises me. She is blond and gorgeous, her breasts unnaturally large, her husband a plastic surgeon twenty years her senior.

No, my writers' group, I say.

It is her turn to look surprised.

I should feel that way at home, I know, but at home I am cautious. Anything I say can invoke seething anger, or worse, rage.

Certainly defensiveness. In my writers' group, though, I don't have to be careful. I am not competing. I read my work aloud and listen to my friends' reactions. They laugh or they tell me a piece didn't quite work, but they don't attack me. I am never on trial.

At home I am. I know that. I know because my husband and I criticize others. We talk about other people's weight, the bulge over a belt, the pooched belly. They are not us. They are not superior. They do not have our money or our education or our style. Others do, of course, they have it all and more, but they're no good either, because they're too persnickety or their marriage is boring or they don't have any juice. We have juice. We fall into bed. We grope each other in restaurants. We make out in parking lots. When we ride up escalators he is behind me. Right behind me, so that his front runs up my backside as we get to the upper floor. We think maybe no one sees us, the move or the contact or the glazed look in our eyes.

Even more often, we scream. We fight, we yell, we accuse. I hit him. I slam doors. He clenches his hands and tries not to hit me.

You think you've got it so bad? he says, his jaw clenched and his face inches from mine. Then leave. You'll get nothing.

He has been making the same threat for years. We have sat in marriage counselors' offices and thrashed it out, him cooly polite, me frenzied. He looks rational, I look crazed, what Kurt calls "desperate." One therapist says I should embrace my desperation. Acknowledge it, accept it, consider it part of who I am. She is the one I call Dr. Weaver. My husband calls her Lisa.

She thinks I should accept that I do not feel safe, that I have come from a place of skewed perceptions, that I do not trust anyone, myself included. My husband is pleased. If I would calm down, accept that I am desperate, give myself over to trusting him, to becoming what he would like me to become, we would have a happy marriage.

Every time we walk into her office I grab the box of Kleenex. The smooth way she talks, the tall blondness of her, the piling on of her and my husband, both clean and handsome, both calm and authoritative, makes me cry.

My husband sits next to me and puts his arm around me, even though we have been fighting for days.

You want to fuck Tim, he says.

Tim is a friend who comes to our home for companionship as his own marriage dissolves. He doesn't confide so much as simply takes solace. He stands in the kitchen as I cook, listens to stories about the kids, about my writing. We debate politics, olive oils, the merits of crushing versus mincing garlic. Tim cooks. A man cooking is as exotic to me as a llama. Sometimes we meet for racquetball, leaning against the gym walls between games, sweating, getting our breath.

He does not talk with me about why his marriage is falling apart. He talks to himself, he says, and that's enough. I suggest perhaps he should seek a second opinion, which makes him laugh.

His reticence keeps me from saying much about my own life, although I occasionally spew over a spat or squabble, or beat the racquetball with unusual violence. He is our friend collectively, though, and I don't want to put him in the middle. He has no desire to take sides. We are both good people, he says. He does not want to choose.

I do not want to have sex with Tim. I have, however, thought about what it would be like to be married to him. What it would be like to be treated gently, with respect, to cook side by side, to have friends over and relax into their warmth.

In that I have been unfaithful.

I do not know if I would be happier,

though, with Tim. I think *I might*
with someone who is just *nice.* *I lik*
like lots of edge, and I do*n't know*
has any. I watch with fond*ness as he*
to my child, and then feel *guilty for*
feeling fond.

He is one of the few people *who come*
our home. Kurt does not like *guests.* *If we*
invite someone he worries abou*t it all day,*
dreading it, even if the guests are *family.*

What made you think you could *schedule*
my time? he asks.

It's just family, I say. It will be fun.

But he hates it. Hates having people *over*,
hates anticipating it, hates the very *idea of*
making small talk or being casual or pic*king*
up the house before and after.

The therapist has us take the MMPI, *the*
Minnesota Multiphasic Personality Inventory that psychologists use to define patients' personalities. I am an extrovert,
which means I get energized by people. He
is an introvert. He is energized by solitude
and quiet. People drain him.

So we rarely socialize, and when we do I
spend the day reassuring. It'll be fine, I say.
It'll be fun.

It has taken me a decade of marriage to
realize that he is afraid of messing up, afraid
of not knowing what to say, of not getting

the jokes, of embarrassing himself. He is that way when I introduce him to skiing, that way when I suggest scuba diving. He doesn't know how to do either, and he's afraid of looking dumb.

The therapist makes me say I understand, but I don't. I understand rationally, of course. But isn't it better to look dumb than to not try anything new?

After fights — daily fights — I go to my office, fuming, wanting to cry. I can't work. I can't read. I can only obsess. What did he say, what did I say, does he still love me, can he still love me, can anyone love me, really love me, if they know me?

I will not go to him. I will not call him. I will not send him an email. He can just sit down in his office and worry. Worry that I don't love him. Worry that we will end it. Worry that he will lose me.

I look at the clock. I will not go to him, will not contact him. I pace around my office, a huge room with windows overlooking the backyard, the pond. I look at the clock. I will not contact him. I lie on the floor, do sit-ups. Look at the phone. Look at my email. The icon is not bouncing. The icon is not bouncing, the instant message icon is not bouncing, no one is writing to me, getting in touch.

I want to punch something. I want to scream. I want to run down the stairs and down the hall and scream at him. Scream at him and call him a fucking rat bastard. Get it out, get it over with, tell him to leave, leave myself, get into my car and drive, go to a friend's, go to the gym.

Instead I stare at my computer monitor. I should work. I have a deadline coming up, I have interviews to do. I look at my motto, taped to my monitor: All you have to do is something.

All I do is nothing. I sit and stare at the screen or out the window and I seethe.

I make it an hour. Then I go downstairs to the kitchen. I look in the pantry. He did his biannual spring cleaning a week ago, stripping every room of everything, then cleaning from the ceiling down, chasing crumbs from drawer tracks with compressed air, getting on his hands and knees and using a toothbrush on the juncture between the floor and the baseboard. For years I worked by his side, but this year I refused on the grounds that I keep the house clean the other fifty weeks of the year.

The canned goods are still alphabetized, still in straight rows, small cans in front, big ones in back, pasta and rice tucked into a new shoe box that does not yet contain crumbs or end pieces or torn-off labels. I want to rearrange it the way it belongs — the waffle mix next to the syrup, the tomatoes with the mushrooms, the canned pears next to the macaroni and cheese. I am the one who cooks, I used to argue; shouldn't the pantry be arranged the way I want it? Your way makes no sense, he'd say. It's messy. It's not organized. My way is better.

I got laid, Amy says.

I laugh. It has been years, in part because she has been so obese and in part because she keeps going after men who are married or too young or too something that makes them unattainable.

Who was the lucky man?

My roommate's little brother. He's visiting.

Little brother? How little?

Not little at all, she says, with a deep, guttural laugh.

Good for you, I say, laughing with her. But I meant how old.

Old enough, she says. I'll send you a picture.

She emails a photo of him in a climbing harness. He is shirtless. The harness frames his crotch. He is in his early twenties at most. I call her back.

Okay, give, I say. I want to hear the story.

There's no story, she says. We were having a few beers, we got messing around, and today I'm one happy woman.

I wince, both because it sounds like she took advantage of a young guy and because I'm pretty sure she's going to be hurt.

Congratulations, I say. Do you think you'll see him again?

I hope so, since he's staying here for a couple of weeks.

To save money Amy has taken in roommates — a couple in their late twenties who are saving up for their wedding. She likes both of them, although she complains sometimes about the thud thud thud of their headboard against the adjoining wall. The brother apparently is sleeping on the couch, which is where Amy found him after everyone else had gone to bed.

I'm going rock climbing with the whole family, she says. It's what he's into.

I'm impressed. Amy has lost something like fifty pounds in the past year, her cancer scans are clear, and she's getting adventurous.

Over the next week she calls a couple of times, getting quieter each time. Eventually I pull it out of her.

So was there a repeat performance?

317

No, she says. Not for lack of trying.

Ouch. You okay?

Oh yeah. I'm fine. I would have liked more, though.

I'm quiet for a moment.

He was kind of young, you know.

I don't want to sound like I disapprove. First of all, I've done plenty of dumbshit things myself, and Amy knows it. But also because I don't want her to stop telling me things, and I'm afraid she will if I get judgmental.

Who else would want me? she asks.

Lots of men, I say. Smart men.

Be serious, she says. You have no idea what it's like.

Lots of men would feel lucky to be with you, I say. What about hockey fans? Why don't you go out with hockey fans?

She snorts.

Amy is past president of the booster club for the Atlanta Knights. She goes to all of their games. Screams, cheers, runs meet-the-player events. She loves her team.

They're fat, she says.

I don't know what to say.

I want to do an NPR commentary, I say.

You don't have a chance.

I am surprised. This is the only time he

has ever said he didn't think I'd get whatever I went after. It makes me just mad enough to send an email to the host of the show, whom I had met at a luncheon redolent with cologned businessmen. He and I were the only writers, and we leaned toward each other, talking about the craft and the business and the challenges inherent in making a living with words.

Send me a script, he says. I'll let you know.

I send it.

Pretty good, he says. Where can you do the taping?

I am gleeful when I tell Kurt.

He just wants to fuck you, he says.

CHAPTER 17

After twenty-two years in Atlanta, Amy moves to Knoxville. She enrolls in graduate school at the University of Tennessee, where she studies comparative religions, trying to understand the impact of organized religion on society and cultures around the world. She wants to find her spiritual center.

They have a hockey team, she says.

I laugh.

What about your job?

They're transferring it to their Knoxville offices, she says. I'm that good.

Amy is a pricing analyst for the Kimberly-Clark corporation. She's been there for fifteen years, working her way up from a temp job to a position important enough that they'd relocate it to keep her happy.

I'm really excited for you, I say.

A couple of days later she calls again.

I'm going to buy a condo, she says. Will you co-sign?

Of course we will, I say. Amy has borrowed money from us before, paying it back exactly on schedule, each check accompanied by a cheery note about her life.

Thank you, she says. I love you.

The next day she calls back.

I got it by myself, she says.

Got what?

The mortgage. I got it by myself.

I do the happy dance with her over the phone.

She is ebullient. She is thirty-six and buying a home under her own credit rating and earnings and proven responsibility.

I'm so proud of you, I say. I've never qualified for a loan by myself.

She giggles.

She buys a small condo in a neighborhood of condos, each half a duplex. Hers has two bedrooms and two baths, a kitchen and a living room, a patio out back with a privacy fence. Pat sends her morning glory seeds from her own garden, and Amy plants them to climb up the fence.

This is so exciting, she says.

We talk almost daily. One day we are chattering along, about everything and nothing.

So I was telling Scott about my yeast infection, she says.

Scott is her former boss, a married man who has become her confidant.

You told him about your yeast infection? Gross.

Heck yes, she says. I tell him everything.

I laugh. I'm glad she has him. She needs a male friend.

She goes on about her classes, about how she loves mixing it up and arguing and learning. She loves feeling part of a community of people who are determined to know more.

I can't believe this, she says. These people are fierce.

I'm sure you're jumping right in with them.

Of course. It feels great. Like I'm finally

really using my brain.

Hey, I say a few months later. Kurt and I are going to Charlotte for a conference. Want to get together?

I don't tell her that this is yet another last-ditch effort to save our marriage, this trip to another state. We have fought for years over whether we'll stay in Missouri. I need mountains, lakes, oceans. A good airport. I don't belong in central Missouri. He does not want to leave. Ever. Not even after the kids go away to college. The trip to Charlotte is a compromise on his part; he's doing it to make me happy, to appear open-minded.

From the map it looks like Charlotte, North Carolina, and Knoxville are neighbors. In truth they're four hours apart. Amy and I split the difference and meet near Asheville, at Chimney Rock State Park.

Tawanda! Amy says, as she leads the way up the steep trail.

Tawanda is her new screen name. She got it from the movie *Fried Green Tomatoes,* in which Kathy Bates plays a woman awakening to her midlife strength.

Amy's eyes sparkle and she laughs often. I had never seen her look so healthy.

I've lost eighty-five pounds, she says.

Wow. You look fantastic.

We climb a trail to the top of the rock, where an American flag flaps in the wind. Amy raises her arms triumphantly, and I take a picture. It is just a few months after the attacks of September 11, and we are feeling patriotic.

Back at the hotel room I take another. In it she is sitting on the couch in a blue velvet top that matches her eyes. She looks straight at me, her chin proud. It is the photo we will use on her "Missing" poster.

A couple of months later Amy meets a man. In an internet chat room, I think, although she is vague. She says something about webcams and seductive talk.

His name is Ron, she says, her voice effervescent. He's a house painter, living in a cheap motel room in Tuscaloosa. He doesn't have a place to stay.

Why not?

She says something about him losing his last job, about a girlfriend, about two kids in Florida he rarely gets to see. I don't pay close attention.

Amy is excited, and I'm happy for her.

Within weeks she invites him to move into her condo, to set up his computer next to hers, to share her bed. It has been a long time since anyone has shared her bed.

We're trying it out, she says.

He leaves me love notes, she says.

We set the alarm for a half hour early so we can lie in bed and cuddle, she says.

He respects me too much to have sex with me, she says. I've persuaded him to let me . . . you know.

She giggles.

You persuaded him? I ask, involuntarily raising my eyebrows, even though she can't see me over the phone. I'll bet that was hard. Does he reciprocate?

There is a pause.

Not yet, she says, but we're working on it.

I shake my head. Why does she accept that? But I also think I don't know the story. I know he holds her when they watch movies. I know he sometimes does the cooking, and that when he does he pays attention to her Weight Watchers portion exchanges, measuring out the oil, encouraging her to go to her meetings. Each of these things make her feel loved, and for that I am happy.

She takes him to her company Christmas party. The next day I call her.

How was it?

Good, she says. We wore our cowboy hats.

I laugh. Ron is a rodeo cowboy, and Amy has bought herself a cowboy hat so they match. Within weeks she'll start volunteering at a therapeutic riding school so she can become comfortable around horses.

So how'd he do with your co-workers?

Okay, she says. Although we were expecting dinner, so he got a little drunk. He said it'll never happen again.

I hope not, I say. You've had enough of that in your life.

No kidding.

A few days later she tells me he has priors.

Priors?

Yeah, she says. I never thought that would be part of my vocabulary.

No kidding, I say.

Nothing bad, though, she says. Money stuff.

I take that to mean there's no violence. No rape, no murder, no armed robbery. I try to be open-minded, to not hold it against him. I learn later that he has served time. Two and a half years here, a couple of years there. Grand theft auto, burglary, passing bad checks.

He went to test drive a truck and just didn't give it back, she says.

Seriously?

Seriously.

What was he thinking?

She is silent, and I don't probe further, thinking she'd tell me if she wanted to, thinking she must be embarrassed.

There is no way this is good.

Kurt and I are lying in bed, talking our way toward sleep.

You know what I want for Christmas? I ask.

No idea, he says, trailing his fingers up my arm.

I want to do an Outward Bound.

His fingers stop.

How come?

I hear the edge in his voice and I roll onto my side to reassure him.

I want to stop being afraid of stuff, I say. Especially heights. I was reading about the one in North Carolina. White water, rock climbing, solo nights. I want to do it.

He is silent. He knows how terrified I am of heights, and of being alone.

I'll look into it, he says after a pause.

I'll send you the URL, I say.

I have read the program's website carefully, my heart thudding in fear and excitement. Thinking about it makes me sweat. I am afraid I'll become paralyzed halfway up a rock face, unable to go up or down, or that I'll lie awake all night, alone on the mountain as wolves howl. I fear the wolves, of course. Or the coyotes or mountain lions or whatever it is they have in North Carolina, but mostly I fear the man who will come into my tent. The man who will come in and seduce me or worse.

My fear is irrational, and I want to face it down, erase it from my life.

My family is gathering at my house for the holidays. Amy is coming, too, even though it will keep her away from her new love.

You know you're welcome to bring him, right?

Maybe I will, she says.

A few days later she calls back.

I guess he's not ready for the Latus mob scene yet, she says.

Smart guy, I say. We can be pretty overwhelming.

You'll get to meet him someday.

Well, he's welcome if he changes his mind.

Amy arrives a few days before Christmas. Ron is not with her, but her eyes are bright, her smile wide. She has flown from Knoxville to St. Louis and then caught a ride to my house with Mom. I rush to the door when I hear their rental car in the drive.

Hello! Oh my gosh you're here! I hug

Mom, then wrap Amy in my arms, kiss her, and pull her into the house.

You look fantastic! I say.

Thank you, she says, pirouetting. Ten more pounds.

Wow. I'm impressed.

I hug her again.

The Christmas tree towers eighteen feet, from the sunken living room up into the cathedral ceiling, its angel barely upright. There is a fire in the fireplace. Christmas music is playing, and my home glows. The mantel is draped in white, the nativity scene arrayed in its china splendor, the painting over the fireplace replaced by a glittering wreath. The ficus twinkles with tiny white lights, a counterpoint to the fat colored bulbs on the tree.

The house, the family, the world sparkles.

I've got you in the downstairs back room, I tell Amy. You'll have privacy. And internet access.

We both laugh.

It's only a month since she met Ron Ball. It is hard to be away from a new love for a week, I know. Still, her step is buoyant, and even though she spends hours in her room checking email, her laugh is deep and real, and her hugs are heartfelt.

You okay? I ask often.

I'm fine, she says.

At night the family plays poker.

Hit me, Amy says, then laughs her guttural laugh at the card.

Again? Steve asks.

No, I'll stay, she says.

My sister-in-law is in the living room, reading a book. Kurt is in his office, where it's quiet. The rest of us are gathered around the table, covered with a tablecloth to keep coins from rolling, the children leaning over their cheat sheets to remember whether three of a kind beats two pair.

During a break Amy runs downstairs and logs on to her laptop. She comes back up, subdued.

Everything okay? I ask.

Sure, she says. Everything's fine.

Later I walk down to her room. She is staying in the workout room, with its wall-size mirror.

Everything okay?

He's not online, she says, frowning. He's not answering the phone, either.

You worried?

Not really. Sort of.

Where do you think he is?

I don't know. That's why I'm worried.

I sit quietly. I don't know how to ask, but

I feel like I should.

Do you think he's gone?

I don't know. She rubs the ridge between her eyebrows. I don't think so.

Then she smiles.

He's probably just at the store or something, she says.

You hear anything? I ask her quietly at breakfast. She shakes her head.

I'm sorry, hon.

I am worried that he has wiped her out, that he has stolen whatever she has of value, her computer and her jewelry. I look at Amy's hand. After her divorce and her ex-husband's death and the long slog out of the debt he left behind, she had melted down most of her gold jewelry and combined it with the monster diamond from her engagement ring to create a piece so big it could be a weapon. She is wearing it now, so at least he hasn't taken that.

Amy maintains her game face, playing with her nieces and nephews, sitting often and close to her sisters and brother. She doesn't talk much about her man, which doesn't make sense to me. When I am infatuated I talk constantly, giggly and gleeful. But she is being quiet, and I'm concerned. This isn't like her.

At midnight we put the last of the Santa presents under the tree. The pile comes up to my waist and spreads out into the living room. It is bountiful, nearly obscene. We go to bed content, sure that the children will feel loved.

In the morning we open presents one by one, everyone watching and oohing and ahhing. It takes two pots of coffee and a break for cereal and eggs — anything to offset the candy canes and chocolate the kids are digging out of the toes of their stockings.

We take turns opening, the kids first and the grown-ups intermittently, my mother smiling gamely as round after round passes her by. She knows we have done something big, she just doesn't know what.

The children find a gift for me. It is a small slim box. A jewelry box. The family watches. Kurt has a habit of buying extravagant gifts, so all eyes are on the box, even though most days I wear only a small opal necklace and a pair of gold hoop earrings.

I open it, smiling expectantly.

It is a black thong.

I crumble it into my hand and blush, while the family laughs.

I quickly divert attention to one of the kids, then meet Kurt's eyes. He is smiling, proud.

When my next turn comes around Kurt goes into the bedroom and comes out with a lumpy garbage bag. The gift is cumbersome and unwieldy, and the family clears a space in the middle of the living room and sits back. I tear into the bag.

It is a sheepskin rug, bigger than a man. It is the kind you see in movies, topped by a woman in something sexy, a slinky chemise maybe, her painted toes in feather-festooned mules. Again I wait to meet Kurt's eyes.

My gifts from my family include a cotton sweater, books, a collection of Beatles CDs.

There are gifts of pans and clothing and Game Boys and art. Dozens and dozens of gifts.

Eventually the area under the tree is empty. The children disperse to their toys while the adults sit back, waiting for the moment we will present our mother with her gift. I am secretly still looking around, expecting Kurt somehow to surprise me with my trip to Outward Bound. Finally he produces one last package. It is the size of a shoebox, wrapped clumsily in red and green.

I am grinning, and I open the package slowly, as he leans in with the camera. This is my big gift.

I remember the year he carved a laptop computer out of Styrofoam, complete with a keyboard and a tracking ball, and a giant heart in lieu of a screen. I wonder how he will depict my Outward Bound trip.

Inside the shoe box is another, much smaller. I laugh as I peel away the paper. Will it be a tiny climbing rope? A miniature life jacket? A pup tent made of toothpicks and tissue?

I open it.

Inside are earrings and a pendant of sapphires and diamonds set in platinum, so heavy that I am surprised by their heft in the palm of my hand.

Again I don't want to look at him, but this time it isn't because I am embarrassed, but because I am angry. I asked for independence. Instead he gives me a symbol of wealth and prestige. A symbol I am unlikely to wear, paid for with money that could have bought me strength.

I compose my face and pass the jewelry around, listening to my family's exclamations. I am even madder because I know this display of affluence makes some of my siblings uncomfortable. It makes me uncomfortable. We may as well have hung a flashing sign saying Rich! Rich! Rich!

I want to throw the jewelry, but I smile as if I'm delighted, and tilt my head forward as Kurt clasps the necklace around my neck.

They match your eyes, he says.

I have nothing to say.

The family stays a week, and Kurt and I are relieved when they go. It has been a joy, of course, but we need our space. Kurt in particular. He has hidden in his office nearly every night, or left for work with a little too much spring in his step. I can't fault him. Wasn't it Benjamin Franklin who said, Fish and visitors smell in three days?

Plus we have fought over and over about the jewelry.

You don't appreciate anything I do, he says.

You don't care about what I want, I say. You just care about how I look.

It is an unending, unwinnable argument.

Amy leaves on Saturday.

Let me know what you find out, okay?

I will, she says. I'm sure it will be fine.

She looks worried.

CHAPTER 18

My phone rings.

He wasn't there, Amy says.

She is crying.

I asked him to do this one thing, to pick me up at the airport, and he wasn't there. He wasn't there. Why wasn't he there?

Oh, Amy, I say. I'm so sorry. What an asshole. Do you know where he is?

I have no idea. I don't know if he's dead

on the side of the road or in a hospital or off with some other woman. I just don't know.

Call me when you get home.

Amy asks the cab driver to wait while she goes in, in case she needs help. The house looks normal from the outside. Inside, the electric fireplace is on and the place is like a sauna. There are pizza boxes, too, and beer bottles everywhere. The trash is overflowing.

What about your computer? I ask when she calls.

It's here.

Your jewelry?

Janine, he didn't rob me, she says, an edge in her voice.

Sorry, hon, I say. I didn't mean it that way.

Except I did, and we both know it.

I'll talk with you later, she says.

I love you, I say.

I love you, too.

I call her the next day.

Do you know anything?

She is quiet for a minute.

Are you there?

I'm here, she says. I hear her take a deep breath. He's in jail.

He's in what?

Silence.

Jail.

For what?

I can't believe this. What is she doing? What is she doing with a man who has priors, who is in jail, who embarrassed her by practically pushing people aside to get to the bar at her company Christmas party?

DUI, she says. He was just so sad and lonely with me gone that he started drinking. Then he needed more beer, so he got in his truck to drive to the store, but he crashed and they took him in.

Wow. Was anyone hurt?

No, but the truck is totaled.

Wow.

Again there is silence.

What else?

I know there's something, or she would keep talking.

It's his third, she says.

Holy shit.

I know.

Amy doesn't tell me that Ron has been extradited to Alabama to serve time, a stipulation from his two prior DUIs, nor that she drives down to Tuscaloosa to bail him out.

She writes a check for $1,765 to the bail bondsman, another for $2,500 for an attorney.

Her friends ask her where Ron is these days, and she says he's back home in Tuscaloosa, helping his dad on the family farm. Later they ask why he's driving her car, dropping her off in the morning and picking her up at night, after she goes to the gym, which she's been doing ever since Ron told her he doesn't like her this fat. She tells them it is because his father needed his truck back at the farm.

She doesn't tell them — or me — that she has decided to take him off her AOL account because he's using it to troll for women. In the process, she reviews his out box to make sure she isn't throwing away anything valuable. She finds two emails to other women. Both include nude photos. Of Ron.

He loves me, she tells me.

He leaves me love notes.

It's true. We will find them, written on scraps of paper, on ripped-out notebook pages, on napkins. But not until later, when we have to look.

She doesn't tell me that she has bought him

a new truck, nor that he persuades her to buy one that's even bigger. So she goes back and gets him a Ford F350 with dual tires in the back, a truck so big she can't climb into the cab without help, and Ron shows no sign of helping. It costs $36,000.

I'm keeping it in my name, she tells her friends. That way if we break up and he drives off with it, I can report it stolen.

She buys him a utility trailer, too, and everything he needs to start his own house painting business. A sprayer, seven ladders, air filters, a Sawzall, a circular saw, levels and screwdrivers and gallons and gallons of paint.

His birthday is in the spring, and he wants to go to a strip club, so she is a good sport and goes along. He still doesn't want to have sex.

She gets cell phones for both of them. Every once in a while he goes out after work with his friends, then calls her to come pick him up. In the morning they go back to get his truck.

One Friday night she goes to happy hour with her friends.

I'm drinking tonight, she says. This time I'll be the one calling for a ride home.

She does. He doesn't come.

A friend tells her to dump him. She stops

talking to that friend. A sister expresses concern. She slows contact with that sister.

Meanwhile I have become a virtual hermit. I go to the grocery store, to Little League games, to the gym, but I do not socialize. No dinner parties, no meeting friends at a coffee shop, nothing. I make excuses to the few friends who still try to get me out. I'm busy, I say. I wish I could, but the family needs me. The truth is, it's too much trouble to go out. Too much trouble to stay up all night justifying who I talked to and when.

I do, however, accept an invitation to speak on a panel about my profession. It is at the local university, and there are five of us on stage. I wear all black, except for a swing jacket covered with elephants and hieroglyphics. I look like a stereotype of a writer, colorful and eccentric. The students are enthralled. They wave their hands in a "pick me! pick me!" way, asking about my bylines, my adventures, the famous people I've interviewed.

I don't tell them about the hours spent staring at a blank computer screen, or the shin-sweating tension of deadlines. I tell them instead about the first time I saw my byline in a major magazine, and how my husband stood in the predawn cold waiting for the truck that would deliver the first copy to town. I tell them about how he brought it home to me and served it with coffee in bed.

I tell them I have enough rejection letters to wallpaper my bathroom. They think I'm joking.

I don't say that when I get home from a trip I am grilled about who I met and who I talked to and whether I screwed around or thought about screwing around or met someone I might consider screwing around with if I weren't married, because even thinking about it is infidelity by our rubric.

The bell rings to end the lecture session, and the students cluster around us, throwing out ideas, asking more questions, intoxicated with the possibilities. Do you think I . . . ? What magazine do you think might . . . ?

When I finally get home I am euphoric.

They want to grow up to be just like me, I say.

I prattle on, excited about what they asked and how I answered, heady at having been the center of their attention.

My husband looks at me.

You met a man, he says.

I pause.

I *have* met a man. Oh my god! There was a new man on the panel, a visiting professor. He was age-appropriate and good-looking, and he wasn't wearing a wedding ring. Further, I noticed that he was good-looking and that he wasn't wearing a wedding ring, which means I wanted him. I look up, my face growing red.

Wow, he says, you did.

He storms off, and I barely resist following.

I got invited to speak at my alma mater because what I do is fascinating and I'm good at it. I went and spoke well. The students liked me. Why isn't that what we're discussing?

I want to run downstairs to his office and yell at him.

But I don't. I know I did something wrong because I feel queasy, like I did as a child when I exaggerated or told a white lie, or made something up to tell the priest in confession, both because I didn't know what else to say and because I didn't want the priest to know that I lay awake at night wondering what my body was like down there, where I wasn't allowed to look or touch.

I clutch the counter, holding myself in place. If I run downstairs now I don't know whether I'll spew in anger or grovel for forgiveness.

Instead I slam around the kitchen, getting out the mixer and the pans and the bowls for making bread. Pounding dough will be therapeutic.

We're going to the Bahamas, Amy says.

Wow. That should be a blast.

I know. Just me and my cowboy. I'm so excited.

Her voice is up half an octave and she's talking fast. They have been together now for nearly half a year.

It's a present to him, she says. He's never been out of the country.

After they get back she calls again. She sounds despondent. He got drunk on the first day and spent the whole vacation sick or passed out.

Are you okay?

She is quiet for a moment.

I'm just disappointed, she says.

But something changes then. It changes in how she talks about him, to me and to her friends. She doesn't bring him up. Or when she does she is cautious.

He's fine, she says when I ask. But she doesn't expand. Normally she would tell me the salacious details.

We're great, she says. I am too wrapped up in my own world to probe. I don't ask enough questions.

Later friends and co-workers and siblings share what we know, which isn't much.

Something happened, we say. It had to be something bad, something worse than passing out drunk. That's bad, of course, but it feels to all of us like it might have been something more.

A few weeks later Kurt and I are lying in bed on a spring morning, the windows open.

Honey, I say, there's something I want to do.

I pull out an adult ed brochure and show him a page describing a day of belaying each other as we climb a challenge course. It is not Outward Bound, but it is a small chance to overcome my fear of heights.

It will strengthen our relationship, I read from the brochure, help us reach new heights together.

I think it would be good for us, I say. It's been a long time since we've done anything new together.

He looks at the description.

It's a whole day, he says.

I know, I say. But it'll be fun.

I don't know if I have to work.

You don't, I say. I checked.

Why are you always scheduling my time? he asks.

Please, I say, I want to do this.

He rolls away.

Fine, he says.

I know "fine" doesn't necessarily mean "fine," and that the morning of the event might find me at the couples course all by myself, but I sign up anyway.

When the morning comes he grumbles that he doesn't know why he's wasting his time on this shit, doesn't know why he should give up a perfectly good Saturday to do something dumb and meaningless when he could be playing basketball or edging the lawn. I stroke him, with words and with my hands, and persuade him to do it. For me.

It is springtime and I think it will be fun, I say.

In truth I don't think it will be fun. When you are afraid of heights, it is paralyzing just to think about climbing.

The day is run by a robust Outward Bound-trained instructor who insists that before we go up our group must bond. We must learn trust.

So we bond. We bond with each other, we bond with the other couples, we bond with

346

the instructors, we bond with our gear. We bond for nearly two hours, as the wind rises and our instructor wishes for rain.

It builds character, he says.

You don't have many friends, do you? I say.

The others laugh, but I am sharply and painfully aware that my husband has heard me. I squeeze his hand and smile into his eyes, trying to communicate that I didn't mean anything. I wasn't flirting.

We decide that Kurt will go up first, and he does, easily. To him it is easier to go up than to stay down and make chitchat with the others. He beams down at me from the top.

I lower him slowly.

You make it look easy, I say.

That's because I knew you had my back, he says. He kisses me.

I smile. I'm relieved that he's having fun.

When it's my turn to climb I put one foot in front of the other, inching up about ten feet before clinging to the pole, my lunch rising in my throat.

Look down at your feet, the instructor says.

Look down? I thought if you were afraid of heights you were supposed to look up, to not even think about how it would feel to land after a free fall. I look at my feet.

Okay, he says, now trust your toes. Put your buttocks up over your foot and straighten out your leg.

I look at him. I look at my foot. The tip of my worn Nike is hooked on a pebble.

I look up. The nearest handhold is just beyond my reach. Of course.

Straighten your leg, the instructor says patiently. Just take the step, and see what opportunities unfold.

I take the step. A handhold appears. I take another step, and another handhold appears. Ever upward I advance. This isn't so hard, I think, as the wind whistles through my helmet. I can do this. People much less athletic than I have done this. My niece has done this. My paraplegic neighbor has done this. All I have to do is trust in the rope. I cannot fall. This is not life or death. This is not like real life. There is only faux risk. You fall, the rope catches you.

It all becomes rather mantralike — step, look for the next opportunity, reach — until I reach the belly of the beast, the section of the climb that requires me to go out and over the edge of the platform. My options are unattractive.

There is no easy way. I want desperately to go down. I am with a warm, friendly, well-bonded group. I can go down and lie back on the fresh green grass and watch the other climbers. That is what I want to do. I want it much more than I want the bile that is now rising in my throat, the bile that comes from the same fear that is turning my legs to liquid, unable to hold me up. Instead I take one more step, just to see what unfolds.

It takes half an hour of coaching, of neck-wrenching belaying, of titanic patience on the part of the instructors, but I make it. I haul myself up over the lip and into what now feels like a gale force wind. I do not stand up, I do not let go, I do not howl with victory. I barely remember to breathe. But I do look, however briefly, at the view, which is no better than what you could see in hundreds of photographs. I wonder if over-coming my fear of heights is worth it. Maybe it is enough to stay on the ground, stay with the familiar, not force myself ever again through anything quite so scary.

I can't get on to AOL, I say.

It is two months later and we are in his office, deep in the lowest floor of the house, the morning light pouring through the French doors.

Sorry, he says. It's my fault. I was trying

to adjust our account, but the password doesn't work.

Oh, I say, my heart starting to thud. I changed it.

How come?

No reason, I say, stalling. I just read that you should change them up once in a while.

He looks at me expectantly.

So what is it?

My mind spins for traction. If I give it to him, he'll be able to read my email. If he reads my email he'll find out about Mark.

Mark is an old friend, a colleague, a man I travel with often on business. This last trip, though, we had gone out to dinner, had a few too many drinks, kissed, Mark and I. It was a release, an exoneration, an escape from being perpetually accused. Afterward I felt guilty, but also excited, like the clamps had been loosened.

We shared occasional emails after my return, and not always about work. Sometimes it was about how much I loved the city, or how much fun we could have if we flew off to a tropical island together, chosen for its randomness, its differentness from who and where we are, chosen with the knowledge that isolation and quiet would drive us both insane.

Want off the hamster wheel? I'd write.

Come to Tahiti with me. We'll lie on the beach and sip umbrella drinks all day.

We weren't going to actually *do* anything, but still, Kurt cannot find out. Ever. And now he is looking at me expectantly, waiting for the new password.

I hesitate, then give it to him.

Bathroom break for me, I say, then dash for my office, taking the stairs two at a time.

Early in our marriage we had shared an office — me with the window open, he with a space heater at his feet, the ceiling stained from the Taco Bell nachos he threw at me once at the peak of a fight. Since then, though, we have built offices as far apart as our big house will allow, so far apart, in fact, that our wireless intercom system doesn't carry that far, even though it sometimes picks up the neighbor's baby monitor. So now I run up two flights of stairs, from the east end of the house to the west.

I fall into my chair, open AOL and delete Mark's emails as fast as I can.

I have been too obvious, though, and within moments Kurt puffs up the stairs. I am sweating, my fingers percussive on the delete key.

What are you doing? he asks.

Nothing, I say, quickly opening an email from a friend.

Then why are you acting weird?

He comes up behind my chair, his eyes searching the screen.

I'm not acting weird, I say.

I turn and wrap my arms around his waist, knowing he's reading the screen. I stand and kiss him, reassuring him with my mouth and body, hoping the email I'd popped open is benign.

After a moment he puts his arms around me, and I feel his breathing slow. Finally he leaves, and I turn back to my screen and scroll through back emails, making sure I've gotten every one.

He has told me, though, that hitting delete or throwing something in the trash doesn't make it disappear. I know he can find it again, that I need to do something else, download something, reset my preferences, restart, somehow do something to make the evidence of my disloyalty disappear.

I push every button, risk losing data, try everything. I empty the trash. I clear my cache. I clear my history. I sit back and breathe. I am still sweating.

Late that night I roll over. I reach for Kurt, but he's not there. I lift my head and look around. It's dark. The room is quiet and the clock says three a.m. I get up and use the bathroom, then pull on a robe and start down the stairs to his office. The moon is bright through the atrium windows, so it's easy to make my way. Abruptly the light in the hall to his office kicks on, and I scrunch shut my eyes, cover them with my hands. When I can see again I creep forward. There's no point in trying to surprise him. The light is on a motion detector switch, and he has to have seen it.

But he's not in his office.

I walk back upstairs, open the door to the garage and see his car. He should be here, then. I stand still and listen, but hear nothing but the tick of the mantel clock.

I walk farther down the hall and look up the stairs toward my office. There is a faint sliver of light under the door.

I walk up the stairs and open the door quietly. The light is off, but from the glow from the computer screen I can see that he is naked, hunched over my computer, clicking through email after email. He doesn't hear me.

I wait until I'm directly behind him to talk.

What are you doing? I ask.

He starts, then leans back triumphantly, clicking through screens until he finds the message he wants. It is to my friend Deb, a long, stream-of-consciousness, joking note about me and Mark and how attractive and giddy I feel. How refreshed. How much fun I'm having.

I read it over his shoulder. Shit. Shit shit shit. My stomach churns. I deserve this. I deserve to get caught. I deserve to get caught and to have him outraged, have him do whatever he feels it's right to do. I deserve to have him hit me. Or leave me. I should never have looked at Mark, should never have gone out for drinks, should never have let years and years of small intimacies — notes about co-workers in the margins of papers, a sport coat over the shoulders on a cold evening, a hand into a taxi — should not have let them add up to a night of intoxicated kisses. I have cheated, and now he is going to leave me. He has to leave me and then I'll be alone and I don't want to be alone. I don't want to live without him. I can't live without him. I am desperate to hold on to him, to have him in my life always. He is the other half of me. I am not complete without him. I will not survive.

Then I get mad. He has no right to go through my emails. No right to read what I have written in confidentiality to my friend. Yes, I have done something wrong. I have considered a life that doesn't include him. But wasn't it also wrong to invade my emails? Don't I have the right to an autonomous life?

Of course I didn't. Don't. What was I thinking? It is not harmless for me to have felt a spark for someone else. It is a disloyalty, a failing. I am a slut.

I cry. He cries. I apologize. I tell him it was nothing, that it didn't matter, that I will never contact Mark again.

But our vows have been broken. I have broken them. I have looked at another man. Worse, I have given another man some of my precious kisses.

I instant message with Deb about what happened. It's more secure than email, I think. It disappears. By phone and instant messaging I can run everything past her, get perspective. Am I horrible for what I did? Did I cheat?

She reassures me.

Get serious, she writes. Everyone's attracted to others, even when they're married. It's called being human.

I know, but Kurt isn't going to see it that way.

You kissed the guy, forchrissake, she writes. You didn't have sex with him.

Kissing is bad enough.

Seriously, she writes. Get over it. You don't need to keep beating yourself up for something stupid.

But I do. I do have to keep beating myself up. I have to earn him back. Earn his trust. I have to, so I seduce him in the kitchen, in the pool room, in the shower. I wear the clothes that I know make him happy. I fawn on him in public. I bake bread and spend hours on elaborate dinners. I watch basketball and action movies. I give massages and wear stilettos and underwires and lingerie.

It takes weeks of groveling apologies to put it behind us. Weeks of begging, of flinching, of accepting the heaped blame, until finally things return to normal. I start to breathe deeply again, to risk occasionally saying no, I'm too tired.

I do not contact Mark again. Not then, anyway.

It is a few weeks later that I realize something is wrong with my computer. It is logy, saving things slowly, and I can't find a piece I'd been writing. I hit the "file" button, looking for my most recent ten documents. There's something odd. It is showing things I haven't opened in months. One called "marriage." One called "early memories." One called "mental multivitamins," which I used to collect the good things Kurt said about me, to bolster me during the bad times. I remember asking for them, specifically.

Tell me three things you love about me, I had said. Every day this week. I want to know.

On good days he had listed things of substance, like how smart I am and how I get him to try new things. He said I am funny, that I have a good sense of humor. But mostly he listed superficial things, about body parts or being good in bed. One day he listed that I know how to make up from fights. I laughed when I read that last one, although a part of me wished and wishes that we didn't fight so often that make-up sex was a standard of our repertoire.

I look down the list of documents. The computer must be getting glitchy, because what should open are files to the stories I'm working on for various magazines. There should be one on how to save money for retirement and another on teething. Notes, drafts, invoices. That's what should open, but this is old, personal stuff.

There also is an unidentified document, something that saved without a name. I click on it.

Am I horrible for what I did? Did I cheat? it says.

I know, but Kurt isn't going to see it that

way. Kissing is bad enough.

It has my instant messaging password. My email password. The URLs I've visited. The content of every email I've written all day.

It is capturing every keystroke.

I am outraged. I am frightened. I am violated.

Kurt has put a keystroke tracker on my machine, and now he can read everything I write. My complaints about him, my rants about chores, about friends and family and politics, my every spilled thought. Everything I've put into writing. He can read it.

He can and he has, because this is clearly only one day's rantings. He has to have come up every night and cleared this document.

I panic. What has he read? Has he read my justifications? Has he read my journals about how pissed I am at him for reading my email? Has he read my wonderings, my worries that the marriage isn't worth it, that I am giving up too much in order to have him? Has he read that I think I'm past compromise and well into sacrifice, that I've traded in my self for him? What has he read?

I call Deb.

Holy shit, she says.

I call Amy.

Have you ever heard of keystroke-tracking software? I ask her.

No, she says. Why?

I tell her.

Why do you put up with this shit? she asks.

Because he loves me. Because I cheated and he's right not to trust me. Because I deserve it. Because he wouldn't do it if he wasn't so terrified of losing me, and that terror is a piece of love, isn't it?

Not in my experience, she says.

Her experience is pale, though. I know better. She and Ron sit at home and watch movies. They snuggle. They don't even have sex, as far as I know. True love is electric and fragile and forever in need of patching and repairs and begging and make-up sex. It is as dramatic as a tango, vibrating with tension.

I understand why he has done it, why he has violated my privacy. I understand that between us there should be no secrets, no private life or experience or pleasure that does not include the other. I understand, but it still has to stop.

How long has this been on my machine? I ask.

How long have you been cheating? he counters.

He has me there. I am forever guilty.

I make him take it off my computer, but still I am skittish. I check every time I log on. Are my documents in order? Are things as I left them? Are there any unnamed documents floating around? Is my email password protected?

What are you trying to hide? he asks.

Nothing, I say. I just have the right to some privacy.

Why? he asks. I thought you loved me. Why would you want to keep secrets from me?

It is a good question, but still I hold my ground.

Good Lord, Amy says, you aren't allowed to talk with friends without him listening in? That's nuts. Doesn't he talk to his friends?

He doesn't have any friends, I say. I am his friend.

Un huh, she says.

There is a pause, then I remember to ask. How's Ron?

Fine, she says. He's fine.

She is back in the gym, back on Weight Watchers, excited about her classes. Her voice is deep and vibrant when she talks. And then it trills upward into giggles. I think it's because she is in love, although something about it sounds anxious.

It takes me weeks to relax, to stop checking that my documents are in order, my email private. Kurt and I return to normal, to squabbling and making love and admiring each other's work. Then one day I find a piece of paper half buried among the notes and papers on my desk. It is a list in his handwriting of the last ten documents I'd opened the day before. The keystroke tracker is gone, yet still he is reading every word I've written.

I want to scream.

A few days later there is an index card propped up against my computer monitor. You promised, it says, in Kurt's handwriting. The screen is open to the phone directory for Mark's company. It is half a year after September 11 and I had looked it up, wanting to see if he was okay. I hadn't, however, called.

I call Amy. I don't know whether to confront him or to let it go, I say. I must be doing something wrong for him to need the reassurance, so maybe I should just let him keep reading until he's comfortable that I'm not doing anything to risk our marriage.

What do you think? I ask Amy.

I think he's nuts, she says.

I decide to try not to talk to her for a while. That way I can pretend it isn't a big deal.

CHAPTER 19

Wow, the deer have decimated my hostas, I say to my next door neighbor Ken.

It is May and he is on his knees, weeding.

Ken is tall and handsome. He's great, as are his wife, Jean, and their three children.

I'm thinking of putting a sign up — Salad Bar. But I doubt the deer can read.

He laughs.

I heard Cathy up the street uses urine to

keep them off her plants. She pees into a cup, pours it into a spray bottle, and spritzes her plants with it.

Does it work? Ken asks.

Apparently. Her yard looks great.

Of course, I wouldn't have to use the spray bottle, he says. I could just run from plant to plant.

I laugh. Just don't do it on our side of the house, I say. The motion detector lights'll catch you.

We laugh.

That evening I laugh as I tell Kurt.

There is a pause.

So you were talking to Ken about taking his pants down.

Later I call Amy. Ron Ball answers the phone. It is the first time I've heard his voice, and I try to reconcile it with the picture she had emailed to me earlier.

Hi, I say, this is Amy's sister, Janine. Is she there?

Nope. I cut her up and buried her in the backyard.

I am silent. What an asshole.

Right. Where is she really?

Naw, she's at the grocery store. Want me to have her call you?

Please.

I hang up. I don't like Ron Ball, and I

haven't even met him. What is Amy thinking?

The restaurant has a glossy marble floor. I walk carefully in the shoes Kurt chose to go with the outfit he had laid out on the bed. Across the room I see a man I know from the gym. I smile and nod.

Who's that? Kurt asks.

A guy from the gym.

What's his name?

Greg.

Greg what?

I don't know. Already I am recoiling, knowing from his tone that this is going to take a while.

So how do you know him?

I told you, from the gym. He works out at the same time I do.

Is he in good shape?

Pretty good, I say, leaving out that Greg is all muscle. He also is funny, but I don't tell Kurt that.

So you've noticed.

Well, it's a gym. He's there a lot.

So you want him.

No, I say patiently, I don't want him.

You want him.

I don't want him. I want you. Although if this is going to be the night's conversation, that could change.

Kurt fumes. Our food comes and I change the subject. Over his shoulder I see Greg stand. Please don't come talk to me, I think. He walks over.

You're eating that? he says.

Every bit of it, I say, laughing, and I'll still kick your butt tomorrow. This is a continuation of how we talk to each other at the gym. I goad him to lift more, taunt him for having arms smaller than mine, even though his are as big around as my thighs. It is gym rat trash talk, and I love it.

I make the introductions. Kurt, this is Greg. Greg, this is my husband, Kurt.

They are cordial, make small talk, then Greg turns to go.

See you at the gym, I say.

It is a mistake.

You want to fuck him, Kurt says, as Greg walks away.

I look at him and shake my head.

You want to fuck him, he repeats.

No, I say, I don't. He is my friend, that's all.

I'll see you at the gym, he mimics in a falsetto. You want to fuck him.

I excuse myself to go to the bathroom. On the way my heel slides out from under me. I stumble and feel the hot flush of embarrassment, although I right myself before Kurt can notice.

In the bathroom I sit on the toilet and rest my face in my hands. I breathe deeply. I want him to just love me. I want him to trust me, to accept me, to let me relax. I want so much to relax. But if I do he won't love me. He won't love me if I get fat. He won't love me if I say something stupid. He won't love me if I look at another man. Please just love me, I think. Please.

I go back to the table. Kurt has paid the bill and is standing by the table. He takes my arm as we leave. In the car he leans over and kisses me deeply. I'm sorry, he says. I just love you so much I can't bear the thought of you leaving me.

I melt. I understand. I can't live if he leaves me, either.

We make out in the car. We drive home, barely making it into the garage before we're peeling each other's clothes off.

Hours later I wake in bed. He is standing over me, his fist cocked and quivering.

You want to fuck him, he says. You probably already are fucking him.

I cover my head with my hands, but the thing about Kurt is that he never hits me anymore. He holds back. Resists. Barely keeps himself from slamming his fist or his forearm into my face. But I know this always: he could.

A part of me is grateful that he has so much self-control that he doesn't just bash my face in.

And that is what happens now. I am on my back, the covers clutched up over my chest, his cocked fist a foot from my face, quivering. I don't think he will hit me now, but I am not certain. He shakes his head and drops his fist.

You're not worth it, he says.

Early in our marriage I would have jumped up and confronted him, taunted him, slapped him, or thrown something. In the early days I would have somehow stood up for myself, felt like I was defusing the situation, that I was at least as in charge as he, riding on the glee and the thrill of the drama. Back then we both threw a few punches, but most of that is gone now.

He jabs a finger into my chest.

You're fucking him. Tomorrow. I heard you say so.

I am confused.

Who am I fucking tomorrow? I ask, still half asleep.

Greg, he says, stretching it out in a sing-song of contempt.

I'll still kick your butt tomorrow, he mimics, his voice high and flirtatious.

I shake my head, my fear and anger making me sweat.

You're out of your mind, I say.

It is hours before he stops accusing, stops jabbing his finger into my chest and insisting I am screwing another man.

Again he threatens to leave. With him will go the children, the life we've built, our history and our future and our dreams. I cannot lose him. I must do whatever it takes to make him stay.

Finally he storms out. I let him, too exhausted to continue to beg.

In the morning I get up to tend to the kids while he sleeps. I drag through my day, guilty and sad and depressed, unable to let go of what happened.

When he wakes up he comes to hug me, but I pull away.

What's your problem? he asks.

I look at him.

You don't remember last night?

He steps back.

You're still obsessing about that? he asks. Get over it.

He said he was going to kill me, Amy says a week later, but I told him it wasn't funny.

He said what? You're shitting me.

Well, he's not going to say anything like that again, she says. I got pretty forceful.

Still, what a bizarre thing to say.

It was bizarre. But he was only kidding.

I assumed he was kidding. If he wasn't kidding we'd be having a much different conversation.

No shit.

Amy, I say, you sure about this guy?

He was only kidding, she says.

It is afternoon and Kurt is leaving for a late shift at the hospital. We kiss good-bye — a lingering, seductive, can't-bear-to-be-apart kiss — and he leaves through the garage. I watch through the front window as he pulls out onto the street, his red sports car gleaming. He turns to wave. Then he stops, slaps the car into reverse and squeals back up the driveway, fishtailing as he does when panicked or angry. I hear his car door slam and the garage door open. I am cringing by the time he storms in.

Who sent them? he demands, ripping open the front door so I can see what he means.

There on the porch are a dozen yellow roses in an orange glass vase. I collect colored glass — bowls and vases in tones of Jell-O — and the asymmetrical vase is the sort of thing someone who cares for me would choose.

I pick up the vase and bury my face in the flowers.

Who sent them? he asks again, grabbing them out of my arms and pawing for a card. There is nothing.

I scramble through my memories. Had I met someone at the gym? Had I let slip in the course of work that I liked such things? What man had become so enthralled by me that he had risked sending flowers? There is no one. For weeks I have gone out only to the grocery, the gym, to Little League.

I don't know, I say, already backing from his jabbing finger. I can't think of anyone.

My face, though, is red. It is possible I had smiled at someone somewhere, possible that a gym buddy had taken my friendly joshing as a come-on.

He comes forward and stands, shoulders broad, face always above mine, looking down, leaning in.

Who is it? he hisses, his voice more frightening in its near whisper. Who sent them?

My denials become weak and weepy.

The inquisition lasts fifteen minutes, until I am in tears and he is late. He storms out, assuring me he will wake me to finish the conversation when he returns, and demanding that I call his colleagues and take the blame for him being delayed. I tell them I had run out of gas and he had to come rescue me. I lie for him.

Mom calls. She had called Amy's house, and Ron answered the phone.
He said he kicked her out, Mom says.
But it's her house.
I know, Mom says. He was joking. He's got a really warped sense of humor.
No kidding.

Days later I run into our old friend Tim, who recently has married and combined households with a delightful woman.
Did you get the flowers? he asks. We had that vase and we knew you'd love it, so we wanted you to have it.
Tears well up, and — in a rare lapse — I tell. He looks at me with pity, so I correct myself. He was tired, I say. He was stressed from work. He loves me.
I can't tell if I'm lying to Tim or to myself.

Give me another chance, Kurt says.
I look at him. The fight has been bad, even by my standards. Days long and grueling and painful. Sleep-depriving, anxiety-inducing. I have been walking through the

days with nerves exposed, vibrating, waiting for him to do or say the thing that is going to tip this. Toward or away from the marriage.

He is not hitting me, only hissing and yelling and turning his back, punishing me in the ways he knows best. He more than anyone knows that I am desperate to keep him. Without him I would be what? A failure, of course. A quitter. A loser who chose poorly. Or maybe a woman who just can't take the lumps of marriage. Everyone has fights. Everyone has irritations. Everyone has times when their husband turns on them and makes that face like he wants to kill them.

We are going through what I euphemistically call a "rough patch," and as usual the lovemaking has been intense. Passionate and desperate, a grasping attempt to connect. Somehow connect. Somehow make up for the words and the actions and the things that make me so afraid.

I call my friend Vickie.

How often do you and your husband fight?

She is surprised.

We never fight, she says. Why would we fight? I mean, we have disagreements, but nothing we can't talk through. Why?

■ ■ ■ ■

I talk to Amy.

I need out, I say.

If that's what you need, then do it, she says. Trust yourself. I don't think women trust themselves enough. If you have a gut feeling, there's a reason.

I tell her I'll talk to her later.

Let's go back to Florida, he says. We can celebrate Sarah's birthday there.

It won't exactly be romantic with a three-year-old along, I say.

We can invite Jane along to watch her. She'd do it, wouldn't she?

My sister Jane is a watercolor artist living in the coldest reaches of Montana. She would love the sun and the sand, and the chance to bond with her niece. I am wary, though, about exposing her to our real dynamic, especially our bad dynamic. I am hesitant, yet I ask her.

That will be fun, she says.

So we set up flights and motel rooms and a rental car and a rental car seat and the traveling playpen and clothes for the baby and fewer clothes for us and we go back to Lauderdale by the Sea, although not to the

Little Inn by the Sea. Instead, since times are a bit tight, we decide it will be fun to stay somewhere unfancy.

As long as it's clean and safe, I say, I don't mind.

I know just the place, Kurt says. It's called the Castle by the Sea. We arrive in the hottest crush of midafternoon, bleary from travel and desperate for a cool room, squabbling over directions because the pavement in front of our motel is being ripped up and relaid by behemoth machines, their tires taller than a man.

Oh, this is grand, I say, my eyes watering from the simmering asphalt fumes.

What? Kurt yells, his voice and mine lost under the screech and shudder of the scrapers and shredders and tar melter, and the pounding bass of the workers' radios.

The motel itself is **L**-shaped and deserted, two stories tall. There is a pool in the courtyard and plants everywhere. A twelve-inch TV is hidden under a scrap of mildewed carpet by day, plugged in and its rabbit ears aligned at night. A Day-Glo skeleton missing a hand hangs from a ficus. Even though it's April a lit reindeer and angel perch on the veranda roof, which drips Christmas icicles from its edge. A gas grill — minus the legs or gas connections — is balanced on the tubular aluminum legs of a webless chair.

We collapse in rusty lounge chairs by the pool for more than an hour, waiting for the office to open. I must have dozed, because I wake up being stared at by a man who reveals a paucity of teeth.

I own the place, he says. I'm expecting you, it is a lovely, lovely day, make yourself at home.

All of this he rattles off as he lets us into the lobby, where the E on the Enter sign is really a W up on end, as if the owners ran out of stick-on letters or lost the E. All transactions are in cash, he says. Kurt reaches for his wallet while I look at the tourist pamphlets, most of them cracked at the creases and yellowing, for businesses in Miami and Dade County, an hour or two away.

He shows us to our rooms, one on the short end of the L for Kurt and Sarah and me and one on the long end for Jane. I'm relieved that they're not neighboring units.

The rooms are decorated in Early Garage Sale, the silverware in the kitchen a mish-mash of metal and plastic. The shower, we learn, has the pressure of a car wash. The linens are dried and stored outside and smell of salt and dampness, and the window air conditioner units work endlessly and mostly fruitlessly, whining over the grinding of the asphalt shredder.

I unpack our bags and then go downstairs to ask about a sheet for the playpen, but the owner has once again been replaced by the Out to Lunch sign.

A woman, bored, walks her beagle around the pool. Both are overfed. I go back up to the room.

Not exactly the Ritz, I say. I think I'm being a good sport.

You can't be happy, Kurt says. You have to find the negative in everything.

I look around the room.

It's a real challenge to find the negative in this place.

He steps forward.

You're such a bitch.

I look at him.

And you're a dick.

You don't appreciate anything.

Really? I don't appreciate anything? Or is it that maybe I'm pissed off because I had to pack everything for you and me and Sarah. And make the plane reservations. And take care of her on the plane while you took your precious nap. What did you do for this trip, besides pick this splendid hotel?

He steps forward again. Now he's leaning

over me, and I have to look up. My throat feels exposed.

I earned the money.

He glares at me, his lip curled. Sarah makes a noise. She is watching from her playpen.

I'm taking Sarah to Jane, I say. She doesn't need to see this.

Fine, he says. Go. I want to nap anyway.

I call Jane's room and warn her that I'm coming. I don't tell her that we're fighting. Instead I imply that we want some time alone. I imply it like it's a good thing, like we want to be intimate.

She is happy to take her niece.

Bring her bathing suit, she says. And sunscreen. I'll take her down to the beach.

When I get back to the room Kurt is lying on the bed, his eyes open.

You're not trying, are you? he says.

I look at him for a long moment.

Is this the behavior you think will win me back?

Come here, he says. He opens his arms, beckoning me to lie down next to him.

No, I say. I'm not making up that way.

Come here, he says, smiling.

He is handsome, muscular, and familiar. I relent. I lie down and find my place in his arms. We lie there quietly for a few minutes, breathing.

Do you love me? I ask.

You know I do, he says, stroking my hair.

I press myself tighter against him.

I'm going to go take a walk, I say after a while.

Fine, he says.

I get up and put on my sandals. I know it isn't fine, that he is angry that I'm leaving, but I don't care. I am exhausted from guessing what he wants and needs, from tiptoeing up to whatever I'm going to do wrong next. We are in Florida by choice, to recharge our love, to relax, but I know that if I wear a bikini I will be criticized, either for my chronic patch of cellulite or for not having it, for my obsessive beach workouts or for eating too much, for having other men look at me or for dressing so that no one looks at me, for comparing myself to younger women, for not noticing how great Kurt looks or making him self-conscious by noticing too closely. The trip is strewn with Bouncing Betties — both the beachfront babe kind and the shrapnel-laden land mines — and the only thing between detonation and me is time.

I'll pick up supplies, I say.

It is okay for me to do tasks, to shop for

groceries. It is less okay for me to just want a few minutes to myself, because claiming that time may mean I enjoy myself or have a delight, a new experience, without him.

I close the door gently, knock on Jane's door just as gently. She opens it and we whisper quietly, even though there can be no quiet with the road being stripped in the background.

How's she doing? I ask.

She's almost asleep, she says, and I make a face. My visit has probably knocked the process back by half an hour.

Sorry, I say. And thank you. I'm heading to the grocery. What would you like?

I'll go later, she says.

I know she is finding her role, balanced as she is between guest and nanny.

I'll get whatever you want, I say. Really.

She gives me a short list. Apples and bananas and juice, maybe some Vanilla Wafers.

I leave just as quietly and walk down the street through the asphalt haze.

When I return, Kurt is gone. He hasn't left a note, but I guess he is at the basketball courts, and I don't much care to check. Instead I walk down to the courtyard and read. When Jane and Sarah emerge, we play in the pool, which is surprisingly clean and cold, and into which Sarah throws herself over and over, so that Jane and I have to take turns standing in the icy water.

Catch me! my little girl yells, before launching herself trust first into the water.

By the time Kurt gets back we are pruny and shivering and he is post-basketball relaxed and happy. We go to dinner — all four of us — and then Kurt and Jane sit out by the pool while I settle Sarah in for the night.

After she falls asleep I join them. The air is still acrid from the asphalt, but the destruction noise has stopped for the night, replaced by the sound of gulls and wind and the occasional siren from the fire station a block away.

Kurt reaches over and holds my hand, and I lean back into my chair. The night is warm and his touch is loving. I am with my husband and my sister, and I belong. I close my eyes, even though a worry worm niggles under the surface. Is this safe? Am I going to make it through the night without tripping a trigger? Relax, I think. Enjoy. Don't ask for it. Don't make it a self-fulfilling prophecy. Kurt loves you. You love Kurt. Everything is going to be okay. I sigh.

Not long later Jane says good night and Kurt and I go up to our room. I kiss him and start to undress in the darkness.

Why didn't you come watch me play? he asks.

I reach for a T-shirt.

I didn't know where you were, I say, pulling it over my head. It's better not to be naked during conversations like this, I think.

You knew exactly where I was.

You didn't leave a note, I say.

He flips on the light and I slap my hands over my eyes.

Turn that off! I say in a hissing whisper. Sarah's sleeping.

I was where I always am in the afternoon when we come here, he says, stepping toward me. You knew I was playing basketball.

I just wanted to relax and read, I say, walking over and flipping off the light. Sarah whimpers and cries out in her sleep, tired from the travel.

So you lied, he says, climbing into his side of the bed. You knew where I was.

I climb into bed without looking at him.

I thought that's where you probably were, I say, but I wanted to read.

How am I supposed to trust you if you lie? he asks.

It wasn't a lie, I say. I just didn't know.

You didn't care.

I care.

Not enough to come watch me play, he says. Or did you have something more important to do?

Here it comes, I think, and then try to quash the thought.

I have no idea what you're talking about, I say, rolling onto my side and pulling the covers up over my shoulders, which turns out to be a mistake.

He jumps out of bed and stands over me.

Where'd you go? he asks, pointing a finger into my chest.

Quiet, I say. Sarah's sleeping.

I can't believe you can even think about going to sleep right now, he says. We have to talk about this.

I open my eyes again.

Jesus, can't we just sleep? I ask. We're not going to settle this tonight. I need a break.

He leans over me.

Tell me you love me.

I love you, I mumble, pulling the covers up tighter.

He takes my shoulder and rolls me onto my back, his face over mine.

Tell me like you mean it.

I look up at him. I am exhausted. I want nothing more than to fall asleep.

I love you, I say. Okay?

He smiles down at me.

Okay, he says. That's all you had to say.

He lets go of my arm, walks around to his side of the bed and gets in, then cups himself against me. The air conditioner is wheezing, he is breathing into the back of my neck, and I can't fall asleep even though I am exhausted. I push back against him and he wraps me up more tightly. I sigh.

Can you move over? I ask. I'm hot.

There is a pause, and I hold my breath.

Fine, he says. He gathers up his pillow and flops to the other side, and I exhale.

We clutch our separate edges of the bed. The détente only lasts a minute. Then he flounces back over, making the bed shake.

You've been a bitch all day, you know, he says.

I don't answer.

You have, he continues. You've been a bitch all day.

I try not to get drawn in, but I answer anyway.

I was not, I say.

You were.

I think about it. I flew all day with a toddler, drove in a convertible in the simmering heat to a crappy motel with a repaving crew in the front yard, took care of everything for the baby. Was I a bitch? I was probably a bitch.

Eventually we both sleep, clinging to our separate edges, trying not to roll together into the middle of the sagging bed.

In a few hours Sarah is awake and smiling.

Mommy, she calls. Mommy mommy mommy.

I adore her, but all I want to do is cover my ears.

Instead I get up, lift her, change her, take her outside to run among the palms so she won't wake Kurt.

Jane opens her door and I take Sarah in, then sneak back to our room and get a box of cereal and the bottle of milk. Kurt is still sleeping.

You okay? Jane asks.

I look at her.

It was a rough night, I say.

I'm sorry.

Thanks.

I lie back on her bed and close my eyes. Sarah calls for me again, but Jane distracts her with Cheerios and a song about three little fishies in an itty bitty pool. Sarah is delighted.

Anything you want to talk about? Jane asks.

I look at her. Do I tell her the truth? Do I

tell her that I'm threading through land mines, that he will blow up today and there's nothing I can do to keep it from happening?

I flop back on the bed.

No, I say. I'm fine.

Jane keeps singing to Sarah.

Okay, she says. But if you need to talk . . .

I'm fine, I repeat. I'm going to go check on Kurt.

Kurt is still asleep, his so-familiar face deep in the pillow. I slip out of my clothes and climb in next to him.

Good morning, I say, when he opens his eyes.

He puts his arm around me and pulls me in.

I'm sorry about last night, I say.

He grunts and pulls me closer.

How sorry? he asks.

We make love before breakfast and before coffee and before the road crew starts its daily pounding.

CHAPTER 20

Later I knock on Jane's door.

Do you mind watching her while we go to the beach? I ask.

No problem, Jane says. We'll play.

Kurt and I gather our things and walk the block to the ocean, where we set up our towels next to each other, facing the water. We open our books and read, side by side. After a while Kurt says, I'm going down to the water. Want to come?

I'll just stay here, I say, shading my eyes as I look up at him.

If I doze off, will you wake me up in about twenty minutes? I ask.

Sure, he says, and walks toward the water. I look back at my book.

Here's a good one, I hear a man's voice say. Six ways to tell if she's faking it.

I lift my head and shade my eyes. A group of twenty-somethings sprawl on towels about ten feet away. The girls are long and lanky and the boys have tattoos and the beginnings of beer bellies. One of them is reading *Maxim* out loud.

Number Six, he says, then pauses and looks at each member of his gathering. She sounds just like a porn movie.

The group laughs.

I know that one, one of them says. He throws back his head and groans — Oh God Yes! Yes! Give it to me! Yes!

The group laughs again.

I stand up and pointedly gather my stuff, then move far enough upwind that I can't hear their inanities.

I plump up a pile of sand for a pillow, stretch out on my back and let my eyes drift shut. A moment later a shadow falls over my face.

What the fuck are you doing? Kurt asks.

I look up at him, squinting at the corona of sun around his head.

What do you mean? I ask.

I mean, he says, speaking slowly, what . . . are . . . you . . . doing?

I stare at him for a moment.

I moved because that jerk was reading *Maxim* out loud, I say. It was annoying.

Sure, he says.

I am too drowsy to defend myself, so I let my eyes drift back shut.

Wake me up in twenty, will you?

I doze off before I hear his answer.

When I wake my lips are dry and cracked. I can't work up enough spit to run my tongue over my teeth, and my eyes are gritty and tender from the sun. I grope for my sunglasses and look around.

Kurt is gone. Shit, he's really gone. I stand up, then quickly bend back down, my ears ringing and my head swimming. I must have been asleep for quite a while, because I am dehydrated. What time is it? I press my right fingertips into my left forearm. When I pull them away four white indentations appear, then turn quickly pink. He had said he would wake me after twenty minutes, and now I am sunburned.

Asshole, I think.

He has stalked off, I am sure of that. Pissed about something, though I can't guess what. Until recently I would have run after him like a Pekinese, begged, pleaded, apologized. Now I don't bother.

I rub the ridge between my eyes and try to clear my head.

A minute later I see him coming toward me, shoulders back, fists and jaw clenched.

Where is he? he shouts, his words half carried off by the wind. Where's your boyfriend?

What? I ask, grabbing a towel to hold in front of myself as I stand. What are you talking about?

Your boyfriend, the guy you were just talking to. Where is he?

I take a step back. I don't know what you're talking about, I say, not defiant, but placating. I was asleep.

You were talking to someone. I saw you. I was sitting on the wall over there, by that tree. He waves to a spot up the beach. And you were all animated talking to some guy.

He puts his hands on his hips and tilts back his head, mimicking a woman flirting. I am still not fully awake, but I know I wasn't talking to anyone.

Something clicks then and I straighten to my full five feet, one-and-a-half inches.

You're nuts, you know it? You're out of your mind.

I start off down the beach, but he catches up with me.

Yes, let's walk, he says, scrambling breathlessly beside me. Let's take a nice walk down the beach. Let's share the fucking joy.

I stride on, silent, him scrambling along next to me in the soft sand. Half a mile later he grabs my arm and stops me.

Tell me you weren't talking to anyone, he says, and I'll believe you.

I look him in the eye. Mine are hidden behind dark lenses, but his are exposed, the crinkles around them deep as furrows.

I wasn't talking to anyone, I say. I was asleep.

I shake him off my arm and start walking again. Again, he catches up.

Okay then, he says. I must have been looking at someone else. It must have been a mistake.

I stop, turn slowly to look at him over my sunglasses. My lavender bathing suit glints in the sun.

Show me, if you would, I say, someone else on this whole damn beach in a purple bikini.

He looks down at his hands, apologizes. Promises to never do it again.

I take him back.

That night I put on the tight pink sweater, miniskirt, and spike heels he likes so much. We leave Sarah with Jane and drive in the convertible to an Italian restaurant. It is a beautiful night, and we are flirtatious, light and happy.

We hold hands, laugh at each other's jokes, eat off each other's plates. I love it when he's like this: attentive and happy, relaxed, excited to be with me. I try to let down my guard. His hand finds my thigh under the table, slips up under my skirt.

When we're done eating he heads to the restroom and I head for a bench out front. Two men are leaning up against the building. I send them brain waves. *Don't talk to me, don'ttalktome, don'ttalktome,* I think. They talk to me.

Excuse me, one says. But are you from Canada?

I laugh. No, I say, but I am from Michigan, and it's close.

Ah, he says, punching his buddy on the arm. He owes me five bucks. We bet that no one would be that sunburned unless they were from Canada.

I am laughing when Kurt comes through the door, takes one look, and stalks off across the parking lot to our car. I scurry behind him.

I get into the car and he peels out of the parking space before my foot is in and my door closed. I grab my seat belt, but inside I am screaming. What have I gotten myself into? What happened that five minutes ago we were headed to a night of lovemaking, a lifetime of lovemaking and sharing and being entwined and now he is screeching around corners and slamming his palm into the steering wheel? How is the trigger so tight, so abrupt? How can he go from loving gazes to this look of contempt, of betrayal, of wanting to wrap his hands around my throat and shake me?

We get to the motel and storm up to the room.

It's over, I say.

It has to be over. I cannot take the ups and downs anymore. I can't take it that at any moment he is going to blow up. I just can't.

I say it's over, but beating staccato in my head are the questions. Do I mean it? Is it so bad that I'm willing to be broke and alone? Is it worth tearing apart my family, making my daughter the rope in a relentless tug of war? I don't want that for her, the instability, the strained loyalties, the feeling that no place is safe.

But she doesn't have that now. Not stability, not peace. I don't want her to see her father and mother fighting and hating and arguing, don't want her modeling her life after mine, with its drama and its disrespect and the stomping off and slamming doors and yelled epithets and insults and belittling comments. I don't want this for her. Even more than I don't want it for myself.

But still.

Fine, he says. I'll leave right now.

Our trip is supposed to last two more days, but I can't spend the time with him.

Fine, I say, but Sarah and I are staying.

He throws his suitcase onto the bed, then scoops his clothes out of the drawers and crams them in.

I'll just call a cab, he says.

Fine, I say again.

He storms into the bathroom and gathers up his things, then closes his suitcase and drags it to the door, where he turns to look at me.

You won't get a no-fault divorce from me, you know, he says. You'll have to call the sheriff to drag me out.

I don't respond. I don't care. I'll call the sheriff if that's what it takes, but I don't think he's going to put himself up for that kind of humiliation. I think he's bluffing, so I just look at him.

I'll call the sheriff if I have to, I say, but you're going.

I stick out my jaw and clench my teeth to keep from shaking. Is he going to go? I am terrified, but also — deep inside — serene.

He glares at me and I stand up straighter. Finally, through his teeth he says, Fine. I'll go.

He waits a beat more, then shakes his head and walks out the door. I let it close behind him, then watch through a crack in the curtains as he thumps his bag step by step down the stairs. When he's out of sight I drop the curtain and sit on the bed. It is one in the morning.

I can't figure out what I'm feeling. Mostly relief and lightness. Mostly freedom. Mostly like I've leapt off a cliff and I'm flying, trying to enjoy but also afraid of the landing. Mostly I am feeling like I have finally done something that should have been done years ago, and I'm wondering what took me so long.

I make sure I have a room key and then walk down the outside balcony and knock on Jane's door.

Hey, I say when she opens the door.

Her pajamas are twisted and her hair is

flat on one side.

Sorry to wake you, I say. How's Sarah?

Jane opens the door and steps back. Sarah is sprawled on Jane's bed.

I'm sorry that went so late, I say.

She squints at me.

Are you okay?

Yea, I say. He's gone.

She closes her eyes and then opens them again.

He's gone?

I nod.

I told him to leave. I can't stand the fighting anymore.

You okay?

Yeah, I say. It's good. I'm going to carry her down to my room. Do you mind getting the doors?

Jane is not like Kurt. She sees what needs to be done and she does it. I am used to doing everything by myself, so it takes me a while to get used to the kind of help she provides.

I gather Sarah's arms and legs and everlonger body and her beloved stuffed elephant. She is still small enough for me to carry her with ease, but I have to turn sideways to get her out the door.

Thanks, Jane, I say when we get back to my room.

I kick the door closed and lay Sarah down in her crib, then lie down on my bed and look at her. She is beautiful. Beautiful and at peace, and I will give and do anything to keep her that way. My eyes fill thinking about it. I'm frightened at paying my own bills and being alone and sleeping by myself and being the only one there to fill my daughter's relentless needs, but I also am at peace.

The door opens.

It's Kurt.

The cab didn't come, he says. I ran into the owner and he said he'd call a cab, but I've been standing out there and no cab.

Why don't you call one yourself? I ask.

I thought he had, he says.

Call one now.

I know he is waiting for me to beg him to stay, to say I can't live without him, but I just want him to leave.

He pulls out his cell phone and makes the call.

I don't want you waiting in here, I say.

He doesn't move.

Seriously, I say. I want you to go.

He glares at me, then turns and slams out of the room. As soon as the door closes, I put on the security chain. He probably can hear me do it and it will hurt him and make him angry, but I don't care. I don't want him coming back in.

I sit on the bed, pull out a notepad, and write.

"Sarah turned three today. Kurt and I are getting a divorce. For her birthday I am giving her a tension-free home, one in which her parents aren't angry and wary and ever cautious."

An hour later he calls. He is at a high-rise Sheraton. He is lonely. He wants to come back.

No, I say.

He tells me he loves me, that he will change, that he will do anything to keep me. He jokes, tells stories from our marriage, talks about our daughter.

I relent and let him come back. For the next two days, he is the good Kurt. He is charming, loving, funny. Neither of us storms or stomps or sulks.

We make it through the vacation.

A week later I call Amy. He is nice now, I say. She has been hearing my daily vacillations. I think maybe I should let him stay. It's not really his fault. I know he's jealous, and I must be doing something that makes men come on to me. Maybe I need to tone it down, interact with people differently.

Uh huh, she says.

I don't know, though, I say. I don't know if I believe he'll be the Good Man in the long run.

How long has it been since he blew up at you?

Nine days, I say proudly.

Uh huh, she says.

His pleasantness lasts three more days, then he snarls and apologizes. It was a small thing, I tell Amy, and at least this time he apologized.

Yes, she says. I remember back when I was married to Jim. He had been sober for a couple of months. One night he had a beer with a friend. I said, It's only a beer. A week later, he had two. Who am I to begrudge him a couple of beers? He works hard. He's an adult, he can have the occasional beer. Then it was every night, and before long I was back to finding bottles under the couch.

I understand, although I don't want to.

You know what to do, she says, so do it.

The next day Kurt blows up at me and I tell him it's the end. He storms out. An hour later he comes back and hands me a letter.

Give me a month to make you fall back in love with me, it says.

I am emotionally cold. I don't care.

Fine, I say.

The next week we are again at the marriage counselor's.

I'm sorry, I say to both Kurt and the counselor, but I see no hope. Not because I don't think it would be wonderful to stay with this good-looking, intelligent man — if he controlled his anger, if he kept working on his own issues, if he became sociable, if he learned to embrace the occasional risk . . .

Kurt looks at me with sad eyes.

I can do all of that, he says.

I walk out of there confused, rooting in my mind for even a wee smidge of hope. I am ambivalent and conflicted, even though I'm 98 percent positive. No, I'm 100 positive I couldn't be with the man I was married to. But could I be married to the man he swears — cross my heart — he could be?

I tell Amy I'm going to give him another chance.

Why?

I don't know, I say. Because I'm tired. Because maybe I'm wrong.

She is quiet for a long moment.

You there?

I'm here, she says.
You don't think I should.
I didn't say that, she says.
Un huh.

Amy canceled again, Mom says. She and Ron were supposed to come down, but Ron has to go paint at his parents'.

Didn't the same thing happen a couple of weeks ago?

Yes, and when I offered to come up she said the place was too messy. Have you met him?

No.

We are both quiet for a moment.

Has anyone?

A few days later Kurt and I leave Sarah with a sitter and drive down to Tan Tara, intent on dancing and getting massages and having fun. On the way down I read to him, and we talk about careers and goals and our children. We are happy, although it's tentative, like walking after being on crutches.

Do you know where you're going at the end of the month? I say. I don't want to get to the end of the thirty days and then have you start looking for a place.

He is quiet.

So you aren't going to try, he says.

I thought he knew we were separating. His letter had said he knew the month wouldn't change everything, but maybe it would be good enough to make me want thirty more days, and then thirty after that.

You're not even going to try.

It's not that, I say. I just want to know that there's a plan in place, so we don't drag this thing out.

He threatens to try to get Sarah, although later he promises he won't. It is a long, sad drive, although no longer angry. We are both exhausted, I think.

When we get there we agree to just let it go and have fun. We order a pizza, make love, watch a movie. In the morning I sit on the balcony overlooking the lake. I drink my coffee.

I wonder if we could separate, go out on dates together, have Sarah drift freely between the houses while I figure out if I can forgive and forget and love him again and want him to touch me. Maybe by being apart we can reapproach each other and find a balance that works. I don't know how we can overcome our differences, but I think a separation would be a great thing for both of us.

I watch the boats and the birds. For the moment I am at peace. Soon I'll work out, and then we'll have breakfast and shop for family birthday presents and head home. Tomorrow is the family's spring birthday party. It may be the last such family function for me, and for that I feel sad.

On the drive home he gives up.

The thirty days won't work, he says. Your heart isn't in it.

When we get to the house he packs another suitcase.

You won't get a thing, he says. Not a thing.

I don't care. I just want him gone.

What about tomorrow's party? I ask.

You're going to have to call them, he says.

I can't.

He drives away.

I look around my house, trying to feel what I feel. It's not joy. It's not fear. It's mostly relief. Like I can finally breathe.

I lock all of the doors, but I'm not worried. He isn't coming back.

I call my in-laws and explain to each that Kurt has left, that we're separating, that I'm happy to have the party anyway if they'd like, but Kurt won't be here. They each politely decline.

I know my daughter's life will be disrupted. I know I'll be poor. I'll need health insurance. I won't be able to afford my house. I won't be able to afford retirement. I'll be alone and broke and lonely. Our friends will have to choose between him and me, and some people will think I'm foolish or an idiot or that there's another man. I know they'll think there's another man because everyone always thinks that. They'll think that one of us has to be screwing around or there wouldn't be a separation, not in a couple like us, a couple people look at and aspire to be like.

In truth there are other men. I've started to notice. They're at the coffee shop and the gym. They're at my professional meetings and on airplanes. And sooner or later I'll date. I'll date and I'll have to tell some man about the breast implants and the surgical scars and the loss of sensation and he will be grossed out. He won't want to touch me.

I call Amy.

Kurt's gone, I say.

Gone gone?

Gone gone.

Wow.

There is silence.

How do you feel about that?

Like the struggle is over, I say. Like I can get on with my life.

She is quiet again.

Are you scared?

Not yet. I think I'm still in shock.

I look at my calendar. The date is May 4. My Independence Day.

You think you'll take him back?

No way.

Don't.

Kurt is gone for ten days. Just gone. Without talking with me or Sarah, without calling his family to tell them where he's going. Finally his father reaches him by cell phone. He has been driving around Florida, thinking. For ten days.

When he returns he finds a rental house. His friends come to help move his stuff.

It's okay, I say to them. I'm glad you're here to help him. I am not mad at you.

Some give me hugs. Of wistfulness, maybe, or gratitude that I am not angry.

A few weeks later it rains. It has been dry and hot for months, and the soil has pulled away from the house, so now when the deluge comes the water rushes in around the foundation. It's the smell of rotting carpet that draws me into the workout room, where my feet sink and the water covers my toes. Shit.

I go into the shop and get a box knife, then cut the carpet in three-foot-wide strips.

I use pliers to pull them off the tacking strips, then get down on my knees and roll each strip, from one end of the room to the other. I bring a wheelbarrow to the back door and load it, three strips per load. It takes all the strength in my thighs and back to push the wheelbarrow up the slope, where I tie string around each roll and dump them at the curb for the trash truck.

When I'm done with the carpet I start on the padding. It is heavier and wetter, spongelike and unwieldy. I am furious.

I call the foundation repair guy, who digs on the outside of the house, cuts drywall on the inside, seals the wall from both sides.

A week later it floods again, in another corner of the basement. The water is creeping its way toward Kurt's pool table. If I don't stop it, it will wick up the legs and warp the wood. I want to say "fuck it," but I'm trying to sell the house. I can't let it smell bad. Once again I peel up carpet. This time I call the carpet cleaners, who suck up the water, spray for mildew and set up fans that sound like jet engines.

I decide, too, that the float isn't working on the sump pump, so I buy a new one and install it myself, up to my armpits in the hole, working at the edge of my reach with monkey wrenches and vice grips. It works, although it doesn't solve the problem. The only thing that will solve it is for the earth to absorb enough water so that the soil once more hugs the house.

I call a friend. He and his wife have three daughters, all of whom babysit, and I need someone for Saturday. I've known these girls since they were little, one since I coached her in T-ball when she was about five. Or maybe it was basketball in junior high. It's hard to keep straight which kids I've coached when, or which one was with me on which field trip or played one of my silly games at the classroom holiday parties.

The father answers the phone, and for some reason I let fly.

I am so mad! I stink. I'm tired. The house sounds like an airplane hangar, my arms hurt, the place smells bad.

I tell him the whole story, about the water and the carpet and the foundation workers and the pool table and the sump pump.

Your phone broken? he says.

I pause in my rant.

No. Why?

You could have called us. We would have come.

CHAPTER 21

Hi, sweets, I say. What are you doing?

It is the Fourth of July and I am calling Amy from the hammock swing on my back porch. Kurt left two months ago to the day, and I am at peace.

You caught me in my yard, she says, giggling. I'm planting impatiens.

God, I'm so proud of you, I say.

I'm using my bread maker, too, she says.

She was talking about the bread maker I had given to her during her cancer treatments, when the radiation burns in her mouth had made it too painful to eat and all I could entice her with were loaves fresh from the oven.

I'm making dinner for my cowboy, she says. We're going to rent a movie and snuggle on the couch.

They still snuggle, setting the alarm half an hour early each morning so they can hold each other before she leaves for work. They leave each other love notes on the mantel, on pillows, tucked into her briefcase and his pants pockets. At night he wraps his long arms around her as they watch movies on the big-screen TV she has bought since he moved in. The sound surrounds them from speakers positioned all around the room, their wires snaking along the floorboards.

No fireworks? I ask.

Only the ones we make ourselves, she says, then laughs deeply.

I wince, not because I don't want Amy to have sex but because I don't think they've done that yet, and I know she wants it more than anything.

Hadn't she told me just a few weeks ago that he respected her too much to have sex with her? Maybe things have changed, but I doubt it.

Uh huh, I say.

He has lived there for seven months.

Seriously, she says, we don't need the crowds. Or the noise. What about you?

I'm going to be alone, I say, although I may be able to hook up with some friends. Either way is fine.

We talk for a while longer, saying little of significance. I complain about my ex.

He's an ass, she says loyally.

In truth she probably likes Kurt. He is charming and handsome and generous with the loans. Plus, I have tried to hide the ugly stuff. She has mostly seen the polished, shiny façade, although every once in a while when the anger is too much or I'm tired or I just can't stand it anymore and need a sanity check I have let her peek through a crack, into the emotional obstacle course that is my life.

A year or more earlier, in a moment of weakness, I had told her the truth. It's like you're walking through a house, I said, and two days a week someone steps out and punches you in the gut. You never know when it's going to happen, but hey, you had five good days, right?

As soon as the words are out I wished

them back. I didn't want her to think of him that way.

So where's Ron? I ask.

He's painting, she says. He'll be home later.

She laughs about what she's going to cook for him, about planting flowers at her own home. She is a proud home owner. A proud home owner in love on a sunny day. She is happy, and I am happy for her.

Have a great time, I say. I love you.

Love you, too, she says.

I'll never talk with her again.

CHAPTER 22

That night I picnic and watch fireworks with friends. The next day is Pat's birthday, a Friday. Amy doesn't call Pat, which is odd. She doesn't show up for work, either.

The weekend passes. No one hears from Amy.

Monday comes. It is a work holiday. No one hears from Amy.

On Tuesday I fly to the East Coast for a

magazine assignment. Again Amy doesn't show up for work.

Her co-workers get worried, they tell me later. They hover around her desk, they call each other. Have you talked with her? Did she say they were going away? Maybe she took a vacation day and didn't tell us. Did she tell you? What if she's sick at home? Does anyone know where she lives?

Abby does. She gave her a ride home one day. Abby, can you drive out to her house and make sure she's not sick or something? She and two others — both men, one as big as a bouncer — pile into a car. Someone else riffles through Amy's desk. It is then that they find it. An envelope, taped to the inside of her drawer. On the front are four words, all in Amy's handwriting. Knox County Sheriff, it says. Personal.

The envelope is sealed. It says "personal." Should we open it?

They look at each other.

Maybe it will tell us something, one says.

April 29, 2002

To whom it may concern:

In the event of my disappearance or death I need to let it be known that I advanced Ronald Lee Ball a considerable amount of money on a variety of credit cards, beginning Jan. 15, 2002, and running to the present. Current balances are approximately $25,000, a sum which does not include nearly $30,000 on a car loan for the Ford F150 truck he drives.

Ronald was arrested on Dec. 21, 2001, in Knox County Tennessee for a DUI. The sheriff's office will have his photo and other identification.

To give you an idea of the charges, they break down as follows:

1/15/02 Bob's Bail Bonds (Tuscaloosa, AL) 1,765
1/18/02 Cash advance for attorney 150
    James Standover (Tuscaloosa, AL) 2,500
2/15/02 Knox Co Clerk (truck tag) 1,780
2/16 Townsend Ford (truck repairs) 3,110
    (Tuscaloosa, AL)
2/21/2 James Standover final pmt 2,500
2/21/2 Tuscaloosa Co Court 5,500
    fines on old bad checks
3/2 Lowes — Cargo trailer 3,000
3/2 Home Depot (pressure washer) 2,000

There are other small miscellaneous charges but the above alone account for $22,300!

Today Ron and I are romantically involved, but I fear I have placed myself at risk in a variety of ways. Based on his criminal past, writing this out just seems like the smart thing to do. If I am missing or dead this obviously has not protected me. However, hopefully it will give you enough to go on to at least question Ron and make sure, if he is behind it, that he won't get away with it. We are struggling in our relationship right now, and life would be much simpler (for him) if the financial issues between us just went away.

I really can't believe that this document will ever be needed. But just in case . . .

Amy Lynne Latus

CHAPTER 23

The co-workers in the office call the ones en route to Amy's house. Listen to this, they say, and read them the letter.

Call the police and have them meet us there.

The ones in the office call the sheriff's department. Detective Mike Freels comes. He reads the letter. He looks through Amy's desk. He flips through her Rolodex. He listens to her voicemail.

Hi, Amy, it's Jane, one message says. I'm not calling for anything in particular. Just checking in. I hope you had a good holiday weekend. Call if you want.

At the end, out of reflex and ingrained manners, Jane gives her phone number. The detective calls it.

This is Mike Freels from the Knox County Sheriff's office. Do you know an Amy Latus?

As soon as Jane hangs up, she starts dialing again. Mom? Pat? Kris?

The detectives drive out to Amy's house, but no one is there. They have Ron Ball's cell phone number from her desk. They call and ask him to come and open the house. He does.

I am in my hotel room talking with a friend who is picking me up for lunch when my cell phone rings.

Janine? Jane says. Have you heard from Amy?

No, I say, my skin already prickling from adrenaline. What's up?

I got a call from Kimberly-Clark. Amy hasn't been there in three days.

My eyes dart to the man standing next to me.

What's wrong? he asks.

He killed her, I say into the phone. That

bastard killed her.

My friend looks shocked, then starts shaking his head.

I know, Jane says quietly. But we're not thinking that.

I know what she means. We can't. I understand that. If we let it gel into a thought it might be true, and that is beyond what I can stand.

The detective thinks maybe she just got in a lover's spat, Jane says. He says it happens all the time; people fight with their boyfriend or girlfriend or spouse and just don't show up for work for a few days.

We want to grasp at that, but we can't, because Amy doesn't miss work. Jane and I know that. During her cancer treatments she had raw sores in her mouth and throat. Her hair fell out. She could barely walk from her car to her couch. At the end of the day she couldn't do anything but curl up with her remote control, her incontinent and ancient cocker spaniel panting at her feet. Still, she only missed work when she went in for treatments. The rest of the time she dragged herself in, joked with her co-workers, quietly put her head down on her desk when she couldn't stand it any longer.

I'm going to call the others, Jane says. Love you.

Love you, too.

I hang up and turn to the man by my side.

Now now, he says. Don't overreact. It could be anything.

I stare at him.

It's not "anything" and you know it, I say. It's bad.

He puts his arms around me.

She's fine, he says. It's going to be fine. Don't jump to the most dramatic conclusion.

I push away and look up at him. My ex used to call me the porcupine, all prickly and painful.

I'm right, you know, I say.

He steps back helplessly. He knows my family by name and story, if not by sight, so he knows about Amy and Ron Ball.

She's probably just taking a break, he says.

I turn on him, furious, even though what he has said is reasonable. Already it is seeping in that it might be true, she might really be hurt, and I desperately want to be wrong.

Amy doesn't take breaks, I say. Don't you get that? She's a Latus. She's not going to just not show up.

I pace the room.

Goddamnit, that asshole killed her. I know it.

He tries to calm me, to get me to stop pacing.

You don't know anything, he says. It's going to be fine.

I glare at him.

I call the Knoxville detectives, but I can't get through, so I leave a message. An hour later my mother calls, angry at me. The detectives have told her someone named Janine Latus has called. Could it be Amy calling in under a pseudonym? Mom's hopes flare, but it makes no sense. She calls and chews me out for giving her that second of confused hope.

It is irrational, but I understand. Or I try to understand. Amy is my sister and I adore her, but she is my mother's baby. My fear pales beside that of a mother.

I gather up my things, check out of the hotel, and fly home, even though being home is no better than being away.

CHAPTER 24

Mom calls Ron Ball's cell phone.

We had a fight, he says. She made me move out.

Do you know where she is?

She called me Saturday, he says. She was going to Atlanta. She got mad at me and told me to move out. I used her credit card to buy some paint, but I left it on the dresser.

There are signs of struggle, the detectives say. The house is a mess.

No, Mom says, that might not mean anything. Amy's house was always a mess.

No one can find Amy's car. It isn't at her house. It isn't at work. Mom calls Amy's best friend in California. She calls a friend in Florida. Each of us call everyone we can imagine, except Gramma. We won't call Gramma. Amy may have run to Gramma, in which case we'll know soon enough, but we will not upset Gramma by bringing her in on this.

I keep hoping Amy took off driving and didn't tell anyone, even though she had never traveled without telling someone when she was leaving and when she would arrive. Maybe she was trying to get away. Maybe she has been in a terrible accident and has amnesia. Maybe she is in a ditch and all we have to do is find her and fix her and she'll be with us. She'll be okay.

The next day the sheriff's department canvasses the neighborhood. Have you seen the woman who lives in 7313?

One man remembers seeing her with Ron Ball in front of the garage on the fourth. A woman says Amy had come by over the weekend to borrow baking soda to make bread. Another saw Amy and Ron in Ron's truck.

Wait, she says. I also saw him and some other woman at Amy's house a couple of months ago. Over Mother's Day. Amy wasn't there, though.

The next day the detectives go back to the house. They get permission from Ron Ball, then call a locksmith to let them in. They also get call records from Ron's and Amy's cell phones. The Saturday call Ron told Mom about is on there, but the records show that it was sent and received from the same cell tower. The one next to the house. Amy's phone was at home Saturday, two days after she was last seen.

The sheriff's department sends helicopters up to look for her car.

On Friday Mom and Kris and Pat fly to Knoxville. They are met by Claire Reid, a woman who works in human resources at Kimberly-Clark. She will become the human face of the company.

She drives them to a hotel, where they spend hours talking with detectives, who take them out to Amy's house.

The carpets are freshly cleaned. Mom calls Ron Ball.

When I talked to her Saturday she told me to get the carpets cleaned, he says. The dogs have been peeing on them.

Amy's suitcases are there, so she didn't pack up and run.

The bedskirt is in a heap on the bed. The sheets are gone, the mattress and box spring stained and saggy.

The curtains over her bed are gone, replaced with a tacked-up sheet.

The big screen TV is gone, replaced with a set so old it has rabbit ears. The speakers, too, are missing, although random wires still litter the floor.

Mom and Kris and Pat are standing in Amy's bedroom.

That's not Amy's mattress, Mom says. She has a new mattress.

The detectives look at the bed. Suddenly they hustle the family out the door. They have seen something, although Mom and Pat and Kris don't know what. The yellow tape goes up. Amy's house is now a crime scene.

I stay home. I have my daughter to think of. I have to meet with my divorce lawyer and the accountant and the Realtor. I rush from thing to thing, trying not to think. At night I flail. I wrap myself in a quilt Amy made in the throes of Hodgkin's disease. I pick at the threads, the lines so perfect and straight, so un-Amy, a product of surviving cancer, of a year spent with the dining room floor buried under billows of color, the table covered with neatly stacked strips of blue and green and pink. She had sewn one for each niece and nephew. Purple for one, shades of orange for another, each a work of love and patience and perfection, made for their someday dorm rooms, their marital beds, a tangible wish for them always to be wrapped in their aunt's love.

I sent cards, didn't I? Cards and letters and pictures? Please let it be true that I was there, that I gave her support. Please let her know that I loved her. Please don't let me have been so selfish, so wrapped up in the drama with Kurt, that I missed something. Please please please.

I beg a lot. To whom I don't know, since I'm not a believer, but to perhaps the universe. Please let her be okay. Please do not visit this pain on my mother. Please let Amy walk through the door and laugh at us for our worries. Please please please.

I envy my siblings their faith, their ability to turn it over to something higher. I turn mine over to my friends. Over and over and over. Four o'clock in the morning I call Vickie. And again at seven. I call Andie and Russ and Jim, friends who buttress me in this horror. I try to be rational but I know

I'm talking too fast, saying too much, thinking out loud. I know I risk alienating them
with my obsession. Where's my sister
where's my sister where's my sister? I break
the mantra only to complain about my
soon-to-be ex. He is an asshole; she is missing. That is my message. Over and over.
Every once in a while I ask about their lives,
their children and jobs and concerns, but
I'm not sure I hear their answers.

CHAPTER 25

The detectives search Amy's condo and find boxes and boxes of spiral-bound notebooks. They are Amy's journals, but the current one isn't there. Neither is her laptop. Nothing that will tell us about her life with Ron Ball.

They flip through other notebooks and find out-of-sequence pages. Some are from Amy's visit to my house the preceding

Christmas, when she forgot her official journal and used the notebook at hand. Others are more recent.

Friday, Dec. 21, Knoxville Airport

Talked until late again last night. I love those conversations, even though they hurt sometimes. Last night, for instance, he was telling me about the girl he was engaged to earlier this year. He said <u>she</u> was his dream, but she lied to him about something pretty basic — her age. He thought she was eighteen, but she was only sixteen. What a thirty-nine-year-old is doing with an eighteen-year-old, I don't know, but that's not the point (although maybe it should be).

In any event, I finally told him that I don't want to hear about her. It is threatening. And he's like, "but it's over and done with." But for me it's that he really loved this girl.

And I'm not what he wants, so what is he doing with me?

Why do I feel so sad?

It's because I don't know what I feel and I don't know what he feels and it frustrates me. I continue to assert that

God has interesting ways of taking care of me.

This relationship has — and will continue to — change my life.

Noon, Memphis Airport

If I want a one hundred percent risk-free relationship, I might as well just lose myself in my books again or die, because there is no such thing.

Maybe that's the reality I really have to come to grips with — not that Ron is going to hurt me, but that everyone is. It's managing risk. Having your eyes open. Deciding how far to let someone in. Enjoying the process despite the peril that sits at the end.

2:45 Memphis Airport

Watching couples with kids walking through the airport, and keep thinking of what it would be like to be pregnant with Ron's child. What he would be like as a father. If it was some sort of guarantee that we'd be happy together for the rest of our lives, or if I knew he'd stay forever, I'd do it. That is how much I love his energy.

Sat. Dec. 22, 12:45 a.m. (Janine's house)

Fuck. Fuck. Fuck. It's after midnight back home and he hasn't been answering the phone all night. Where the hell is he? How can I possibly fucking trust him with anything if he can't even keep his word for one day? Jesus I hate this. Just hate it.

Sat. Dec. 22, 10 a.m. (Janine's)

Still no sights or sounds from Knoxville. I sent him an email that he hasn't read yet, which tells me he has not been home all night. What does that mean? If I trusted him, I would be more worried than angry. What if something happened? Part of what's bothering me now, too, is that it's obvious that I'm hurt and disappointed and it's making a bad impression on the family. Not an auspicious beginning, Ron.

Sunday, Dec. 23, 8:20 a.m. (Janine's)

Another quiet evening from Knoxville. I keep praying for help in dealing with this and I woke up with something firmly planted in my brain. Whatever Ron is doing right now has nothing to do with me. Until next Saturday at 2:45 p.m., when my plane lands in Knoxville, he is a free agent. He can do whatever he wants, whenever he wants. I don't think he's cheating. He promised me, and I think he's true to his word. I'm not going to come home and find him gone, either. Unless something bad has happened and he's been hurt.

Mon. Dec. 24, 10:35 p.m. (Janine's)

Still no sight nor sound from him. What I need to know is that he's okay — he's not hurt, or dead on the side of the road.

Tues. Dec. 25, 11:45 p.m. (Janine's)

No word from Ron today. No change in his status on AOL. I'm really mystified. It's nearly 1:00 a.m. there — I just figured he'd be home by now.

"I must think of what I want, rather than what I fear."

I fear that harm or injury has befallen him. I fear that my trust is misplaced. I fear I will be embarrassed in front of my family because of my trust in Ron. I fear he will let me down. (I fear he already has.)

In my heart, I don't see any mean-spirited manipulation on his part. I see innocent thoughtlessness. "Amy's gone.

She's with her family. She won't spend two seconds thinking about me. If I stay or go, she won't care as long as I keep my word and meet her at the airport on Saturday."

I miss him. I miss holding him. And I especially miss him holding me. I'd hate it if it turns out that I'm just some big dumb idiot about him and what's been going on in my world since we met. Oh, God. Please help me make sense of this. I know that whatever happens, I will be fine. But I want to go further with this. I hope I get the chance.

I have such deep fears and suspicions. I just can't seem to shake them. Please God let me be wrong. Just this once, I want to be completely and totally wrong.

Fri. Dec. 28, 7:30 a.m. (Janine's)

It's terrible, but I'm lying in bed thinking, "One more night of this bullshit and then I'll know." I'm sure the family would not be pleased by how detached I am from all that's going on around me.

Sat. Dec. 29, 2 p.m. (in the air)

Finally embarked on the final leg of this rather uncomfortable journey. Who would have thought that I would be so full of trepidation upon returning to my HOME? I feel, instead, like I am en route to meet someone I've never met before — a stranger in a strange place.

What sort of airport reunion — if any — will I have?

It is simple. Will he be there, or not?

My thoughts shift <u>so</u> quickly from, "He <u>will</u> be there. He <u>has</u> to be there," to "Don't set yourself up to be disappointed like that. Be prepared for him <u>not</u> to be there. Expect the worst."

Absence makes the heart grow fonder.

Out of sight, out of mind.

Which is it?

Beginning our descent into Knoxville. I'll have my answers soon.

I feel like I'm flying to my fate. My destiny. My future. And I very well may be. What happens in the next hour could very well change my life.

3 p.m. (in the cab)

He wasn't there. I'm in a cab now, on my way home. No answer on the phone. What the FUCK is happening? Trying not to throw up. Or cry. I'm just crushed with disappointment.

5 p.m. (home)

HO-LY SHIT.

Ron is in jail.

I don't know why, but I'll find out soon enough. I'm on his visitors' list at the jail, so I'm going there for visiting hours at six.

9:30 p.m. (home)

It was good to see him, to reassure myself that he really was alive. But looking at him, framing his loving eyes between the squares in the wire in the glass that separated us was . . . surreal, to say the least.

Now I'm in this impossible, untenable position. This is how I see it: He wants me to wait. He told me he'd marry me if I'd wait. But you know my strongest view of that — if anyone marries for any reason other than love, they're an idiot. Now, he has time to woo me and win me and make me fall in love with him. But I don't want him to marry me out of some sort of obligation. How horrible and bleak is that?

To add insult to serious injury (or maybe the other way around) in my search through Ron's stuff (to find him) I found a note he wrote to his ex-fiancée on 12/17 telling her that he still loves her. In another note to someone else, he says he's moving to Texas in a few months. Says he's at the finals in Las Vegas. Says he's still in a hotel.

If he's lying to everyone in his virtual world, how can I even imagine that he'd be honest with me in <u>this</u> one? Or maybe I'm the only one he <u>is</u> honest with — life-to-life, face-to-face, day-to-day. The layers slip away.

I don't care about the little stuff, but the note to Kris must be explained.

So, back to what I was saying earlier. I can wait for him. "Stand by your man." Let him woo me and win me. God knows we'll have plenty of time for him to write. And if I wait, we start over when he's out. It will be just the same as it has been here. Warm and loving, but filled with insecurities and hiccups. Waiting means days, weeks, months and maybe years alone. More fucking lonely nights. (And what if we still don't match sexually?)

Or I can cut and run now. Save myself from the hassle and embarrassment of prison visits and explanations to family and friends.

Sun. Dec. 30, 10:45 (home)

I hate my bed alone. I find myself getting angry. Last Sunday Jane had asked me if I felt betrayed, and I said no, because I had no evidence that I had been.

Does a DUI count as a betrayal? Do prior DUI arrests count as betrayal? The thing with the truck? A betrayal?

My biggest fear is that I'll wait, he'll get out, and we won't hit it off. That we'll still be a mismatch sexually. That I'll never be able to trust him, or forgive him for this.

5:10 p.m. (home)

So my shrink returned my call and slapped some cold water on my face. Ron _is_ an alcoholic, she's sure of it. Just because of the fact that this is his _third_ DUI. He's a binge alcoholic, not like Jim, which is why I couldn't see it. But I'm pissed again. Damnit, there are things I want to do right now. I want to paint the house. I wanted to go to the rodeo last night. I wanted to go to Oklahoma to see him ride next month. I had dreams and desires that he was central to, and now they're lost.

January 11, 2002

You've said that I have you completely. What changed? I mean, it seemed to have happened pretty darn quick. Is it because you've been drawn up short by your arrest and are now forced to really evaluate your options? Why not settle for me? I'm here. I care. I'm low maintenance. I'm gentle, loving, and giving. I'm smart. I'm good with money. I'm not rich by any stretch of the imagination, but I have a nice home . . . a lot to offer overall. So I'm not a cowgirl. I'm not young. I'm not blond. But I would be alright for a while.

June 4, 2002

Last night was one of my worst nights ever. You said something about deserving punishment and it makes me feel like I'm your parent or something. It's up to you to punish yourself. To hold yourself accountable for your actions. To decide how and where you want to spend every precious day of this life.

As for me, my responsibility now is to protect myself from the bad decisions I have made. I have to hold myself accountable. I loaned about sixty thousand dollars to a virtual stranger. I wanted to believe he loved me, but I don't believe he ever did. Now I have to shield myself and my emotions from further pain. I have to be able to look in the mirror and say, "Yes, I did that. It was stupid, but I did it." And then MOVE my life so that I don't do anything stupid like that again.

I don't know where this leaves "us." I won't support you any longer — no new stuff! And I will get rid of the things that increase my exposure — the cell phone, AOL, and the credit card. You will have to make your own way on those things. Fool me once, shame on you. Fool me twice (or more!) shame on me. If you agree to go to AA (while I go to Al-Anon) every single week, I might reconsider.

But what I want right now is for you to go to one of your "good" friends and see if they will support you, if they will take you in. I am ready to help you move out. I would want you to leave my investments, though, which I know threatens your livelihood. I don't know what the solution is to that. Perhaps your mom could help . . . ?

I don't know. All I do know is that last night was my last night like that.

CHAPTER 26

On July 13 they find her car. It is in a lot behind a business near the college, a pale blue '94 Toyota Corolla, indistinguishable from dozens of other students' cars. In the front seat is a newspaper. Her laptop is not there. Neither is her journal. The floor is littered with beer cans.

She was alive on the sixth, the detective says. That's the date on the paper.

No, Mom says. Amy didn't read the paper.

There are press conferences. Mom is calm, gracious. She looks straight into the camera, with tears in her eyes.

If there's any way you can help us, she says. Please. Help us find Amy.

The sheriff's deputies dust the car for prints. It's clean except for the button you have to push to shift gears, which retains one perfect thumb print.

Ron Ball's.

CHAPTER 27

HAVE YOU SEEN AMY?

AMY LATUS
MISSING SINCE: 7/6/02
5' 4", 200 LBS.
HAIR: BROWN, CURLY
EYES: BLUE

$2,500 REWARD
FOR INFORMATION
THAT LEADS TO AMY'S WHEREABOUTS
PLEASE CALL
865-215-3590

I design a "missing" poster using the picture I'd taken during our North Carolina trip in the fall.

Mom announces a $2,500 reward for information that helps us find Amy. Kimberly-Clark raises it to $25,000 and lets Amy's co-workers off during working hours so they can tape the fliers up at every business along Cumberland Avenue, the main drag near the college. At the bookstore, the coffee shop, Mellow Mushroom, Amy's favorite pizza joint; at the deli, the Indian restaurant, the bank, until her picture strobes in your peripheral vision as you drive down the street.

Please please please.

Mom walks into a sandwich shop. Her baby daughter's picture is on the front window. It is on the bulletin board inside. She can barely order lunch.

Officers go out on horseback. They ride jet skis and look for snagged bodies in the river. They take search dogs in ever-widening circles.

This guy is lazy; she's going to be close by, the detective says.

Ron Ball had another girlfriend, we find out. He was splitting his time, lying to Amy, telling her he was going to Tuscaloosa to paint his grandmother's house. Really, he was with Karen, who tells us he left her on the afternoon of the fourth and came back at night with a cut on his head and blood on his shirt.

Amy threw a lamp at me, Ron Ball said.

On the sixteenth, sheriff's deputies pick up Ron Ball. They can hold him for forty-eight hours for driving with a revoked license. They put him in the local jail, in the basement beneath the sheriff's department.

Mom and Kris and Pat go back to Amy's house, but they can't get in. They go around back, where morning glories twine up a wall, grown from seeds from flowers in Pat's garden.

Do you think we should?

They use a spoon to dig them up. Each will plant a few in paper cups and take them home in their carry-on luggage. The next Christmas we each will find their seeds in an envelope in our stockings. "From Amy" it will say, in Mom's handwriting.

Investigators tear up Amy's carpet. They take the trap out of her sink.

The forty-eight hours are up too quickly. Ron Ball is released. He flees to Alabama. Deputies follow.

For sixteen days I pace and rant and live half in and half out of my life. I go to the gym. I work. I talk with friends. I eat I sleep I shower and bathe and walk and breathe.

Kurt sends me an email saying that he understands how upset I am about Amy, but asking me to move forward on the issues between us, even if it's hard.

I am sorry I cannot reconsider, I write

back. I am completely wrapped up in finding Amy, and while I appreciate your offers of help and your willingness to be flexible in covering our daughter, I am not willing to discuss the past or future of our marriage. I am sorry this disappoints you.

He writes back quickly. Apparently my fear of reconsidering our marriage, or even discussing it, is "weird," but he hopes that whomever I'm dreaming about is worth ending the marriage and that our lawyer will get things moving. He expressly says that he knows I have a lot on my mind, but he'd just as soon get the divorce done.

He threatens to withhold spousal support, to try to get custody. Then he recants. He won't try to take my daughter from me. He calls back again and again and again. Relentlessly. Sometimes he comes over, hoping to charm me back into the marriage.

Each time the phone rings I leap.

Stop it, Kurt says.

It might be Amy, I say.

It could be Amy, and I hope it is, but in my heart I think instead it will be the detectives. The detectives or my mom or my sister or someone who will tell me the cold news.

The call comes on July 22.

Janine, it's Mom. They found Amy.

I know from her voice that she is leaving

out a word. They did not find Amy, they found Amy's body. I know that. I can tell from the dead calm of her voice. They did not find my smart, funny, ebullient sister. Just her body.

I am quiet, marveling that my mother can say those words at all, let alone with dignity. I am stunned, too. Stupefied. I knew it was coming and yet it is incomprehensible.

Are they sure? I ask.

Kimberly-Clark is sending someone up from Atlanta with her dental records, she says, but they're pretty sure it's Amy.

I want to ask details like how and where and who, but instead I say I'm on my way.

Okay, honey, she says.

The conversation is short. She tells me which siblings are flying in, where we'll all meet. We have cell phones, so the logistics don't have to be exact.

I love you, Mom, I say.

I love you, too.

In our family we say it always. Even before. Before we knew for certain that any one of us could disappear. We say it because it is who we are, it is what binds us together as a family. For some reason there is comfort in that, because it means I said it to Amy. I said it to Amy, so maybe at the end she knew. Please God, I want her to know.

I hang up and call Kurt.

They've found Amy's body, I say, and I have to go to Knoxville. You need to keep Sarah.

I'm on my way, he says.

He shows up without a shirt, claiming he's fresh from basketball. He had stopped at his house to get our frequent flier certificates, though, so he is shirtless by choice.

I pack a bag as he makes flight arrangements. He charges the thousand-dollar ticket to his credit card without even asking. I am grateful. I don't have that kind of money, but I can't think about it right now. Right now I have to figure out what I'll need for the trip and what I have to do to make the house run while I'm gone. I am thinking about that and about what Kurt will find if he logs on to my computer. Is there anything that will make him angry? I want to run up to my office to check, to lock my system down with a password, but I don't have time. I have to get to the airport, and it's a two-hour drive.

I roll my suitcase out of the bedroom and thank him for setting up the flight.

I don't know when I'll be back, I say.

He comes to me and wraps me in his arms.

I'm truly sorry, he says, then presses himself against me and kisses my neck.

Stop, I say, and wrench myself out of his arms.

He gathers me back into his arms.

Stop, I say again, struggling. Stop touching me.

I start sobbing. I am screaming, flailing.

I don't want you touching me. I don't want you comforting me, I don't want you anywhere near me. I have to go.

Tell me what is going on, he says angrily.

No, I say. I need to go.

I push past him and drag my bag toward the car.

He snarls at my back — You just can't be nice, can you?

CHAPTER 28

There is no point in crying, no point in screaming. I am focused just on getting to the airport and getting on the plane that will take me to Knoxville to support my mother and be supported by my siblings. We are going to identify and claim my sister's body.

I want to beat on someone or something for the terror, for the belief starting to seep in that my sister is really and truly dead, that she won't answer the next time I call, she won't ever ever ever answer.

Over and over I repeat it. We are going to identify and claim Amy's body.

I call my friends Vickie and Greg, telling them that I'm on the road, flying to identify and claim my sister's body. They marvel that I am calm, that I sound rational. I am rational because it is too early and too late. Too early to let go, too late to save her. I am in the purgatory between the two. The calm, the eye, the moments when I can put one foot in front of the other, breathe in and out, make everything work because there's something to do, and as long as I can focus on the details of booking my flights and packing and catching my plane, I can do it. I can focus on those things, obsess about those things, and not think about my sad little sister, who may never have had a happy span in her life, and how she was brutally murdered by a man she wanted nothing from but love. Amy, who never had a good relationship with a man, nor a relationship with a good man.

Amy, who struggled to be loved, died in terror and pain.

My own two pains combine into blazing furious infuriating anger at men, who somehow in spite of my efforts and the efforts of other strong women somehow run our lives.

I am speeding, passing cars with small children waving, semis with tattooed truckers, buses and FedEx trucks.

I can't figure out what I missed. I replay phone conversations in my head. He leaves me love notes, she said. We snuggle every morning. He makes me dinner, and he does it by my Weight Watchers rules.

I remember a photo of the two of them, in their cowboy hats, smiling. He is wearing cowboy boots and a rodeo belt buckle. There is a gold necklace with the cross on it around his neck.

Surely there was a warning. Warnings. Lots of warnings. Fights, arguments, thrown crockery. Something. There had to have been warnings, and she ignored them. I of all people should understand.

If you tell people the truth, they'll tell you to leave, so you can't tell them until you're ready to get out. Maybe she wasn't ready to get out. Maybe she still had hope — that it'd get better, that this time she wouldn't piss him off, that if she were thinner or wore more makeup or different clothes or a different hairstyle he would love her and the pain would stop.

Any of us would have taken her in. Any of

us would have done whatever she needed done. If she had called, we would have come. We came when she had cancer, and we would have come now. Why didn't she call?

I pound the steering wheel, then open my cell phone and poke the button to call my friend Russ.

They found Amy, I say.

I'm so sorry, he says.

We are silent.

Say "Good-bye, Amy," he says.

Fuck you.

Say "Good-bye, Amy," he repeats. You are going to have to say it, and you can do it alone or with a friend, so say it.

Fuck you. I won't.

Say "Good-bye, Amy."

No! I yell. I won't do it. I won't say it.

Say it.

No.

Say it.

I want to scream more. I want to yell at him, call him a rat bastard. Instead I sniff.

He waits.

I can't do it.

You can, he says. You have to.

He waits.

Finally I mumble it.

Good-bye, Amy, I say.

Say it again, he says.

No.

Janine. You have to.

I pause. He waits.

Good-bye, Amy, I say again, more clearly.

I take a deep breath. The grip I have kept on my heart loosens, and the pain rushes in.

Shit, I say.

I know, he says.

It is hard to drive through my tears.

At the airport I am flagged as a security risk for flying on the day I bought my tickets. They search through my bag, have me stand on the footprints, my arms outstretched as they run a wand over my body and then pat me down with the backs of their hands.

Look, I say, I know you're just doing your job, but my sister was murdered and I'm going to identify the body.

The security personnel look at me blankly. They don't know, don't care, don't believe. It's not their problem.

I grab my bags and bolt for the plane.

Before my second flight I am wanded again.

Do you have any idea what I'm going through? I ask.

■ ■ ■ ■

In Knoxville I walk through security and around the corner to where two sisters and one brother and a spouse are clotted near the wall. We hug deeply, then wait for Mom.

Do we know anything else? I ask.

They shake their heads, and we murmur among ourselves about what little we know. Mostly we shuffle our feet and wait for Mom.

When she clears security we envelop her, her grown children trying to hold her up. This is why I'm here, to do something for this woman who has suffered so much. I want her to be able to break down and know that she raised good and strong and compassionate children who are now adults and who can hold her up if she wants to crumple.

But she doesn't.

En masse we go to the hotel, where we wait in connected rooms. I sleep with Jane, Pat sleeps with Mom.

The TVs in the rooms are turned to different stations, and we rush between them each time Amy's picture shows on the screen.

Police investigating the death of Amy

Latus say she appears to have been involved in a love triangle, the plasticine anchor says.

Mom flinches, like she's going to get up and hit the TV.

How can they say that? she says. How can they say that?

She paces between TVs. We all pace between TVs. It is inconceivable, Amy's beautiful face alternating with that of her man, ugly now in the police mug shot.

The sheriff's department gives us use of their conference room, where we sit eating thick-cut ham sandwiches and drinking sweet tea.

Every time a detective passes we pounce.

What do you know? Is there anything new?

We dive for our cell phones, cram our mouths full of crackers and chips and soda, anything to stave off the emptiness.

On the second day we walk downtown to a deli. We avoid the television trucks set up in front of our hotel, their satellite dishes aimed like alien eyeballs at our hotel. There is the sense always of being watched.

Mom's cell phone rings. Butch, the detective who has taken our family under his wing, has news, he tells Mom. He'll meet us at the deli.

Mom walks faster. It is hot. They are turning abandoned buildings into loft apartments across the street, the power tools banging, the generators louder than our talk. The air smells of melting asphalt.

Butch pulls up in his black Crown Victoria. He is trim and handsome, in his forties, with laugh lines and a goofy grin. Mom introduces us and he shakes my hand in both of his.

I can see the family resemblance, he says. He turns and shakes hands with Kris's husband Michael, too. Everyone else he has met.

He looks at Mom.

Marilyn, hon, we've got a positive ID on the body.

My eyes tear up as Mom looks at him, taking it in. She closes her eyes, then opens them and nods.

Thank you for coming down and telling me, Butch.

Butch opens his arms and Mom steps in.

After he leaves we go into the deli and order Reubens and pastrami and their famous slaw. We talk quietly. Remember the time . . . ? we say, trying to keep her alive.

I stare into my food. The news is not a surprise. I had known since the first phone call. I had known this was going to happen, and yet I am breathless. My mouth is dry, yet somehow the food tastes wonderful.

CHAPTER 29

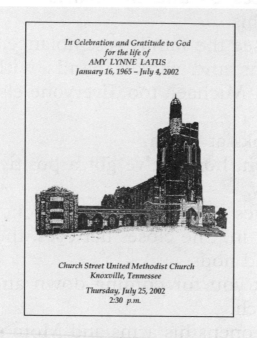

In Celebration and Gratitude to God
for the life of
AMY LYNNE LATUS
January 16, 1965 – July 4, 2002

Church Street United Methodist Church
Knoxville, Tennessee

Thursday, July 25, 2002
2:30 p.m.

Later we drive to the sheriff's office, Butch in the lead. He uses his pass to get us into the underground parking garage, then leads us through a maze of hallways and elevators and anterooms to the conference room. We array ourselves on one side of the table. Mom is in the middle. She will do the talking. We set up easels that hold collages of pictures of Amy. At the last minute Dad and his wife arrive.

The sheriff comes in and stands behind Mom. He is running for reelection and his face is all over local billboards. He nods, and deputies open the doors. Reporters jostle through the doors. Tripods are opened, cameras are bolted in, TV personalities check their microphones.

We have found Amy's body, Mom says.

The reporters start in. How do you feel? they say. Do you think the sheriff's department did a good job? Do you know who did it?

Mom is dignified.

The sheriff's department did a wonderful job, she says.

We are sad, she says.

We will miss her forever, she says.

The cameras pan our faces.

We want to thank the people of Knoxville — and especially her employer, Kimberly-Clark — for their support through this ordeal.

That's enough, the sheriff finally says.

The reporters are herded out through the front door. We go out the other, into an office in the back.

Dad looks at the collages.

God she got fat, he says.

Mom wants to see Amy's body. I don't think she should. I pull Butch into the hallway.

What do you think?

Butch leans in close. Quietly he describes that the detectives had been called by a man visiting a construction site on a remote country road. The man saw the pile of dirt from the newly dug foundation. Next to it was another, much smaller. It had been raining, though, so some of the fresh dirt had been washed away. He saw a painter's tarp, so he cleared away more dirt. The tarp was wrapped around something, then tied with speaker wire. He cut the tarp open, then called 911.

When the deputies got there they unfolded the rest of the tarp. Butch describes, then, what they saw.

A couple of weeks underground in this heat will do a lot of damage, he says. That shouldn't be a mother's last memory of her child.

I nod.

I rejoin the family. Mom again says she wants to see the body.

Butch and I were talking, I say, and we think that's not a sight any mother should see.

She looks at me for a moment, then nods.

We go back to the hotel to gather ourselves. Dad is staying at a cousin's house, and he and his wife go there. I am exhausted. I want to cry. I want to sleep. I want to put on my headphones and listen over and over to Carrie Newcomer singing "When one door closes." I push "play" and hand the headphones to Mom instead. She cries.

Later we pile into cars and drive to the funeral home.

Let me show you our urn selection, the funeral director says.

We look at each other. Amy's body is being cremated, and we're taking her ashes home to Michigan.

We don't want an urn, Mom says.

You can't fly without one, he says.

Kris and I look at each other. We are both reporters, and we're skeptical.

Let me just call Delta Airlines, I say.

I am on hold when Dad comes through the door.

Hello, he says cheerfully, as if this were a block party.

He walks around the room, dispensing hugs and lip kisses. When he gets to me I point to the phone and hold up my index finger.

One sec, I say. I'm on the phone.

Delta gets back on the line. We don't need an urn.

I want to see the body, Dad says.

Steve says he doesn't think that's a good idea. I say that Butch and I have talked about it, and it's not a memory any parent should have.

Yea, he says. I'm sure the maggots and the rodents have gotten to it by now.

The funeral director returns with the forms for the release of Amy's body. Since she wasn't married, her parents will need to sign. Mom does, then passes it to Dad. His hands are shaking. He has had a tremor all of his life, but now they are spasming, jerking uncontrollably.

Want me to fill that in? I say.

Thanks, honey.

I write in his name and address, then pass it to him for his signature, which is a spiky scrawl.

Afterward we loiter in the parking lot.

Now what do we do?

There is a Krispy Kreme across the street. We are all from the north.

Let's go, Dad says.

We buy donuts and coffee and sit in hard cold seats, licking the sugar off our fingers.

There will be two memorial services. We were going to do one back home in Michigan, but Amy's co-workers and classmates ask us to have one in Knoxville first. They want to come together to grieve, to show us how much they care.

Amy's professors call. They want to take all of us to lunch.

She was brilliant, they say.

She was funny.

She was a joy to have in the classroom.

The local Methodist church opens its doors. I am giving one of the eulogies. I want to stand up in front of Amy's friends and co-workers and teachers and celebrate the life of someone I consider inconceivably alive.

That night I sit at the rooftop pool in shorts and a T-shirt. My feet are in the water, a beer by my side. My family is scattered about, mostly in the pool area. We order pizza. I am writing longhand.

Dad wants to come over, my brother says, holding his phone.

If he's coming I need to go put on more clothes, I say.

My brother looks around at us. He

hates this.

You probably shouldn't come, he says into the phone. I don't think it would be comfortable.

We eat pizza, talk quietly. In the morning I'll need a ride to a store, I say.

In my rush to get out the door I have forgotten to pack anything funereal. Or maybe it wasn't the rush. Maybe it was denial. If I don't take funeral clothes, maybe she won't be dead.

I finish writing. After a while I go into the hotel hallway and call Russ.

I finished her eulogy, I say.

Read it to me, he says.

I slide down the wall until I'm sitting on the floor across from the elevators.

I sob as I read.

He listens patiently.

It's beautiful, he tells me when I finish. You have done Amy justice.

Now, he says, read it to me again.

Early on the day of the funeral I walk to Kimberly-Clark's offices, where they give me a desk and a computer and a printer so I'll have a clean copy of my eulogy. The company has chartered two buses for the three-hour drive from Atlanta to Knoxville, and given a hundred employees time off work to come to the service.

Later I walk with my family into a soaring vaulted Methodist church, the sun through the stained glass leaving pools of color. I am wearing shapeless black pants and a tunic, picked up in a hurry at Wal-Mart. The pants are rolled up three times and still I'm stepping on them.

Many of Amy's co-workers and friends are sobbing quietly, blowing their noses into wads of Kleenex. Forever I will insist on Kleenex brand everything, in gratitude to the company.

Her boss reads from emails sent by co-workers. One of her professors speaks. So does a classmate. They praise her for her intelligence, her sunny attitude, her ability to listen.

When it is my turn I slide past my family's knees and walk up to the podium. I put on my reading glasses and straighten my notes. I adjust the microphone, look up, and scan the audience, carefully skipping over my family sitting shoulder to shoulder, hands clasped, in the second row.

I clear my throat and begin.

First, the family would like to thank you for being here, and for being Amy's friends. We are not surprised that there are so many of you, because Amy was exuberant and loving, and she attracted good people. But we are gratified that you came here today to share in this memorial, this celebration of her life.

I talk then about her sense of humor, about hockey, about how much she loved her nieces and nephews, about how proud she was to be back in school.

Amy poured herself passionately into everything she did, I say. You who worked with her know her as diligent, reliable, and endlessly cheerful. You who taught her know her as eager, curious, and intelligent. You who were her friends know her as an endless ear, a wise counsel, a font of caring. We who are her family know her as all of those things, but also as the curly-mopped little girl who followed us, and eventually led us.

Good-bye, Amy. You will be missed.

Dad goes to the podium next. He tells of a trip he took with Amy when she was in her teens and he in his late forties. He and Mom were divorced by then, so he and Amy started off at a regional Parents Without Partners gathering at a campground. One night he was on his way back to his camper and a group around a campfire invited him over.

They were Canadians, he says, and they

offered me a beer, which I took, of course And pretty soon Amy came along. She came over to meet them, and they offered her a beer. She looked at me and I did like this.

He holds up one finger.

After about a half hour I gave her a little wink and I . . . he whistles and jerks his head toward an imaginary campsite . . . and she gets up and gives me a nice kiss and says she'll see me in the morning. I sit there and after a minute they say, Is that the way Americans handle this?

Handle what? I say.

You send your wife to bed ahead of yourself?

At this he laughs, his sun-spotted hands gripping the podium.

The funny thing was, he continues, as people shift nervously, that happened at least six times on this trip, people mistaking us as husband and wife instead of father and daughter. We got to the point where we were living it up, we were making people think that might be the case.

Dad chuckles, then launches into another story, about how a few years later he took Amy to Switzerland, on a trip he had won through his job selling insurance.

One of the comments I've heard here today, he says, is that Amy was a great listener. Well, we had a great trip to Switzerland. We were on top of the mountain, all fogged in, and she was running around like a wild hare. I called her over and said, I want you to stand here and be quiet. She said, What am I listening for? You'll not know unless you'll be quiet, I said. He pauses. How soon will I hear this? she says. So I says, Learn to be quiet and listen.

He pauses again.

So we stood there and, My god, what's that?

I said, when Julie Andrews was singing "the hills are alive with the sound of music," what it is is the cows down in the valley. Each farmer has a different pitch to his cow bells, and if you listen, you'll hear them.

That's absolutely beautiful, she says.

He looks at his audience.

So when these Kimberly-Clark employees said she's a good listener, that's because she learned to shut up and take my advice.

I look at Jane, who is sitting stiffly, her hands clenched. Steve and Ruth are holding hands. Pat is sobbing. No one will meet my eyes.

Afterward, the pastor says a blessing, and then tells the congregation that the family will receive mourners next door, if they will just give us a moment to ourselves. We file out of our pew and into the next room, where we have set up the collage of photos. We hug, we marvel at how many people gave up their day to honor Amy. Then we find our places, and the pastor opens the door.

I have misjudged how many people are here. The line stretches from the front of the church to the back. There are women and men and children. They want to touch each family member. Hug us. Shake our hands.

I know who you are, they say. Amy talked about you all of the time.

They know details — that Kris was once on *Oprah,* that I have a lovely adopted daughter, that Steve is hearing-impaired, that Jane is a watercolor artist. After a half hour we try to disperse, to move down the line so that people won't have to wait. The guests won't hear of it, though. They each want to talk to each of us. It is overwhelming.

A woman hugs me. She is Amy's therapist. I've heard so much about you, she says.

That can't be good, I say. We both laugh.

A tall man comes up, his teenage daughter in his shadow. It is Scott, the man Amy told me she told everything.

Did you know?

No, he says. I had no idea.

It takes nearly an hour for everyone to move through, and still people are clustered around the photos. Remember when she . . . ? I loved the way she . . .

The line dissipates and still we stand around in pairs and clusters. I am talking to Amy's therapist again when my father moves into my peripheral vision.

My dad is coming toward us, I say quietly. Do you want to be introduced?

No, she says, turning her head away from him.

CHAPTER 30

The second memorial is a week later, in the outdoor chapel of the Michigan youth camp we attended as children. The wind whispers in the cattails that serve as walls, topped here and there by red-winged blackbirds. It is a late summer morning, sunny and warm. Steve has arranged for a microphone and a podium. On its front hangs a framed photograph of Amy, the same one that had been on the "Missing" posters. Beneath the picture I've propped the Badge of Courage, along with a bouquet of flowers. Dozens of people sit facing it on half-hewn logs, all wearing Mardi Gras beads.

Dad and his wife sit in the front row on the right. The rest of us sit on the left, the little girls wearing so many necklaces they can barely turn their heads. Kurt is here, too. He drove up separately, to pay honor to the family he is leaving, to do what is right.

The plan is for each of us to do a eulogy. Pat goes first, explaining why the ceremony is here, at the youth camp where Amy was happiest. Mom speaks proudly of Amy's strength, her joy in life, her love for her family; and with regret for the things she wishes she'd done differently. She puts a home-made rainbow on the podium, because Amy loved rainbows. She puts an old hat on her head, too. It is the one Amy wore most often when she had lost so much hair from the chemotherapy.

Steve holds up a cross-stitched plaque Amy made for him when he went away to college. "P.O.R.," it says. It stands for "press on regardless," a phrase made famous in our family during a summer hike. With Amy, though, the P stands for perseverance, he says. The O for optimism. The R for remarkable. She was remarkably smart, funny, loyal, and observant. He draws from her letters, saved in a plastic sleeve in a three-ring binder, one section for each of his sisters. When it is Jane's turn she talks about Amy as an inspiration, a role model who had finished college just a few years earlier and inspired her big sister to do the same. I talk about her pizzazz, and her pride in her weight loss and graduate studies and new home. Kris talks of their antics from high school, and about her joy when Mom and John married and she gained Amy as a sister. Gramma couldn't come, so Pat's husband reads a letter she sent reminding everyone that Amy was her little Zsa Zsa, always diving into Gramma's bureau for silky nightgowns and scarves she'd wave like boas.

Then it is Dad's turn, and he repeats the eulogy he had given in Knoxville. It was bad the first time. It is horrifying the second, in part because we know what's coming.

When everyone is done speaking, we form a half circle in the front of the camp chapel. "I caught you, sir, having a look at her, as she went strolling by . . ." we sing, just as we had at her wedding. "Now didn't your heart . . . beat . . . boom da boom da boom? And didn't you sigh . . . a sigh? Once in love, with Amy, always in love with Amy . . .”

We can barely sing through our sobs.

When we are done we invite everyone to stand and hold hands in a circle. Because this is camp and because it is a tradition, we sing "Kumbaya." The linked circle, the familiar words, the wind in the cattails combine to bring me peace. For that moment I am not alone.

At the end of the service Mom gathers us kids behind the podium. Our cousins and aunts and uncles and long-lost friends are still milling, murmuring about the murder and the memorial.

Do you think it would be okay if we scattered some here? Mom asks.

It has to be, we agree.

Better to ask for forgiveness than permission, Mom says.

She opens the box that holds Amy's ashes, unwinds the twist tie of the plastic bag inside and sprinkles out half a cupful. The hard pieces drop to the ground; the gray dust drifts on the breeze, into the cattails.

Mom and Dad had divvied up the ashes, and Dad had buried his share in the Catholic cemetery, at the foot of my twin sister Janette's grave. Both took little room.

I had not gone to that ceremony, because

Catholicism creeps me out and Dad creeps me out and I have not yet discovered that his side of the family is peopled with generous and loving souls. When I left home I left them, too, and only now am meeting my cousins as adults. They surprise me. They are kind and loyal. They will do anything for us, just because we are family.

Amy wouldn't want to be buried in a Catholic cemetery, I say to my siblings.

I've thought about that, Steve says, but I think Amy would be happy to be anywhere that was sacred to the ones she loves.

I try to be as open-minded. What keeps me from objecting more strongly is that I don't think Amy's ashes embody Amy. I'm glad they're going back to nourish the earth, but Amy isn't in the gray powder and bits of bone. Still, it feels sacrilegious to me to have her buried there.

I decide it doesn't matter. It's just a place. A place under a tree, as I remember it, although I've visited fewer than a dozen times in my life.

After the service we all drive to Uncle Sandy and Aunt Darla's, where their family has put out hamburgers and potato salad and deviled eggs and brownies and cookies and cake. Kurt is moving among the family members, saying his good-byes. It is embarrassing for him to be here, I know, because he knows that they know that he is on his way out. He talks with my aunts, Sue and Darla, both loving women who have stood with their husbands for better or worse, richer or poorer. He says good-bye to the family that has become his. When he has talked to everyone, he hugs me, crying. Then he waves and walks away.

I can only stand there, my heart torn open by the twin mournings, my marriage and my sister.

My aunts fill his void.

Are you sure? they ask. He's handsome. He's smart. He makes a lot of money.

For a moment I am angry. No, I'm not sure, I want to say. I was affluent and now I'll have to struggle; I was the center of his world and now I'm alone. I just thought it might be a lark to end my marriage, see what fun there is in flying solo.

I'm sure, I say. I'm sorry, but I'm sure.

They each hug me.

We're behind you, honey, one says, whatever you decide.

For a moment I lean against her. I am grateful.

My cousins mill around, talking, watching each other's children. My stepdaughter is there, among the young adults. My daughter is there, run amok in the hammock and sandbox and underneath the feet of adults who will not pause in conversation as they steer her away from a hot grill or scoop her off the ground after a spill.

I have lived so long in isolation that I marvel. It is like a foreign country to me, this place where my daughter is embraced by so many. So many people there to pick her up if she falls, physically or metaphorically. My sight is blurred by tears of gratitude.

Thank you, I say to Uncle Sandy. He is presiding over the grill, his adult daughters coordinating the movement of food and drink and children.

We're just so proud of you, honey.

He puts his arm around me and I lean against him. I don't want to bawl, but it would be okay if I did. This is family.

The next morning the family caravans down to Lake Michigan. We're heading to Hagar Township Park, where Gramma would take Amy whenever she'd visit. The park itself is a shady space just off Highway 33, the old two-lane that runs along the Lake Michigan shore. I remember when I was in high school and I'd drive my rattling Pinto down to visit Gramma. I'd go to the beach along this road, worrying about bumper stickers that read "Pray for me I drive 33."

We unload our coolers and cookies and sandwich fixings, our soda pops and lemonades. It occurs to me yet again that we are the aunts now, the ones who make Thanksgiving dinner and Christmas pies, the ones who buzz in the background of family functions.

We grab cameras and kites, bubbles and towels, and parade nineteen strong down the hundred-plus wooden steps that will take us to the beach. The children burst free, running toward the water. The adults lay out blankets and towels.

Finally Mom calls us to order.

I think it's time, she says.

We need a picture, someone says.

Of course. We are together. We must have a photo. Before Amy it was funny, our need to take a picture no matter what, but now we know this could be our last. It could be our last photo together.

Finally Mom takes the plastic bag of ashes out of the box. The water is gentle today, and she walks in up to her waist, even though she's still dressed. The smallest children stay on the beach, but the rest of us wade in behind her. I am standing nearest Mom when she opens the bag, so she offers its open maw to me. I had thought she would tip it and let the ashes blow and sprinkle. But she is holding it out as if I am to reach into the grit that is all that remains of Amy's body. I do not know how to do this. I only know that the young people are watching me. My mother is watching me.

I reach in and scoop up a handful. It feels like the remains at the bottom of a fireplace. Fine ash, slivers of bone. I step away and search inside myself for something sacred. I close my eyes and remember Amy's laugh. I see her gleefully racing the balloon-powered race car I gave her one Christmas. I see her surrounded by quilt fabric. I see her cheering for her hockey team. I see her blowing bubbles and flying kites and telling me, Trust your instincts. You have great instincts.

Good-bye, Amy, I say again, as I let her ashes filter through my fingers.

Around me are the people who love me best, stepping forward, taking their handfuls, performing their own rituals of absolution and farewell. Mom looks around.

Has everyone had a turn?

She closes her eyes for a moment, then tips the bag and lets Amy's ashes slide into the lake she loved.

There is a moment of silence, and then

the in-laws and young people walk back up to the beach as Mom's surviving children step in to encircle her. We wrap our arms around each other and bow our heads, Steve and Jane and Janine and Pat and Kris, standing together in the gentle swells, each of us quietly crying. I hope again that our strength will somehow hold up Mom, who never looks like she needs anyone.

We sob, but we stand strong. Mom reaches into her pocket for a tissue, then makes a sound that is half laugh, half sob.

What kind of idiot, she says, walks into Lake Michigan with her Kleenex in her shorts pocket?

We all laugh, then break apart. I walk to the beach and into the arms of my step-daughter, so tall and strong. We get out the bubbles and the kites, because those are the things Amy loved. We play catch in the waves, throwing the ball high so the other person has to leap, or ditching it straight into the water in front of the other person's face, to make a splash. Steve throws it toward shallow water, for Claire, who dives sideways to make the catch. She comes up shaking sand out of her top.

I think I just got some of Aunt Amy in my bathing suit, she says, and we laugh.

Later we'll sort through box after box of

photographs salvaged from Amy's condo. Remember this? We'll say. Ooh, let me have that one. We divvy them up. I am struck by the memories, but also by the sheer number of pictures and cards. We cared about her. We kept in touch. We shared our lives. We were a good family. And yet this happened. This happened and she didn't tell anyone. The photos show she was loved. Look at that one. We are touching her. Our arms are around her. She knew. So why did she think this man was okay? Why was he her version of the best?

I can feel the anger welling up again. I want to be here to celebrate and share, but I am feeling rage and guilt and a screaming anger. I am angry at Amy. Are you? I ask my siblings. Sometimes. But not right now. Not today.

I try to let it go.

And then I am crying again, feeling the abyss of loss. The drama of her murder has kept it from me, but now it is bottomless. She is gone. She will be gone tomorrow and at Christmas and on the days of my daughters' weddings. She will be gone forever, for the rest of my life.

CHAPTER 31

You owe me a thousand dollars for that plane ticket, Kurt says. And when are you going to make up the extra time I took Sarah?

I have been home for less than a week. The house echoes with emptiness and memories, of my lost marriage, of my sister's visits. I wander through the rooms. This is where I baked bread and lasagna and Christmas cookies. This is where we took a marker and wrote "An author works here" on the floor of my office, right before workers laid the new carpet. This is where we served bagels after the kids' sleepovers, and pizza during the boy-girl parties that would have us patrolling the perimeter, switching on the overhead light just often enough to keep things PG. This is where the birthday candles set off the smoke detector, and where I sewed Halloween costumes and dress-up clothes and party dresses.

Around the corner the motion detector light flips on. I freeze, my heart thudding in my ears. He is here again, just down the hall, ready to stand over me and poke his finger into my chest, accusing, calling me names. I lean over a trash can and gag, my body not listening to my mind, which is chanting, "motion detector, motion detector." I hold still so long the light turns off. I want to call Amy but she's still dead. That's how I phrase it in my mind — still dead — as if that is ever going to change.

In August I get an email from my mom. Today I got tired of not being able to walk because of the rain, it says, so I just put on my raincoat and went anyway. I figured the rain could mix with my tears and nobody would know the difference.

I understand.

The house is for sale. Our pictures are off the walls, the kids' misshapen art projects are stored away. Our divorce is final and Kurt has found his next wife. She is one of his babysitters, twenty-one years his junior.

I am lonely, grasping for someone, anyone. I want someone to care when my plane lands. I want someone to want to read my stories. I want someone to somehow make me enough.

That has to come from inside, Vickie says.

I know, I say. I know.

But I don't know. I give speeches on how to be an effective writer, and people applaud.

I publish in bigger and better magazines, and people write letters to the editor, who call me back. Write for us some more, they say.

I teach part-time at my alma mater, where students vie for my sections.

It all should be enough, but it's not.

At a coffee shop someone asks me, Has Amy's death made you reconsider your divorce?

I look at her, thinking. I sip my coffee.

Yes, I finally say. It has made me even

more sure. Life's too short to be afraid.

Over the next few years I date, but gingerly. One man tells me not to worry my pretty little head about a thing. Another says he likes to be in charge. By that he means dominant. By that he means sexually dominant. I take his word for it.

Another meets me for a walk on the beach. He refers to his daughter as a tramp, then says a passing woman shouldn't be allowed out in public in a bikini.

Another man sees me in my reading glasses and says, Ooh, you're going for the sexy secretary look.

I look at him over the lenses.

That would be "sexy boss" to you, I say.

Another man gives me a monologue of his trip to Europe, droning about each hotel, each train ride, each mediocre meal, until finally he gets to Amsterdam and takes a breath. I break in.

There's a progressive country, I say.

Progressive? It's the only place where the prostitutes actually turned me off. Normally I like to talk to a girl before I do my business, but there you just pick them out of a shop window, do your business, and leave.

I stare at him.

■ ■ ■ ■

There are good dates, too, with men who would have potential if only they weren't still married — but I *feel* divorced — or creakingly old, or paunchy, or incapable of witty conversation.

I push at the ones who come near, looking for anger, for jealousy. I do not trust them. I do not trust myself. I tease one about his accent.

I'm going to kill you for that, he says.

He doesn't mean it.

I tease another and he makes a choking motion with his hands. He is kidding, but it isn't funny. Later he realizes what he's done, and he apologizes.

I have a swirling engulfing infatuation with one man, a dancer with the hands of a craftsman.

Are you going to murder me?

I try to believe his answer.

I am writing, but the scramble for assignments and paychecks and uninterrupted work time is too much, so I apply for faculty positions at a handful of universities. I get two offers. One is from Miami of Ohio, where a professor named Kerry drags me from interview to interview, and later out for a drink. The program could be great, he says. You'd be a fantastic addition. You have great energy.

The other offer is from East Carolina University, which wants to hire me sight unseen, on the strength of my credentials. The school isn't as good, and it's in the middle of tobacco country, where I am unlikely to find kindred souls. Still, no one there has met me, so they can't be offering it because they want to fuck me. Even though I know that's Kurt's voice reverberating in my head and it has nothing to do with Miami's interest in me, I take the job.

Kurt tries to stop me from taking our daughter, but in the end offers me a deal. If I give up assets that amount to a year and a half's salary, I can take her and go. I sign, and we are free.

I am alone and broke and in a strange town, and life is good. Peaceful and good.

One day I get an email. Ron Ball's sentencing hearing is set for April 5, 2004, almost two years after he killed my sister. He is pleading guilty to second-degree murder. I call Mom. I call Jane. We call each other, we call the lawyers, we call the liaison to the prosecutor's office, a bulldog of a woman who is supposed to be our advocate and instead runs interference for the lawyers. We fly once again to Knoxville.

It is in the courtroom that I first lay eyes on the man who killed my sister. I stare at him. He gazes back. I see no remorse, nor do I see malice. He's just a forty-one-year-old guy with normal hands that wrapped around my sister's neck and squeezed until she died.

In my mind I add "kicking and screaming," but there's no point. Every time I slow down to think about her death I come to that point, and it's too obvious to delineate. Obviously she was kicking and screaming.

Your honor, in Case 75586, Ronald Lee Ball will be entering a plea of guilty to the first count of the indictment charging second-degree murder. That's a Class A felony. It is a one-hundred-percent, violent-felon felony. And the agreed sentence would be eighteen years.

He will also be entering a plea of guilty to the second count of the indictment charging abuse of a corpse . . . The recommended punishment would be two years, to be served consecutively to the first count, making a total effective sentence of twenty years.

The prosecutor says something about the

possibility of sentence reduction, giving statutory details, and I do the math. Ron Ball could do just over sixteen years. For taking my sister's life. He will get out between the ages of fifty-seven and sixty-one, young enough to love again, young enough to kill again.

It is unsatisfying. Later the assistant prosecuting attorney tells us that to get a conviction for first-degree murder in Tennessee you practically have to write a letter that spells out when, where, and how you're going to kill.

If Ball had shot or stabbed her the charge would be even lower, he says, because you can do those impulsively, in the heat of passion. It takes a long time to hold someone's throat shut, which gives you plenty of time to reconsider. You're lucky to get second.

The judge listens to the charges, then turns to Ron Ball.

Is your plea given freely and voluntarily?

Yes, sir, it is, Ball says.

And are you guilty?

The courtroom is silent. The family leans forward. There is a hesitation.

Yes, sir.

The family freezes. I want to jump over the railing and claw his face with my finger-

487

nails. The feeling is primitive and I am ashamed, but that's what I want to do, claw him until he bleeds. I grip the seatback in front of me.

This is our only consolation: We no longer have to wonder.

Mom stands to give a victim impact statement. It is a formality, since Ball pled guilty, but at least we can feel like we have had a say, and maybe it will be considered when he comes up for parole. Mom's voice is calm and strong. She looks him in the face.

You have a daughter, she says.

Ron Ball looks away.

The judge taps his gavel and asks Ball to stand. The deputies come for him then, and he walks from the table with his hands behind his back, anticipating handcuffs, which don't come. As he walks out of the room Ball snaps his fingers and then claps his hands, in a rhythm both casual and contemptuous.

He could have as easily flipped his middle finger.

I am exhausted from a day of pulsing poisonous adrenaline. I just want to lie down.

We shuffle out of the courtroom, an unsatisfied jumble of sisters and brothers and spouses and parents, a cousin and her husband. Mom takes a right, toward the television cameras. Her voice is measured as she answers their questions. Yes, there is some satisfaction, she says. But it will never bring our Amy back.

My cousin comes to me. It has been more than twenty-five years since I left home and my father's side of the family. This woman is a stranger to me, yet I recognize her as kin.

Her name is Diane. Until four years ago she and her seven siblings lived in Denver, within a pizza circle of their parents, my Midwestern aunt and Italian uncle, the kind of people who pinch cheeks, who talk always loudly, come in! come in! Welcome!

I know that now.

But then I didn't. I thought only that they were my dad's family and therefore tarnished by the same brush that painted him. Not my people.

Diane comes to me and opens her arms.

I'm so sorry, she says, and I dissolve, there in the hallway of the courthouse, my stranger cousin's arms around me. I lean against her solidness as the dam breaks. Tears run down my face.

I was in Denver and I got beat up really bad and I didn't call you, I say, sobbing.

You should have called, she says, her tears

mirroring mine.

He broke my nose and my ribs and I didn't know you were there, I say. I got beat up and so did Amy and I didn't save her.

I feel like I will burst, explode, erupt. Diane holds me tighter.

You should have called, she says. We would have come.

I know you would have, I say. I know that now.

I am bawling. I hate bawling. I hate attracting attention. I hate being ugly. She holds me tighter.

We would have come.

1965–2002

AFTERWORD

If you see yourself in this book, you are not alone. I thought I was. Amy thought she was. But we weren't. I know now that if we had asked, people would have come, as they will for you.

It takes courage to change your life. Day in and day out, over and over, you have to decide to take the small, brave steps that change your future. Amy had that courage — tons of it — and she fought until the end. I wish I could rewind time and fight with her. I'd add my courage to hers, and together, perhaps, it would be enough. Instead I will help other women by donating money to Amy's Courage Fund. The Fund, administered by the National Network to End Domestic Violence, gives grants directly to women who need to flee — money for a month's rent, a bus ticket, a car repair, or any of the myriad small things that can stand between a woman and safety. For more information, to apply for a grant, or to donate with me, go to www .amyscourage.org. In Amy's name, we can save lives.

Another worthy organization is the National Coalition Against Domestic Violence. It supports shelters and advocacy programs, provides financial education, and coordinates a reconstructive cosmetic surgery program to remove at least the physical scars of domestic abuse. To contribute or find out more go to www.ncadv.org.

At minimum I ask that you join me in a national conversation about abuse. Let's talk to women when we don't like how they're being treated. Let's tell men that hitting is never okay, that belittling is never okay. Let's set an example for our own children, so the marriages they aspire to, those that look familiar, are ones of love and respect.

For other resources or more information about this book, visit www.IfIAmMissing orDead.com.

If you or someone you know needs help, please contact the National Domestic Violence Hotline at 1-800-799-SAFE(7233) or TTY 1-800-787-3224. They'll listen as you figure out what to do, and then direct you to resources — including shelters — in your own community.

ACKNOWLEDGMENTS

I wrote this book alone, sinking deep into my memories every day. My family and friends propped me up, both through the events in this book and through its writing. I am grateful.

My thanks first to my family, especially my mom, for recognizing that the good we can do by speaking out outweighs the pain of going public.

To the many generous members of the American Society of Journalists and Authors who shared both friendship and expertise, especially Jim Morrison, for telling me (over and over) that I'm brave, and Andrea Warren, for love, encouragement, and professional advice. To Chloie Piveral for her spot-on edits, and Bridget Bufford, who ran the writing workshops where I first put some of this into words. To Chuck Grant, for believing not only that I could do this, but that I would, and to Greg Frost, for setting the bar so high. To the people at Elliott's Fair Grounds, who knew when to respect my silence and when to lift me from the dark place. To Chris Williams, for quiet pride. And to my little girl, for always being a bright spot.

My thanks to my agent, Katie Boyle, who cheered for this book every step of the way, even though it made her cry. To my editor, Marysue Rucci, who brought out the best in my writing. To her assistant, Virginia Smith, for handling so many details. To Elizabeth McNamara, for her time, patience, and legal expertise. And to Simon & Schuster, for its enormous commitment to this project.

My gratitude, too, to the Knox County Sheriff's Department, for helping us find Amy, and the people of Kimberly-Clark, for caring.

Most important, my thanks to the people who do the real work — the advocates, the ones who run the hotlines and the shelters, who create safe harbors for women who have to run. I am proud there are so many and saddened that there is such a need.

Let this book be a call for change.

ABOUT THE AUTHOR

Janine Latus lives in Virginia, where she is at work on her next book. You can learn more about her at www.janinelatus.com.

The employees of Thorndike Press hope you have enjoyed this Large Print book. All our Thorndike and Wheeler Large Print titles are designed for easy reading, and all our books are made to last. Other Thorndike Press Large Print books are available at your library, through selected bookstores, or directly from us.

For information about titles, please call:
  (800) 223-1244

or visit our Web site at:
  www.gale.com/thorndike
  www.gale.com/wheeler

To share your comments, please write:
  Publisher
  Thorndike Press
  295 Kennedy Memorial Drive
  Waterville, ME 04901